Trauma Recalled

Trauma Recalled

Liturgy, Disruption, and Theology

Dirk G. Lange

Fortress Press

Minneapolis

TRAUMA RECALLED
Liturgy, Disruption, and Theology

Cover image: *Crucifixion* by Graham Sutherland © Scala / Art Resource, NY.
Cover design: Paul Boehnke
Book design: Publication Services

Library of Congress Cataloging-in-Publication data
Lange, Dirk G.
Trauma recalled : liturgy, disruption, and theology / Dirk G. Lange.
    p. cm.
Includes bibliographical references and index.
ISBN 978-0-8006-6462-6 (alk. paper)
1. Liturgics. 2. Luther, Martin, 1483-1546. 3. Jesus Christ—Crucifixion.
4. Theology of the cross. 5. Life change events—Religious aspects—Christianity. 6. Post-traumatic stress disorder—Religious aspects--Christianity.
7. Reformation. 8. Event history analysis. I. Title.
BV178.L35 2009
264.001—dc22

                              2009018282

Manufactured in the U.S.A.
14   13   12   11   10   1   2   3   4   5   6   7   8   9   10

To Ilona

With deepest gratitude and affection

Disclaimer

Even if nothing but bread and wine were present in the Supper, and yet I tried, simply for my own satisfaction, to express the thought that Christ's body is in the bread, I still could not say anything in a more certain, simpler, and clearer way than, "Take, eat, this is my body." For if the text read, "Take, eat, in the bread is my body," or, "With the bread is my body," or, "Under the bread is my body," it would immediately begin to rain, hail, and snow a storm of fanatics crying, "You see! do you hear that? Christ does not say, 'This bread is my body,' but, 'In the bread, or with the bread, or under the bread is my body!'" And they would cry, "Oh, how gladly would we believe if he had said, 'This is my body'; this would have been distinct and clear. But he actually says, "In the bread, with the bread, under the bread, so it does not follow that his body is present." Thus a thousand evasions and glosses would have been devised over the words "in, with, and under," no doubt with greater plausibility and less chance of stopping it than now.

—Martin Luther, LW 37:306

Contents

Preface

This set down
This: were we led all that way for
Birth or Death? There was a Birth, certainly,
We had evidence and no doubt. I have seen birth and death,
But had thought they were different; this Birth was
Hard and bitter agony for us, like Death, our death.
We returned to our places, these Kingdoms,
But no longer at ease here, in the old dispensation,
With an alien people clutching their gods.
I should be glad of another death.

    —T. S. Eliot, "The Journey of the Magi"[1]

A Liturgical Disruption of Theology

Alongside a quest for identity comes closely the search for origin. Foundations, sources, beginnings—whether mythical or historical or a combination of both—take on their own meaning. This attraction pulls ever stronger, strangely, I might add, in a culture that names itself "postmodern."

Religion in particular struggles with this search for beginnings. Ancient movements have settled the question in the mythic stories that have shaped entire, global cultures, such as the giving of the Ten Commandments. More contemporary religious movements (I'm thinking of those that have arisen in the last five hundred years in the West) have also quickly institutionalized their spirit-filled beginnings. Multiple manifestations of Martin Luther's and John Calvin's reformation, developments in England and America, and of course counter-reformations have all created their own narratives. Then there are the "seekers" today who find no home in any of these localized, culturally specific stories and create their own homes in self-styled worship and communities, communities that often reflect like a mirror the same entrapment of the older, localized communities.

I may seem to be particularly critical of narratives. Allow me to qualify this position, for the writing that follows arises out of my own story and my own quest for origin. This quest has taken me on a journey—a long journey—that has brought me to the realization that origins escape representation, that beginnings happen over and over again. In fact, there isn't a linear history taking me back (or forward for that matter) to any given, discernible point in time that would illuminate all the rest (the present, for example) but rather a search that leads only to a kind of death from which I set off once again, a new beginning.

This quest for origins in my own case led me to monastic life, but not in just any monastery. It led me to the Community of Taizé, in southern Burgundy, France. A place acclaimed by Pope John XXIII (and reiterated by John Paul II) as a "little springtime." Yes, it was also a source of faith but a unique source, a provisional source, living a provisional witness for the Christian community in its multiple manifestations. The prayer at Taizé is deeply embedded in contemplation and in struggle, in the nurturing of a deep inner life and a dynamic commitment to human solidarity. Practice and theology are one—not something that happens often, whether in church or academy.

Here, worship and life, liturgy and ethics are indistinguishable. They are, in fact, disrupted in an intimacy. Or perhaps I should say, their distinction becomes blurred to the point where the distinction and the primacy that has been argued for either side is questioned. Here, the old aphorism *lex orandi, lex credendi* (the rule of prayer, the rule of belief) takes on a new beginning.

That intimacy and blurring haunt the writing of this book. How to write beginnings, spirit-filled beginnings, that do not once again create a new origin, another localized, institutionalized identity or foundation? How to write the provisional dynamic of the Holy Spirit and maintain its provisionality? How to write beginnings that are also, always deaths?

Martin Luther turned to the liturgy, to the sacraments in particular to write that provisionality. Luther turns to the liturgy to disrupt the theology of his day. He turns to the liturgy not as a new source or origin but as that which attempts, in faltering steps and actions, rituals and words (but all words are a form of ritual!) to continually break open representation, memory, identity, foundation. This may come as a surprise to those who too quickly equate Luther and preaching or proclamation and preaching. The Word for Luther is both preached and distributed. One can certainly argue, based on his Small Catechism, that preaching is to bring us to the sacrament.

In the sacraments, an event—a Christ event—continually returns, but not the event we readily imagine or contrive or desire or create. Rather, and precisely, something that we can't imagine, contrive, create, even desire—something inaccessible in that beginning—returns not to condemn, not to leave us orphans, not to leave us in despair, but to hold us in death and in life.

Sacrament as event

This "something that returns" is the subtext, the context, the text of the writing that follows. At times the writing of history and theology as well as worship practices (no matter what shape or form) that operate in a representational framework are set up as a type of scarecrow. This is not simply a dismissal but an invitation into thinking other frameworks. Again, this writing itself is just one of those proposed frameworks. This "something that returns," that continually returns to both haunt and interrogate, is deeply the question of survival, the question of trauma. "Why did I survive?" I want to say it is: "Why did I survive the death of God?"

The liturgy in itself is that question, that disruption, and as always-failed response, it continually iterates the question anew for every generation, for every culture, for every theology, disseminating meaning, rupture producing life.

I write a profound thanks to my wife, Ilona, who upheld me throughout this study and writing. For guiding me in an ever-deepening understanding of my own search, I express a joyful gratitude to my teachers Don Saliers and Mark Jordan, Cathy Caruth and Gordon Lathrop, Wendy Farley and Geoffry Bennington, Timothy Wengert and Egil Grislis and also to my teachers now departed: frère Roger of Taizé and Father Joseph Gelineau, S.J. I praise God for the whole community of believers at Living Grace Lutheran Church, Tucker, Georgia, and its pastor David Hardy, who supported Ilona and me through this writing project and life's mysterious trials. I also praise God for my pastors—Pastor John Kunkel and Father Robert S. H. Greene. As I neared completion of the manuscript, Michael West's support and insightful comments were extremely encouraging; and Jennifer Grangaard's assistance gave me much-needed last minute help and assurance. Thank you! Finally, thanksgiving and praise are given for my family: my mother Ursula and my sister Brita, my aunt Annemarie, and those who have not lived to know this book as a published event but have known it inscribed in my life—to my father, Gerhard, and my grandmother Charlotte. They have embodied, since my earliest childhood, a questioning of the myth of origins.

Introduction

An Event

THIS BOOK CONCERNS ITSELF WITH BEGINNINGS even though that word does not appear in the title and appears only infrequently in the text. Another possible title could have been "Liturgy and Beginnings," as it is through the liturgy that I wish to approach the enigma of event, of emergence, of beginnings.

Beginnings happen—or don't happen—in time. The Reformation was a type of beginning. It began with an event, with a rupture. An event is always in some ways a rupture, something that happens and changes the context that we currently inhabit, an unexpected emergence. Historically, of course, we think of political revolutions that apparently constitute a type of beginning—for example, the American Revolution or the French Revolution or the Russian Revolution. Beginnings are deeply associated with revolutions. When such a rupture occurs, there is a rethinking of time and history. A new time "begins" or a new history. In the case of American historiography, an argument has been outlined for the beginning of a history that was against history.[1]

What is curious about these beginnings, however we might struggle to define them, is their link to repetition. Those who are part of a revolution want to continue it, to repeat it. Those who were part of the Reformation sought to continue it, to repeat it in ways they thought were the most "authentic." This struggle of repetition, particularly as it pertains to the Lutheran reformation, is still very much alive today.

"Beginnings" and "event" and "repetition" are embedded in our human experience. Of course, a rupture, an event, a beginning that is then repeated, also requires a memory. We need to remember that first event or those first intuitions. But the remembering as repetition always happens in a different context from the singular "beginning." The

1

remembering happens in a different space and time and by different people. It raises the whole question about the possibility of remembering something: What does it mean for us to remember? And then, what does this remembering mean for beginnings?

An event, a beginning, a remembering, and a repetition are all characteristics of ritual action, and specifically of Christian *liturgy*. But here is also the dilemma: the liturgy (and the possibility of a liturgical spirituality) apparently suggests something very clear and precise about event, remembering, repetition. There was an event, however we define it (for example, the Last Supper or the cross). There was a beginning (a "resurrection," if you will, an Easter and Pentecost). There is a memory (Scripture, tradition). There is a repetition of that memory (ritual, liturgy), and this repetition curiously combines all of the above.

Liturgy as we have come to know it, especially through practice, embodies these four things. It becomes the bastion of a type of religious culture that gives participants comfort and reassurance and perhaps also a sense of identity. It takes our realities, our lives, and reflects them through the gospel, through the event, the beginning, and the memory of a culture and people. It points back to a story, to an event. It has a center, a core, a heart, a beginning. And this beginning or center has defined all of our liturgical activities and theological thinking.

The way we "remember" has stirred up much debate. If we were to study denominational differences from the angle of memory, I believe we would discover that the various faith expressions come primarily from different ways of remembering the so-called "event." When we ask "How do we remember the Christ event?" we are usually asking: How do we *connect* with it? How do we make it real? How do we actualize it? Do we develop an elaborate theory of remembering and name it after a Greek word like *amamnesis* as if the celebration of the sacrament actualizes something of the cross event today? Or do we simply go to a film, like *The Passion of Christ,* and participate visually and emotionally in a torture? Perhaps we believe in a mystic reenactment of the sacrifice? Or do we sweep all of our questions under the table, away from view, and hide behind a proclamation of the Word alone as if we were the immediate inheritors of Christ's testament and all we need to do to endure ritual purity is establish the correct direction (from God to us)?

The questions multiply. The center of focus has become not the Christ event itself but the way in which it is "communicated" to the believer. How is the new testament or covenant (Matthew 26) communicated to us? How are we connected to the event?

We take communication for granted, and the metaphor of communication as self-evident. We have inherited this notion that communication is possible between two people or two groups of people when a common language and common presuppositions exist. The liturgy also falls into the naive belief that through the Word and the sacraments something of God is communicated, as if the Word and the sacraments were like instruments channeling grace. Theologians use another metaphor for the role of the Word and sacraments that adds to the confusion: the "means of grace."

When we speak about the sacraments as "means of grace," we evoke certain images. Through these "means" something comes down to us, or through the proper celebration of these means we somehow have access to God. I am arguing against this rather medieval metaphor that is surprisingly still operative today. It is operative in all of our churches and in many spiritual movements. It is operative wherever "God" is placed in one realm and we are placed in another. It is operative wherever anything of God's realm is called "sacred" and anything in our realm is called "secular"—or in any other such nominal distinctions we may make.

A metaphor of communication—for it is simply a metaphor, a tool of language—is defining the way we approach the event and how we remember and how we repeat it. This book will question this metaphor and begin by asking how we know event. Can we define it? When event is understood as rupture, there is an obvious questioning of all forms of communication.

But what happens to communication when there is a beginning, when, in a revolution or reformation, something new happens that breaks the context of communication, that breaks the context of language and thought? In the political and social realm, we then see an outburst of creative energy. We witness moments like the *Declaration of the Rights of Man and Citizen* in the French Revolution or the *Declaration of Independence* in the American Revolution. We see a restructuring of life. But this restructuring almost always and very quickly falls back into a reified system. The emperor comes back but in different clothes. It requires a bloody civil war to end slavery in the United States, but the trauma of slavery continues to manifest itself. And today, in the "name of" a declaration, or a constitution, or a mythified history, injustice is allowed to reign. Despite the creative beginnings, one system replaces another. Religion is not exempt. Christianity is not exempt and, as a Lutheran myself, I need to confess that Lutheranism is not exempt.

Is there a way in which the beginning is always a beginning? Is there a way in which the event is always a rupture, something disruptive? Is there a way in which we can keep the provisional nature of beginnings?[2] I will not presume to know whether Luther asked these questions, but I want to argue that they permeate his writing.

Luther immediately saw the danger: the Reformation needed to happen, the Ninety-Five Theses were posted, but then the rest of his life was spent combating primarily other "protestant" manifestations that wanted to turn the Reformation into a new system, that wanted to turn a provisional beginning into a new law. After the initial years when Luther needed to distance himself from Rome, he spent most of his time debating his fellow reformers who were trying to narrow down the Reformation to just one insight, who were trying to systematize the insight, who were trying to centralize everything once again.

Where does the concern about ever deepening systematization and the deconstruction of theory begin for Luther? Witnesses are already found in his early polemical treatise against Rome entitled "The Babylonian Captivity of the Church." But in this treatise Luther is attacking the way Rome—not the church but Rome—has captured and restrained and reified and systematized and memorialized the sacraments. Luther begins the Reformation by freeing the liturgy, by freeing it from the baggage of metaphors that have bound it down. A theological disruption begins in and through the liturgy.

For Luther, the water, bread, and wine are physical entities that confront us with God's return. They are not elements that get magically transformed so that they are not really physical anymore, nor do they remain simply elements without any other significance than as a reminder of some past event. The sacraments invite us into a space that defies our logic and rationally coherent worldviews. They make us aware, first of all, of our connection to the earth (as a good thing) but also of how God continually returns to us through these created gifts.

Resisting the capture of the sacraments, resisting the capture of the liturgy, by a hierarchy—allowing the "return" of God—became, so I will argue, a leitmotif of Luther's writing, though a leitmotif that is hardly acknowledged by historians or theologians. This resistance for

Luther begins in calling back the liturgy of his day to the gospel, to the life and witness of Jesus Christ, to death and resurrection. It also begins in Luther's insistence that the sacraments arise out of event. For an action to be a sacrament, for Luther, the promise of God must be connected to a sign accomplished by Jesus, to something that happened.

If a resistance takes that is understood as a liberation—if the sacraments, liturgy, theology, are freed from the grips of a metanarrative— *is this a hermeneutic* then another question arises: How do we remember and repeat that resistance, that confrontation, that disruption? The question is not "What is this 'something' that returns?" or "What does it mean?" but how does the disruption of systems of meaning, and of therefore "verifiable" meaning, find an expression without becoming once again newly systematized or encoded? How is the inaccessible event itself remembered, enacted? How is the event, how is rupture, the beginning, expressed linguistically and ritually without once again becoming law?

Trauma Theory, Event and Liturgy

Following Dietrich Bonhoeffer's suggestion that a new language for theology will be perhaps "quite non-religious,"[3] coming, we might say, from outside theology, the rewriting engaged in this book has appealed to a language—to voices—from outside theology, in particular, the voice of trauma and trauma theory.

The two words that I have already mentioned several times— *remember* and *repetition*—are also focal questions in poststructuralist thought and in trauma theory.[4] Sigmund Freud's initial reflections on trauma, found in his work *Beyond the Pleasure Principle*, arose out of observations he made of a repetitive ritual game enacted by a little boy (his grandson) who, as Freud ascertained, was trying to recall or remember his absent mother.[5] I want to suggest that the impact of trauma theory on contemporary philosophical thinking and on literary works cannot and should not be ignored by theologians. Trauma theory has something to say with regard to the repetitive ritual action we call the liturgy. This book explores the intersection of liturgy and trauma and particularly the ways in which trauma theory may help us not only rewrite our understanding of ritual but also open up avenues for thinking about a liturgical hermeneutics.

Trauma theory has become known to most readers through its clinical diagnosis of post-traumatic stress disorder.[6] Post-traumatic stress disorder is not, however, confined only to the clinical domain. As read by an eminent scholar in the field, Cathy Caruth, post-traumatic stress disorder not only is a clinical or psychoanalytical category but also offers a means of reading history.[7] Using the insights of psychoanalysis, trauma theory reveals a way in which we can approach meaning and reference in history that moves beyond an empirical and representational prison. Because liturgy is about remembering and, particularly, remembering God's acts in history, a consideration of a new reading of history will have significant implications understanding the term *remembrance* and what the liturgy is actually enacting.

A reading of history through trauma theory implies, first of all, the disruption of representational forms of remembering (or reference). This disruption, however, does not mean that we cannot "know" history (as some critics of postmodern thought contend). Rather, knowing itself is redefined. There is a blurring of the distinction between knowing the (traumatic) event and the way in which that event is remembered. The traumatic event escapes accessibility—it cannot be fully known either by memory or by intelligibility. As Caruth writes: "The shock of the mind's relation to the threat of death is thus not the direct experience of the threat, but precisely the *missing* of this experience, the fact that, not being experienced in time, it has not yet been fully known."[8] The traumatic event is a missed event, a missed encounter with death. The very fact of "missing" the experience disrupts an empirical notion of time itself. The traumatic event is not experienced "in time"—that is, the event is not experienced consciously in fullness of time or space, of time or context. It therefore remains inaccessible to knowledge. The fact that the event was missed creates a demand. This missed encounter demands, as it were, the continual repetition of the traumatic event. For those who suffer from post-traumatic stress disorder, this repetition is not a conscious remembering of the trauma but, first of all, the "return" of the traumatic event continually experienced as if for the first time, as if trying to capture the moment in time for the first time.

Something, however, in the event remains inaccessible to consciousness. This inaccessibility points us to a characteristic of history: there is something "latent in the events of history."[9] Events carry within them and "pass on" from generation to generation a traumatic character, as if human beings were condemned to repeat the very events that trauma-tized persons and communities. Communities are condemned to repeat the violence of their origins, the violence that they, at one point in their history, committed or suffered. In this sense, violence begets violence begets violence. Though the return of the past event within the living community can also be witnessed in sublimated forms. For example, in *Moses and Monotheism*, Freud argues that the repression of the murder of Moses returns as a sense of chosenness in Jewish tradition.[10] And, as Caruth highlights, this "history of chosenness, as the history of survival, thus takes the form of an unending confrontation with the returning vio-lence of the past."[11] As the biblical injunction has it: the iniquity of the parents is visited "upon the children and the children's children."[12] This "visitation" however can take on many forms and, most commonly, not one that involves conscious knowing.

Despite the apparent dismissal of the past event as an object of knowledge, at the beginning of her chapter on Freud's *Beyond the Pleasure Principle,* Caruth asserts that the notion of trauma does not eliminate the possibility of reference in history. This is a crucial move and one to which any critic must pay close attention. Trauma theory is, rather, a rethinking of reference and history that brings "event" back into writing, into theory, and, I want to add, into ritual. However, this "return" of event into theory (and ritual) is not the return of a perceptually confirmed and cognitively verified fact or "happening." The event is known not simply through description or a tracing of its causes and effects but is witnessed as the continual return of some-thing that was not understood.

There is "something" in experience, in event, that cannot be grasped by understanding but which arises and asserts itself beyond the categories of rationality. Immediate understanding (knowing defined as immediate perception of the "here and now," knowing defined as simply representational) is displaced in this assertion. We could say that history is "known" by something latent, something unobservable, something that *makes itself known,* that imposes itself in unexpected ways on the student of history, the participant in history, the reader—something over which we have no control. That which is latent is precisely that which was not known in the first instance, in the first "happening," in the moment of encounter, event. Because this latency cannot be framed within the field of rational knowledge, it is like a force that continually returns to haunt the field of simplistic historical vision, breaking in to disrupt established meanings though not negating the possibility of meaning or reference.

The latency within event is not in opposition to reference or the possibility of meaning. In fact, it is the condition of such meaning. That which is latent in event is known through a struggle with the traumatic experience (the train crash, the bombing, for example). The opaqueness of event (that which historians attempt vainly to "clarify") gives rise to something latent between the lines, between the empirical "facts" of history. The question that trauma theory raises for us is then a question of focus. Should we not be more attentive to that latency that returns, that haunts and read the reference of history through it? This exercise might produce a history of the unrecognized, the voiceless, the unvoiced. It might enable a history of peace rather than the perpetuation of a story of violence.

telos? [handwritten margin note]

What is repeated is the fact that the traumatic event was not known in its happening or was not fully experienced in its happening. Based on this insight of trauma theory, I want to argue that what gets repeated is that which was missed, what I will call the inaccessibility of *every* event. What is repeated is not the event itself but that which made the event traumatic in the first place—the fact of having missed something, the fact of having survived.

The traumatic event is experienced as a shock of survival—why did I survive? The shock of survival is the shock that "death" was encountered and missed. Something in the event was missed and is continually experienced, *after* the event, as something inaccessible, as something that haunts. It is the inaccessibility that also renders the event singular and strangely not repeatable (unique). The "singularity" of the event (to use Jacques Derrida's expression) at one and the same time both demands and yet denies the possibility of repetition. The singular cannot be repeated. The inaccessible cannot be known and imitated and *yet* continually returns as the question of survival—and as a question that demands ritualization.

Trauma theory reveals a realm of knowing that is not representational but that is itself continually interrogated by the violence, by the trauma of a past event, a knowing that is never complete. In the words of Caruth: "Trauma . . . does not simply serve as record of the past but precisely registers the force of an experience that is not yet fully owned."[13] Trauma, in this sense, is a continual awakening to an event that was not fully understood and that, because of this incompleteness, is being continually made present. Repetition is not the repetition of a known event or deed but an impossible repetition—an iteration of something that is absent, something ✳ that was missed and is inaccessible. This iteration is lived ritually as well, not as an attempt to master the inaccessible but simply in order to survive.

Trauma Theory and the Christ Event

The event I name as traumatic is the Christ event. As event, it was known not in its happening but only afterward, in a moment too late. It raises the following question: How is this traumatic event—an event that we cannot fully grasp, an event that is only "registered" as a force of experience—remembered, repeated, and therefore, of course, ritualized? In other words: What does trauma theory imply for liturgical action that is itself focused on an "event"—God's saving act in history?

A reading of the Christ event through the lens of post-traumatic stress disorder suggests that the repetition or ritualization is not a remembering on a facile, representational level. It is not simply the remembering of a past event in and through an established ritual pattern (for example, through a proper ritual enactment of the Lord's Supper). The ritualization of the Christ event cannot simply capture it in the present context, in the present moment. The event—the traumatic event or, in this case, the Christ event—is inaccessible, in its totality, to the mind. It continu- ✳ ally returns as a resistance to meaning, to ritual, to language. The Christ event returns as a force that continually disrupts our usual forms of remembering and ritualizing.

The return of something inaccessible in event is perhaps best witnessed in an early church document, the *Didache* (see chapter 5).[14] The chapters that refer to an early eucharistic celebration were probably recorded fifteen to twenty years after the event known as the crucifixion of Jesus. It is therefore astounding that the way in which Jesus is remembered in this liturgical document is not by images of the cross but by a sharing of bread and wine. In fact, the eucharistic celebration in this document makes no (explicit) mention of the cross.

The *Didache* as event of writing disrupts our remembering, and it does so at that critical moment in the liturgy when the celebrants (ordained and lay) think they are at the most crucial and intimate moment of "remembering"—at the recitation of the Words of Institution. The absence of the Words of Institution confronts the reader/participant with the following question: How is the Christ event "remembered" in the eucharistic liturgy? By its silence on the Last Supper and, in particular, on cross symbolism, the *Didache* disseminates the sense of access to the Christ event that our current liturgies attempt to foster. "Remembering" of the event is disrupted liturgically, and at the same time, the inability of our liturgies to ensure a permanent "access" is revealed.

This early church order pushes the reader/participant to reformulate the notion of liturgical or ritual repetition as the force of a return. Liturgical iteration, already in this church order, which is chronologically the "closest" to the event, is not a remembering of "the" event but the continual return of that which cannot be captured in the event; it is the continual disruption of all forms of remembering in the disorientation and reorientation of a radical commensality. The place of commensality becomes a place of dislocation, of disrupted access.

The source of ritual remembering is a sharing of bread and wine. It is not the violence of the cross. Ritual, in this document, breaks the spiral of violence, notably, the spiral of religious violence—sacrifice, But ritual itself is a manifestation of law. It provides order if no other way than through its insistence on a particular sequence of communally enacted practices. How can ritual break the violence of law when it embodies a form of law and imposes that form? Jacques Derrida asks a similar question. In his article "Force of Law," he points out that, at the heart of the law, there is always an imposition, a violence: "There is no law without enforceability and no applicability or enforceability of the law without force."[15] How do we distinguish between the legitimate ritual (as celebration of God's promise) and the imposition of ritual, which is always, in some form, a violence? The question is critical for liturgical theology (and for all thought that deals with laws, rituals, or systems). However, this question leads to another. Derrida then asks: "How to distinguish between the force of law, of legitimate power and the allegedly originary violence that must have established this authority?"[16] The repetition that is the basis of ritual, the remembrance that is continually engaged in liturgy, is continually challenged to ask how it distinguishes between ritual action and an originary violence. Are we, in our liturgies, merely propagating, passing on, a violence that established the rites in the first place? I believe not. Rather, through trauma theory, we are able to understand ritual not as passing on violence but as pointing toward, as repeating, something inaccessible, something that breaks the cycle of violence.

10

Of course, if we remember the Christ event as the sacrifice on the cross, we are "remembering" that event through its violence. At the source of sacrifice is an originary violence, such as the sprinkling of blood on the doorposts to avoid the angel of wrath. Or, there is also a violence done to oneself in the pursuit of some goal. The cross is understood as originary violence/sacrifice that demands, in turn, "sacrifice" on our part. It is as if the "sacred" required some form of violence. As the monumental study of René Girard (*La violence et le sacré*) has pointed out, violence—the violence of life, death itself—is brought under human control by turning it into the sacred. Has not the classical theological/liturgical narrative of the cross event succumbed to this desire to control the violence of the cross and in that desire actually immortalized its violence?

look at this...

Martin Luther understood, long before Girard, this human tendency toward sacralization. The term *sacrifice* itself is our way of controlling death. An enormous danger arises when we turn the violence of the cross into something sacred (through ritualization, for example): over time, it results in the sanctification not of what Jesus accomplished on the cross but of violence. Violence is always conceived as a viable option. Wars continue to rage. The death penalty is still considered just. The holocaust happens.

With Luther, we want to move into a different territory far from violence (even though we might still use the "wrong" word *sacrifice*). If the source of the law is some form of originary violence, what is at the source of the gospel? How is the gospel ritualized without becoming violent? The cross has come to symbolize the gospel for us, but what are Jesus' instructions? "Do this in remembrance of me . . ." Jesus points not to the cross but to the meal as the place of remembering. The sharing of bread and wine— not the violent death—becomes a form of ritual remembering that disrupts violence. The sharing of bread and wine is like an utterance that displaces the violence of the cross. In the sharing—in the practice—something that was inaccessible in the event returns and engages the participant in an impossible but continually demanded responsibility, into discipleship.

Event and Language

This book begins with a curious study of an event—not the Christ event but an event in the life of Martin Luther. Or, perhaps it would be more accurate to write, with an unknown or indefinable event in his life but one, nonetheless, that has taken on an incredible life of its own in

scholarly writing and debate: the moment of Luther's discovery of justification through faith alone. I describe this exploration as a "curious" study
because this unknown event, this invented event, haunts both Luther
and the writing of scholars, historians and theologians alike. It continually
returns, if you will.

Luther's resistance to any form of systematization is not a resistance
that happens on only a theological or liturgical level (such as redefining
what church is or what the sacraments are). The struggle with event (and,
particularly, the event of origin) is witnessed in writing, in and through
language. Luther's resistance is expressed in his very approach to reading
and writing. In other words, Luther realized that to change the way we
think, the way we pray, the way we relate to God, we have to begin with
the way we understand the event of writing, the event of the word.

Luther's reform was therefore and very deeply a revolution of
language—a revolution of the way we read and write. For example,
Luther breaks the mold of medieval exegesis. Luther argues against the
idea that there is a literal meaning and then a deeper, hidden, spiritual
meaning. Words themselves are not just instruments that communicate
a deeper hidden meaning. Already in their literal sense, he argues, words
engage us in a struggle.

In his commentary on several chapters of the "Second Book of
Moses" preached in the years 1524–26, in a section entitled "Allegory
or Spiritual Meaning of the First Chapter," Luther writes: "I pray that
you hold to the kernel, the good treasure, the worthiest treasure in Holy
Scripture, namely, that you learn Holy Scripture according to historical way."[17] Further, in that same commentary, he develops this radical
statement by writing that the kernel is not the inner, spiritual meaning
but the shell, the historical meaning, the event. Language, words, event
already confront us with what they are, not with what they hide.

Language itself, as we will discover, becomes a place, a location
of an impossible repetition, and in that impossibility it becomes event
itself. Language is understood not as a mere description (as if we could
know or represent the event) but as an inscription, as if the contours of
the event (its violence and its latency) are surfacing in words. Any grade
school student has learned that one revolution of Luther's reformation
was the use of new technology—the printed word. This revolution of
accessibility to language, however, is far overshadowed by Luther's revolutionary approach to the interpretation of language and his search

free from metanarrative

for a theological grammar that would free language, words, from pre-established meanings, from the hands of scribes, from the sequentially ordered, hierarchical structures in which faith was imprisoned.

Luther engaged a freeing of speech so that the event—not the event of his discovery of justification through faith alone but the event of Christ—might become the language of the masses.[18] This freeing of speech, however, did not happen without a struggle with meaning, without a confrontation with words. This struggle is witnessed in Luther's account, in a Table Talk, of his discovery of the sweetness of words (see chapter 1). The sweetness of words is tasted through the discovery of a theological grammar, through a way of reading in which that inaccessible or absent thing in event is continually rendered audible, tactile. The repetition, if you will, of the traumatic (Christ) event haunts every location of reading and writing, every location of life. The Spirit kills (in the letter) and makes alive (also in the letter).

"The *event* engages the *structure*."[19] The Christ event engages not only the social and political structures of life but also, perhaps even more fundamentally, the structure, the grammar of language. It therefore also disrupts the simple forms of communication that we attribute to language and meaning. Luther witnesses to a grammar of absence within language itself.

The study of an absence that confronts, that cannot be delineated or known, is inscribed in these pages. An event that continually returns to haunt and, paradoxically, to give life is approached and repeated through liturgical enactment. It also haunts that enactment and gives it life. The traumatic event points us toward the failure of both ritual and language, of both action and word. It points us toward liturgy as failed speech, and that "speaks" precisely in its failing.

An Outline

Since liturgy is about an event, chapter 1 begins by analyzing the construction of "event" through writing—that is, how have historians written "event" in the life of Martin Luther? Though Heiko Oberman had already dismantled the fascination with the idea of "reformation breakthrough" (a "tower experience") strangely enough, this breakthrough continues to remain operative in writing about Luther and, in fact, even in Oberman's own writing. I explore the implications of the fascination with a tower experience and the ways in which it has blinded the reader to another movement in Luther's writing—precisely, his turn to the liturgy to write the events of his life. The chapter disrupts both traditional understandings of event as well as traditional approaches to meaning by demonstrating how Luther's use of the liturgy confronts both subject and context. Luther, in effect, pushes the reader away from a simple appropriation of "event"—even the so-called tower experience. Luther's own experience of a liturgical confrontation prepares the reader for his amazing statement that in "things" (event and language) there is always something absent. This absence, which cannot be captured, will figure largely in Luther's understanding of liturgy as the locus of a demolition of towers (both liturgical towers as well as metaphysical towers) and subsequently in my own argument for the disruption of theology.

Luther's turn to the liturgy reconfigures the ways in which meaning is accessed, especially meaning in Scripture. Luther, in his analysis of "letter and spirit" (2 Cor. 3:6)—an analysis that then develops in the distinction between law and gospel—demolishes the illusion of a direct access to meaning. Chapter 2 develops Luther's understanding of language itself as an event that confronts the reader. Luther's disruption of the simple metaphors for the communication of meaning is significant. This disruption comes to the foreground in the actual event of his own writing. The focal text of this chapter is Luther's autobiographical statement written several months before he died: the preface to the Latin edition of his works. This preface has been variously used by scholars, primarily to uncover the actual "moment" of Luther's reforming breakthrough. I argue that the text does not point the reader to any "moment" or precise event. Luther, in this text, is rewriting his life from the perspective of baptism. Through the use of baptismal metaphors, Luther is able to grapple with those things that remain "absent" in all events; Luther is able to write the confrontation with what is not known in every event. This rewriting of event leads Luther to a shocking conclusion: those things that theologians sometimes call theological loci (for example, justice or mercy or forgiveness) simply establish new towers when they are considered "eternal truths." For Luther, the things of God remain strangely "present" and "absent." They cannot be grasped or known. Rather, God immerses us in them; we are continually confronted by and through event and are then led to a new place.

Chapter 3 takes a critical look at the notion of event in poststructuralist thought, particularly in the writing of Jacques Derrida. Derrida's exposé on the singularity of event provides insights for reading Luther's own turn toward the sacraments as singular events that cannot be known but that demand, nonetheless, a repetition—that demand, in other words, a liturgical structure. Derrida argues for the nonsaturability or permeability of context. Theology, especially liturgical theology, has failed to account for this permeability, assuming that the event—the Christ event—can be known, written, remembered, and liturgically celebrated. Our theologies assume a "presence," whereas Derrida assumes, first, an absence. The discovery of this chapter is Luther's own discovery. In the letter written to his father that prefaced his treatise on monastic vows, Luther realized that faith begins with an absence that disrupts all contexts, including religiously grounded contexts. Subsequently, Luther rewrites both context and call (vocation). The disruption of context, however, is not theoretical. It is lived out in Luther's own struggle with vows, his monastic context, and the authority of his father. It is also experienced in the physical disruption of context by the advent of the "other." A further ramification of this struggle is a profound questioning of the very nature of vows.

Following on the previous chapters' having shown how event disrupts both subject and context and, particularly, how Luther turns to the liturgy as disruptive event, chapter 4 explores more in depth the character of this disruption. The chapter turns to trauma theory and the innovative writing of Cathy Caruth, who reads trauma theory as an interpretative mirror of history. Trauma theory suggests that the events of history carry within them and "pass on" from generation to generation a traumatic character, as if human beings were condemned to repeat the very events that traumatized persons and communities before them. Communities are condemned to repeat violence that they, at one point in their history, committed or suffered. Violence begets violence. War begets war. The repetition itself can be traumatic because it appears to be out of human control. What is repeated—the traumatic event—is not the event itself but that which made the event traumatic in the first place. What is repeated is the fact that the traumatic event was not known in its happening. The traumatic event is experienced as a shock of survival—why did I survive? This shock of survival, also named the "inaccessible" character of the traumatic event, demands and yet denies the possibility of repetition.

In this chapter, the event that is named "traumatic" is the Christ event. And the question raised is then, How is this traumatic event—an event that we cannot fully grasp, an event that is only "registered" as a force of experience—how is this traumatic event remembered, repeated, and subsequently ritualized? The Christ event returns as a force that continually disrupts our usual forms of remembering and ritualizing. The insights and questions of trauma theory permit me to explore the ways in which Luther turns to the celebration of the sacrament of Holy Communion (or Eucharist) in order to understand "disruption." Luther proposes that the Eucharist is a literal embodiment of the trauma of the other. This position is most clearly stated in his treatise against Zwingli, "That These Words of Christ, 'This is my Body,' etc., Still Stand Firm against the Fanatics" (LW 37). In this treatise, the force of a return— that which cannot be captured, known, represented, memorialized by ritual—is not some abstract notion of grace or forgiveness of sins or other theological construct but is the irruption of the body, the confrontation with a body, at the heart of the ritual.

In chapter 5, I argue that Luther's eucharistic hermeneutic arises out of the confrontation with the sacrament itself rather than being developed from any preconceived theological or philosophical position. In other words, the event of the meal itself pushes toward a rewriting of theology and of Christian practices. This disruption of theology by the meal-sharing event is witnessed in Luther's odd use of the word *law* with regard to the sacrament. A close analysis of Luther's text reveals that the sacrament of the meal is not a new law but, rather, that which disrupts all law. The implications of this insight are then pursued primarily with regard to remembering. Luther questions the ways we remember by suggesting that the sacrament dis-members before it re-members.

I am able to argue Luther's point not only from his own writing but also from an example in the history of the church: the early church document known as the *Didache*. In the *Didache*, all forms of remembering the Christ event are disseminated. The *Didache* resists the temptation to make the cross something sacred by turning it into a sacrifice. It is as if this early church community recognized that with the term *sacrifice* it would only be trying to control death. Over time, falling to this temptation resulted in the sanctification not of what Jesus accomplished on the cross but of violence. Luther too resists turning the cross—or the Christ event—into a sacrifice. Turning away from the cross as violence, Luther

16

asks this question: How is the event remembered? The surprising answer to his question disrupts both law and, in fact, hermeneutics. The answer pushes the reader toward the sharing of bread and wine as a form of remembering, not as the memory of something past but, rather, as a displaced reliving of what was latent, inaccessible, and absent in the event. That which cannot be known in the event displaces facile remembering; that which confronts us in the event, in experience, is not an object that can be remembered or mastered or theorized. In this reconsideration of remembrance, the rewriting of liturgy has its own beginnings.

In the concluding chapter, remembrance as dissemination is further developed. Dissemination, in popular parlance, has negative connotations—something scattered, dispersed, even incoherent or illogical. And yet, in the *Didache,* for example, the bread is disseminated. The moment of scattering is the moment of promise, promise given. In poststructuralist writing, of course, this dissemination is itself a type of justice. In this chapter, the theological connection is made between dissemination and promise and therefore between liturgy (as dissemination) and grace. The constructive theological move seeks to answer a very simple question: How is the disruptive return to be written (practiced)? Luther attempted an answer by moving away from the notion of event as a simple historical occurrence in a space-time continuum—from event as happening—to an understanding of event as that which continually "returns" (or haunts) in and through ritual, and particularly through the eucharistic celebration. The promise continues to confront the reader/participant through liturgical iteration as addition, as both dissemination and call.

Considering the sacramental act as the encounter with something inaccessible that continually returns, as something that confronts the believer, perhaps frightens or awakens the believer to both a death and a resurrection, allows me to write "that which returns" as grace. Grace is the displacement of God in vulnerability, need, or suffering with which we are continually confronted. Grace is the displacement of all mystical foundation. This grace is the absent thing in every event, the permeability of every context, the dissemination of subject in order to find life through faith alone. The liturgy itself disseminates and disrupts rather than simply remembering, repeating, ritualizing (systematizing), and concluding. Liturgy points to the hole, to the abyss in which the "promise" can be truly promise, truly testament.

Chapter 1

Writing an Event and the Event of Writing

A Haunting Event

AN EVENT HAUNTS THE WRITING OF REFORMATION SCHOLARSHIP. This event, this story of a beginning, is nothing less than the beginning of the Reformation itself. The difficulty of tracing historically a beginning submerges us in the murky waters of tradition and identity. A strong consciousness of identity exists within churches tracing their origin in the Reformation, and yet, as we will see, this origin remains elusive.

The debate, particularly among scholars of Luther and intensifying throughout the twentieth century both in Europe and in North America,[1] attempted to pinpoint, to localize and name, the event that was the turning point in Martin Luther's faith and thought. The unspoken agenda of theologians and historians in pursuing the origin of this particular event suggests a concern (even a worry) to maintain theology's preeminent place in the Reformation narrative. The event, however, has eluded capture. Known as the Reformation breakthrough or Luther's *Turmerlebnis*, it is the story of Luther's supposedly sudden, illuminating insight that occurred during a moment of intense struggle in a room of a tower, an insight that initiated the Reformation and sparked the transformation of the medieval into the modern world. This so-called tower experience continues to raise its head. It continues to haunt Lutheran (and Reformation) scholarship despite a growing consensus near the end of the twentieth century that pinpointing the event to a particular moment in time may be a futile exercise.

The topic proposed here does not have the grandiose hope of resolving this debate once and for all. It even hesitates before stepping into these waters, afraid, perhaps, of drowning. But a question arises nonetheless, a question not about causes and breakthroughs, not about origins and sources of a *Turmerlebnis*, but about simply why this search for the pivotal moment (event) in Luther's life and thought continues to haunt not only Luther's writing but the writing of scholarship? How has an event that remains basically unknown become an event of writing? And even more generally, why does a search for origin persist at all in writing and in life? What are the contours and dynamics of this search?

This question consists of multiple layers. In its more complex form, the question is about the relation between theory and practice, between, in this case, theology and liturgy. In its simplest form, the question is about event and how event is written. There is (or is not) a historical event—that is, something that happened in the course of a life. Life, in its historical expression, consists of a collection of events. But then there is also the event of writing. The writing of event itself becomes an event rather than something that simply represents "what happened" in history. The event of writing often possesses more force than the historical event, for the writing creates a narration that attempts to represent the event through careful repetition and thereby "communicate" its meaning. The writing, in fact, possesses not only the happening of an event but the many possibilities of that event that never materialized historically. Writing opens up the possibility of other options.

Writing itself is caught in the illusion of being able to represent in words something that has had the force of an impact on the writer, especially when this writing is autobiographical. But even when the writing is merely recounting an event as third party, it is subject to a force that it cannot encompass. The inability of writing to "represent" pushes writing into a passive role. The result of this inability of writing results in a sort of revelation: writing as event reveals something that is not captured, something uncontrollable, something that is not understood in the event, something even beyond the intention of the writer. This "something that is not known" continually returns as if inscribed in the writing despite various and ingenious ways (conscious and unconscious) the author may employ in order to control that something in event. Theory (theology) is already destabilized by the actual event of writing.

In the specific case of Luther, we discover the event and the writing of event to be particularly enmeshed. Lutheran scholarship (but also, more generally, academic work on the Reformation and its consequences) has been haunted by the narration of a story—the so-called Reformation breakthrough of "justification through grace by faith alone." Scholarship has been haunted by the story, by the narration of an insight, by something the narration itself cannot explain or capture or pinpoint. The desire to pinpoint an origin, the desire to establish the narrative, is not new either. Traces had already been found as early as the writings of Johannes Bugenhagen, Luther's pastor.[2] Scholarship has been haunted by a narration of its own creation.

The context of Luther's radical proposal—justification through grace by faith alone—is, in fact, the narrative of the human being's relationship to God. With Luther, a major shift occurred in the understanding of this relationship. The story, however, created to ground Luther's proposal in a theological illumination, dilutes the complexity of the event, turning the reader away from the messiness of experience to the simplicity (and attractiveness) of ideas and hagiography. The invented story is in itself rather simple: at some point, Luther turned from his identity as an Augustinian monk to a new identity, that of the great Reformer. Breaking out of the medieval worldview, Luther insisted that it was not by works—not by the things we do, whether those things be labeled spirituality or prayer or liturgy or asceticism or simply good works—that the human would be saved; it was not by human works that a just relationship with God would be found. Justification was a work of God—a gift of faith. God establishes the just relationship.[3]

We will leave aside for the moment the content of this so-called "insight" in order first to examine how the narrative of justification by faith alone has been appropriated—not by Luther, whose narrative was continually disrupted by events, but by theologians and historians of the Reformation. How has it happened that the narrative of justification by faith alone has in one case (Luther's) been disrupted by events and in another case (the writing of Lutheran scholarship) been reinforced by and imposed on events? Lutheran scholarship has written the narrative and then sought its verification in the events of history as if the writing were always a faithful representation of what "actually happened." The narrative, as defined by scholars, has given rise to much debate and many publications—and rightly so, for it is as if the scholarship mirrors the ambiguity of Luther's own narration. Luther's writing witnesses to a disruption of the narrative, a disruption of event, of context and subject. Luther's writing refocuses or re-situates, even rewrites, what is commonly understood as the conscious subject acting (*event-ing*) in an established and knowable context. Luther's rewriting is event itself, not the event of a breakthrough but the event of faith, the event of a continual becoming. The question that is then posed is the following: What writing is appropriate for the event? What writing translates justification by faith alone without inserting it once again into fossilized structures and knowable contexts?

Event obviously cannot be approached as a simple, "historical" occurrence. The still-murky waters of Lutheran scholarship preclude the illusion. Rather, the question about event is approached as a question about writing and what I will call the grammar of event. A new grammar must be sought, one that does not attempt to represent or communicate or faithfully (authentically!) copy the event but a grammar, an approach, if you will, that may permit the event to become for us.

The sources, therefore, for our study are not in the events of Martin Luther's life (as if these could be known to us) but in his writing. This may seem self-evident: some would argue that we can have access to the events of Luther's life only through his (and other) writing. I want to argue that, through the writing, we have access only to the event of writing and a grammar that is marked on the writing that permits something to irrupt, something that reader and writing cannot control. Writing as event has inscribed within it the complex possibilities of the story it is relating. All of these possibilities, even those unrealized possibilities, remain to haunt the text. Therefore, a particularly intense analysis will be made of Luther's language and his own struggle or confrontation with event and grammar (writing), of disruption and the force of "something" that continually returns, that continually irrupts through the text.

Event, for Luther, is not a simple occurrence in time and space; event contains traces of something else, something inaccessible. This "something else" is different from what has been called a hidden meaning or a spiritual sense of an event or text. The something that returns in event and in the written text resists any form of systematization and leads to a disruption of meaning as it is classically understood. Luther's own writing witnesses to this resistance as he reverses a traditional narrative of meaning and as he redefines insight or illumination with notions of struggle and confrontation (and even temptation). Luther turns to experience—more specifically, Luther turns to the liturgy and liturgical language—as a language of confrontation and resistance to theory. This turn to practice, to experience, is not as easily recognizable; it is, in fact, often ignored by scholars who continually attempt to resystematize

Luther's understanding of event through the invented narration of the discovery of justification by faith alone. Unfortunately, the invention of an origin and its narration have consequentially narrowed the meaning of promise.

How does Luther understand event? Of course, Luther is not concerned with event as philosophical category. In the end, he is concerned with only one event—the Christ event—and how this event continually returns to disrupt all construed meanings, all our invented narratives. Through liturgy and liturgical language, Luther witnesses to a force that cannot be theorized but that continually returns in writing and in life.

disrupts our created/devious identities

An Irreversible Narrative Is Reversed

Claims to greatness are usually held suspiciously, especially by those who are subjects of those claims. But I will contend that one of the scholars of Luther and the late medieval period, Heiko A. Oberman, has influenced more than any other the study of Luther over the past half century. His breadth of knowledge, his ability to trace the many nuances within the Reformer's thought, his "geographer's" perspective surveying all the tributaries leading to the great river that is the Reformation, continue to push scholars deeper into Luther's theology. In one of his major books, *Luther: Man between God and the Devil*, Oberman effectively put an end to the debate concerning the Reformation breakthrough.[4] He argued that "Luther's theology cannot be reduced to a single point," that his theology is continually "invigorated and stimulated by the joy of discovery."[5] Oberman argues that there is not a special moment in Luther's itinerary when he moved from being monk to self-confident Reformer.[6] However, despite Oberman's denial of a single breakthrough, the notion of a "discovery" remains operative in his writing. Oberman cannot resist the temptation to pinpoint a "major" discovery (the understanding of the text of Rom. 1:17). "It is in the year 1519; the Reformation 'discovery' of justification by faith has been clearly expressed and worked out."[7] Perhaps Oberman's own amazing ability to trace Luther's thought in its connection and its disconnection from medieval thought sustained Oberman in his belief that there was still a discovery (even if not just "one" discovery)—the discovery of a certitude in Luther's faith and expressed in Luther's writing.

23

Why does the question of the Reformation breakthrough surface persistently in Oberman's writing? References to "Headwaters of the Reformation," "Roots and Ramification," "Reformation Breakthrough," "*Initia Lutheri—Initia Reformationis,*" and "*Immo: Luthers reformatorische Entdeckungen*" repeatedly appear in the titles of his articles, chapters, and books and within the subtext of his many writings.[8] Even a posthumous publication carries the title "Luther and the *Via Moderna*: The Philosophical Backdrop of the Reformation Breakthrough."[9] Despite Oberman's own insistence on the impossibility of pinpointing "one" all-inclusive, all-conclusive moment, the elusive and haunting, the disruptive event, continues to resurface in his writing. The "event" is never fully contained or controlled by Oberman's erudition. His writing betrays his attempt (and the predicament of Reformation scholarship in general—for is not the "breakthrough" or event being sought the reader's own?[10]) at situating the event of the breakthrough or *Turmerlebnis* within the logocentric cloister—a cloister Luther himself attempts to demolish.

In an article written before his popular book *Luther: Man Between God and the Devil*, Oberman develops the theme of a breakthrough with considerable nuance.[11] He suggests that Luther's "breakthrough" is to be found not when Luther first writes about "freely given (unearned) justification in a reforming vein," nor in any so-called tower experience, but when Luther is finally able to fully develop and reconcile within his own faith and thought a distinction important to the nominalist tradition—the distinction between two spheres.[12] One sphere is named variously nature, world, or experience; the other sphere, theology.

Nominalism is itself a part of this narration because of its important role in Luther's intellectual development and struggle. Nominalism (and we use the term broadly, aware of the debate surrounding its definition) was already, long before Luther, a disruptive element in medieval thought. Moving away from the overriding notion of an *analogia entis* (as if there were a continuum of being between God and the created world), nominalism insisted much more on God's utter transcendence. Therefore, to understand God's relation to the world, it was necessary to understand the exercise of God's will. The human creature is utterly dependent on this will, but this will is known only through what God has ordained (creation and its laws).

The difficult task of comprehending God's volition necessitated an imaginary distinction, purely rational but porous. The distinction was invented to account for God's totally free acts in the world. These free acts of God were not to be understood as unexpected acts (they do not crush or annul human liberty) but as acts that, though devoid of necessity, still obeyed certain laws. The imagined construct, the invented distinction between the absolute and ordained power of God,[13] permitted them to argue against any form of necessity in God's action.[14] God is free to act as God wishes (*potentia absoluta*), but God has chosen to act in a particular way through the events and laws of creation (*potentia ordinata*). God is no longer related to creation by deterministic causation. God is related to it by volition, by God's personal decision, rather than by metaphysical arguments based on necessary causal links.[15] This distinction predates the nominalists, but with William of Occam, a reversal (not a negation) is reached: the distinction secures the contingent nature of history rather than simply denying necessity to God. The contingent nature of history signifies that "what God actually did *de potentia ordinata* was not "ontologically necessary."[16] In other words, events simply represent the realized will of God. This does not imply "an arbitrary suppression of human agency" but is a way in which medieval thinkers accounted for God's acts in history.[17]

Though the things and events of history are denied ontological necessity, they remain important as realizations of God's will. They are the means by which the human being knows something of God. In other words, experience in the world receives much greater value, whereas universals as categories of knowing, and especially as categories of knowing God, are diminished. Universals as categories by which God is defined are disrupted by events as they are experienced. Oberman characterizes this point as growing out of a hunger for reality, a hunger that revolts against "the meta-world of heteronomous reality."[18]

One consequence of the imaginary (rational) distinction is the development of two different grammars used to understand or discover God's will—experience/nature on the one hand and theology on the other. They are distinguished primarily through their relation to things (*res*)— history, experience, events. For nominalists, words are understood as "'natural signs' rather than as reverberations of the eternal logos."[19] They are thereby cut off or cleansed from unfounded speculative connotations. They are liberated to "mean" or refer according to context. As

Oberman points out, this freedom opens a new way of relating to the world. We "discern a novel understanding of the way to access information, now geared toward the reliable identification of the singularity of each object of observation *(cognitio particularis rei)*."[20]

What we will retain from Oberman's observation is his use of the terms *access* and *identification*. Access—implying an opening or passage—suggests that meaning or information is discernible within or communicated through *res*. This notion of access to meaning is certainly legitimate and probably unquestioned by nominalist philosophers, for they operated in a universe in which meaning is still attainable if not through metaphysical constructs then through words or experience. Words still refer to something (things, experience, events). This access is closely linked to the identification of the singularity of things. The singularity of an "object of observation" is accessible. In other words, the uniqueness of the *res* is comprehensible to reason. Again, this is not surprising in a world where, philosophically, *res* is still a referent containing meaning. Singularity is itself a conduit, a way of access, to something else. In the worldly sphere, nominalists have perhaps redefined the authority of context and experience but they have not broken out of the mold of logocentric authority, that is, the authority which demands that words refer directly (or have "access") to a reality, hidden or revealed.

What about the theological sphere? We need to return to Oberman's earlier publication. Seeking fresh sources, Oberman leaves behind him the exegetical works (especially Luther's commentary on the Romans and his second Psalm commentary) and discovers the Luther of the Table Talks—the more informal Luther in discussion and reminiscence. In the Table Talks, Luther distinguishes the two spheres epistemologically.[21] In the worldly sphere, clear reason *(ratio evidens)* "exerts its influence."[22] Clear reason is the "discoverer and guide of all things and people" *(inventrix et gubernatrix omnium)*.[23] Reason is knowledge of the world based on demonstrable facts of experience.[24] "In the sphere of the world, experience makes our perception possible, sharpens it and provides the foundation for our understanding."[25] Oberman contends that Luther champions reason in a far more radical way than Lutheran scholars who wish to uphold *sola scriptura* want to recognize. In the theological sphere, however, the human being first submits to God's word. This submission and assent *(assensus)* precede experience.[26] There is an initial assent to God's revelation—a fundamental trust in God's revelation—that then seeks verification within the realm of experience. Luther's reformation "breakthrough," according to Oberman, occurred when he was finally able to make the connection, when his assent to God's revelation (God's word) was connected or verified ("secondly"— but only secondly) with the grammar of God's word (Holy Scripture). According to Oberman: "The real breakthrough required both justification by faith and its exegetically verifiable foundation in the Word."[27] Oberman reads Luther's breakthrough as the moment in which Luther is able to connect the two spheres of experience and theology and yet conceptually maintain their distinction. Revelation, in other words, finds authentification within experience.

"The irreversible sequence leading from assent (that is, the living obedience of faith) to 'grammar' (faithfulness to Scripture) made Luther a reformer."[28] In relating Luther's breakthrough to the nominalist distinction of two spheres, Oberman establishes the breakthrough or discovery in two stages: assent and verification. What is of concern is the subsequent distinction between assent and verification as if they formed a pattern, a chronologically definable connection, a sequence, an ascent into God's meaning (though not a mystical or hierarchical ascent as in the work of Pseudo-Dionysius but, rather, an ascent through experience but an ascent nonetheless). Meaning is verified in and through experience and only then does it become valid.

This sequence or connection apparently bridges a gap—a gap between theology and the world, a gap between faith and reason, a gap between a life in faith and verification in Scripture. What demands, however, some attention is not immediately the two terms of the sequence (assent and verification) but, rather, the figure of speech "irreversible sequence." The metaphor of sequence itself—sequence as possibility, as possible continuum, as possible access to a deeper meaning, as possible reference to a hidden source, as possible reference even to God (God's word)—surprises us. How are we to understand this "irreversible sequence"—not, first of all, in Luther's writing but in Heiko Oberman's writing? Oberman suggests that Luther actually breaks the distinction between the two spheres by *connecting* them, by establishing a link between them, by lifting up experience (object, person, thing, event). Yet Oberman's writing continues to operate as if the two spheres were still rationally distinct and preestablished in a hierarchical relation.

Experience remains only a secondary term, only a place, a location of verification.

Oberman, in this particular article, does not refer to the distinction between *potentia Dei absoluta* and *potentia Dei ordinata*, yet I believe it is functioning as a backdrop or subtext to the main performance. The notion of *assensus* to God's word, submission to God's revelation as something that precedes all experience, suggests that this revelation is itself independent of the things of the world. The *assensus* opens the door, perhaps unknowingly, to a divine revelation not contingent on experience. Only under this condition, only as the move from an absolute *(res)* to a contingent *(res)*, can this sequence be "irreversible." That this assent operates within the realm of the *potentia Dei ordinata*, that this assent to God's revelation operates within the created world, does not matter. The *assensus* as such falls within a sequence, or, more accurately, the *assensus* is at the origin of a sequence—a necessarily irreversible sequence—that leads from the "living obedience of faith" to a faithfulness to Scripture or "grammar."[29] The possibility of this *assensus* reestablishes a chronological sequence, even hinting at a hierarchy. All of this, once again, leads to the temptation of pinpointing Luther's breakthrough as a specific illumination of the divine sphere. As we will see in the next section, Luther does not connect the two realms but, in blurring their distinction, eliminates them.

A caveat, however, does need to be mentioned. In a posthumous publication, Oberman writes that the "God who acts"—that is, the God who acts without necessity yet according to the laws Godself has established in the ordained world—becomes for Luther the "God who acts in Christ." This is the foundation of Luther's *theologia crucis*. This God is unpredictable, contrary to reason, foiling systematic search, and against expectation.[30] The *assensus*, then, could be reformulated as *assensus* not to divine revelation as absolute, originary, source of irreversibility but as *assensus* to the unexpected, in event and particularly in the Christ event. Oberman opens this possibility, curiously, in absentia, with a dead voice.

At this stage in our reflection, we need to ask whether Luther's thought even fits the irreversible sequence *(unumkehrbare Abfolge)* as proposed in the earlier essay, for Oberman's idea of an irreversible sequence, more than his posthumous writing, has influenced Lutheran scholarship and our understanding of the Reformation breakthrough.

We need to ask whether Luther, indebted as he was to the nominalist distinction of the two spheres, is not, in fact, blurring the distinction between a worldly sphere and the sphere of theology? This blurring is not to be found as much in Luther's affirmations as in the strange use of words and certain tropes that continually reappear in his writing, carrying with them multiple syntagmatic possibilities and continually disrupting our reading.

This is particularly true for a passage that serves Oberman as a subtext for the idea of an irreversible sequence. Luther is recorded in a Table Talk as follows: "In nature, experience is the cause on account of which we hear, and it precedes assent; in theology however experience follows assent, it does not precede it."[31] Here, Luther apparently acknowledges a sequence. With regards to God's word, *assensus* does precede experience. But in the world, this sequence is reversed—as Oberman points out. Luther apparently proposes two different paradigms: there is one sequence that moves from experience to assent, and another that moves from assent to experience. These sequences exist as independent spheres with contrary movements that must not be overlapped. It is also to be noted that Oberman characterizes only the second sequence (from assent to experience) as "irreversible."

Three words in this text, however, illustrate how Luther blurs the spheres rather than reinforcing their distinctiveness—*experiential* (experience), *audiamus* (hearing), and *assensus* (assent). What concerns us first of all is Luther's understanding of *experientia* in the theological sphere. According to Oberman, the "living obedience of faith" leads irreversibly to the grammar of God's word (faithfulness to Scripture). The discovery of this sequence from assent to verification brings Luther to the Reformation breakthrough.[32] The second stage of the irreversible sequence (the verification of the assent) happens when God's revelation is confirmed, if you will, in and through the grammar of God's word as revealed in Scripture or biblical discourse or "faithfulness to Scripture." *Experientia* is here understood by Oberman to be revelation's faithfulness to Scripture, faithfulness to the text, to the words, the grammar of the text, faithfulness to experience. Luther, however, uses only the word *experientia*.

Experience is a component in both parts of Luther's statement. It is part of the worldly sphere, and it is part of the theological sphere. There is a metaphor of journey implied in both sequences. We move from experience to assent in the world, but in theology we move from assent to experience. Assent, however, has obviously two different meanings. In the one case, it is caused by the experience(s). In the other case, it simply precedes experience.

This distinction is crucial. In the one case, assent is an act of the will that has come to a particular conclusion based on experience. In the other case, assent is simply something that precedes, something that is "given," perhaps even imposed. It is not an act of will. It is, however, "followed" by experience—that is, it becomes known through experience.

What becomes clear is that the term *experience* is the same in both the worldly sphere and the theological sphere. There is not one type of experience in the worldly sphere and another type in the theological sphere. Luther forces the reader, through a parallelism, to be aware of a similarity, a point of contact, between the two spheres. In both spheres, experience is a confrontation with "hard reality"; it can be an intellectual, spiritual, or physical struggle, but it is also a struggle with things, events, people. And therefore, in the theological sphere, *experientia* must be read more broadly: not only as the grammar of God's word but the grammar of event *(res)*, the grammar of experience in the world that strangely makes assent possible!

The important role of this grammar of experience, this grammar of *event*, is reinforced by the curious appearance of the verb *audio (audiamus* in Luther's text)—"we hear." Experience in the world leads us to hearing; it almost necessitates a listening. But "hearing" is, of course, also crucial to Luther's understanding of the communication of God's word. Faith is born of hearing. As Luther writes: "That entire book [Acts of the Apostles] treats of nothing else than that the Holy Spirit is not given through the Law but is given through the hearing of the Gospel. For when Peter preached, the Holy Spirit immediately fell upon all those who heard the Word."[33] Hearing, for Luther, is a liturgical verb. It is in preaching that the assembly "hears" the word of God and comes to faith. Experience in the world is hearing, and this hearing can lead to assent. But why not simply state that "experience" leads to reasoning, which leads to assent. Why use the verb *audiamus? Audiamus* in this short phrase is particular to experience in the world, yet it is the verb for Luther that occasions assent. "Hearing" is the verb par excellence of the revelation of the word of God. Even though *audiamus* does not appear in Luther's statement as part of the theological sphere, it is nonetheless "heard" as the passive assent to God's word, the means by which God's word reaches the heart. The all-too-tight distinction (and sequence) between the two spheres is obviously blurred, disturbed by, in this case, Luther's introduction of a liturgical word.

Assensus has already been mentioned, though, besides its entwined relationship with *experientia,* it too has liturgical connotations. What is entailed with the gesture of *assensus?* There is, in the worldly sphere, an assent by reason to experience. But then there is, in the theological sphere, an assent to God's revelation. Oberman describes this assent as *"das Beugen vor Gottes Offenbarung."*[34] The published English translation renders this as "submission to God's revelation."[35] The English lures the German back into the realm of incorporeity: submission, surrendering as intellectual or spiritual function—into the purely systematic theological sphere. Oberman, however, writes *"das Beugen"*—a bowing down. The text calls upon a liturgical act, an act of the body (in Luther's text, "hearing"; in Oberman's text, "bowing down"). Oberman uses the bodily metaphor of bowing down to describe the *assensus* in the theological sphere. We would have expected it in the worldly sphere. The unexpectedness of this metaphor disturbs Oberman's text, disturbs the meaning of the irreversible sequence. *Assensus* is not assent to *res* as "substance" (as in the English translation) but assent to words, things, event—assent to *experientia.*

Assent translated as "submission" to God's revelation, assent understood as originating an irreversible sequence (in the theological sphere), once again makes possible a vision of eternal substance or essence. Oberman's use of *assensus* as part of an irreversible sequence opens the possibility of an access to an absolute realm. It reestablishes a hierarchy and even, indirectly, an *analogia entis.* But it is precisely this metaphysical vision and hierarchy that Luther attempts to tear down. When assent becomes part of an irreversible sequence—when even experience becomes part of that sequence—then the old law, the *analogia entis,* is maintained. For Luther, is not assent the obedience of faith as *Beugen,* as bowing down? Is it not an assent to boundaries and therefore an assent, even a submission, to experience, events, grammar? This assent is not a bowing down before an absolute divine revelation but a bowing down before the God who acts in Jesus Christ, the God who acts in history, the God who acts in words, through things, through event. It is the God who acts, as Oberman himself finally points out, "against expectation." There is a profound contrast between the ordered, lawlike regularity of nature, the hidden meaning (substance) of words (understood as God's revelation), and the unpredictable events of salvation history. The former (*res* as substance) is *lex;* the latter (*res* as event) is *libertas.*

Reading and Singing Words

The blurring of the two spheres that eventually leads Luther to find *libertas* on the side of the *res,* the *historia,* even the grammar, is brought to the foreground in another passage Oberman cites (though it must be noted that in Oberman's text the passage serves as the basis for his insight into the "irreversible sequence").

Many of Luther's writings portray the movement of assent to verification as laden with intense struggle.[36] Experience seems almost synonymous with inner conflict.[37] In certain autobiographical moments, Luther expresses this struggle not in intellectual but in emotional terms—for example, he "hated" the words *iustitia Dei;* they were words of condemnation from which he wanted to run away. This struggle has been woven into a narrative by church historians: a "man" is presented, a restless conscience; Luther, consumed by a desire to find peace and certitude, was someone caught in the paradox of God's revelation as both condemning and yet comforting.

Perhaps here, based on this image of Luther's restless conscience, we discover why scholars and popular hagiography still cling to the idea of a definite breakthrough, of an illuminating insight: there is a desire—even in the reader—to find a resolution to the struggle. Oberman, as we have seen, still localizes the breakthrough to a particular moment in time when "Luther succeeds in connecting his 'assent' *(assensus)* to God's word with the 'grammar' *(grammatica)* of God's word."[38] This is the framework of the irreversible sequence.

But what does Luther actually say? And how has it been translated? One of the Table Talks (around 1540) records Luther in this way (since the German is important to the subsequent analysis, I am keeping it in the body of the text and not in a footnote):

Da ich erstlich im psalmen lass und sang[!][39]: *In iustitia Dei tua libera me!,* da erschrak ich alle mal und war den worten feindt: *Iustitia Dei, iudicium Dei, opus Dei,* denn ich wust nichts anders, *iustitia Dei* hies sein gestreng gericht. Nuhn solt er mich noch [nach] sein gestrengen gericht erretten? So wer ich ewig verloren! Aber *misericordia Dei, adiutorium Dei,* die wortt hett ich lieber. Gott lob, da ich die *res* verstunde und wiste, das *iustitia Dei* heiss *iustitia, qua nos iustificat per donatam iustitiam in Christo Ihesu,* da verstunde ich die *grammatica,* und schmeckt mir erst der Psalter.[40]

And the translation used in the English edition of Oberman's essay:

Since I first read and sang [!] in the psalm: "In your righteousness [*iustitia*], set me free!" I shrank back and was an enemy to the words: "the righteousness of God," "the judgment of God," "the work of God"; for I knew nothing other but that the righteousness of God meant his stern judgment. And should I now be saved according to this his stern judgment? If so, I should be eternally lost! But "God's mercy" and "God's help"—those words pleased me better. God be praised that I understood the substance and knew that the righteousness of God meant justice, by which we are justified through the righteousness given in Christ Jesus. Then did I understand the grammar [*grammatica*], and only then was the psalter sweet to me.[41]

In the classical portrayal, Luther, as person, as a conscious self, remains the subject of both the text and the history, of both the narration of the event and the event itself as a localized moment in space and time. Luther, in this privileged portrayal, becomes the discoverer of an irreversible, nonnegotiable sequence; he climbs the very ladder he wishes to deconstruct. The "irreversible sequence" reestablishes a hierarchy between the *assensus* and the *grammatica.* Yes, God is still revealed in the *grammatica* but only "at a second stage."[42] That the sequence is irreversible also frames the sequence within a chronology: there is a temporal succession of events from assent to grammar, from assent to verification. Luther assents; "then" Luther verifies. When the verification is successful, Luther has reached his breakthrough understanding of God's justice.

According to the English translation of this text, Luther is the subject of a struggle leading to a breakthrough. After much anguish ("Since"—at first, Luther shrank away and found himself an enemy of the words *iustitia Dei*), "God be praised 'that' I understood the substance." At some point, Luther understood the "substance," "then" he understood the grammar, and "only then" was the Psalter sweet. The English translation clearly suggests a progression through time (created linguistically by a series of the word *then*). There is a sequential movement. Luther advances from a state of anguish to a moment when the Psalter is sweet again. Luther appears to be reflecting on his own progression (from assent?) toward the verification in Scripture toward the breakthrough in faith and understanding.

I believe, however, that the irreversible sequence is not as evident in the German/Latin text. In fact, what we discover in this autobiographical text is, once again, a distinct blurring of the sequence (just as there is a blurring of the two languages—German and Latin—within the text). This blurring will be heightened when we examine Luther's major autobiographical writing, the *Preface to the Complete Edition of Luther's Latin Writings*, in chapter 2. Assent is, in our present text, not assent to eternal truth communicated through a special, divine revelation to the believer but assent to the events *(res)* through which God reveals God's self. Assent is not simply assent to "substance" but assent to both substance and grammar. Assent arises from the midst of the struggle with the grammar, with the "event" that is the text of the Psalms. This struggle is Luther's experience (the grammar, the word intersecting with his life). The grammar itself provokes inner conflict.

Here, in this text, the moment of imagined communication with God or with God's revelation—the event of prayer—is primarily expressed as the struggle with words, as a confrontation. Luther is not only reading and studying the words but also praying the words (and, in the monastic context, singing the words in the Liturgy of Hours). Luther is addressing the words to someone, to God. But despite this reading and this singing of the words, they remained incomprehensible. The words confronted Luther with a certain meaninglessness, that is, with something inaccessible. This inaccessibility, this absence, confronted both the reader and the singer. It was only through the confrontation, through the dispute with words—with grammar—that Luther was brought to a point ("God be praised!" in Luther's words) of understanding the *res,* of understanding experience (*res* as event, grammar, thing). Only in that confrontation with experience did Luther discover again the sweetness of the words.

Two words in this text and one word absent from this text will again retain our attention. The German *da* and the Latin *res* are both present; *assensus* (the critical term of the irreversible sequence) is absent.

The German text portrays a different space, a questionable sequence. One word is repeated four times—a word of seemingly little importance, though Oberman himself has shown that theological significance can reside even in a simple adverb.[43] Luther uses the word *da* four times. In the English text, it serves as a basis for the irreversible sequence. In the German, I believe, its function varies according to the sentence.

The word *da* in German does not primarily or necessarily denote a temporal relation between objects or events.[44] *Da*, as a demonstrative pronoun, designates place or situation (*örtlichkeit*),[45] though, secondarily, it can also designate an earlier time or event. When Luther writes, *"Da ich erstlich im psalmen lass und sang,"* he is describing (yes) an earlier situation in which the reading and the singing of psalms confronted him with certain words in a certain place, words in the Psalter and in the choir. With the second use of *da* (*". . . da erschrak ich alle mal"*), Luther describes the impasse: *in* the reading and *in* the singing, confronted with the words *iustitia Dei*, he shrank away from the Psalms. *Da*—there, in that situation of private study and communal singing, Luther became an enemy to the words; he struggled with the words.[46] Luther struggles with the imprisonment of words within an ordered system of meaning. And he hates this captivity. He hates these words and their imposed meaning.

The word *da* gives special attention to that particular situation. *Da* is a metaphor of place. There—in reading and singing, in the Psalter and in the choir—"there" I was afraid. "There" I found myself in opposition to the words "justice of God." "There" I found myself eternally condemned. Luther struggled with these different expressions—*iustitia Dei, iudicium Dei, opus Dei*—the event of words confronted him. Though he could paradigmatically place these words next to one another—one over the other—he could not replace these words with words more pleasing to him, such as *misericordia Dei* or *adiutorium Dei*, "God's mercy" and "God's help." The word *da*, as Luther uses it in this text, encapsulates the confrontation. This confrontation with words, for Luther, is not the struggle with "meaning" as "substance"—ultimate, eternal (theological) value. The struggle is with a system in which the words are caught. The struggle with words then becomes the struggle with what the words reveal and hide *for Luther,* with what is present and absent in the words that affects Luther's situation. It is a struggle to contextualize meaning, a struggle to find a new grammar over and against the conventional, official (culturally defined) meaning these words (and especially their underlying theological concepts) had acquired.

And then, in the text, praise be God, *da*—that (there) I (Luther) understood the *res* ("there") in this place, in this story, in the events of this life, in history, in the literal sense *(sensus litteralis);* I understood the passive justice of Christ. "There" I understood the *grammatica.* There, for the first time, did I taste how sweet the Psalter is. There is not a move from assent to verification. Luther does not discover a "substance" out there somewhere and then find its justification within the text. No, Luther discovers what the words could mean for him now. Luther discovers a freedom within the words and is able to free the words from their ordered universe. Luther discovers, we might say, the working of the Spirit in the very struggle with the text.

But what is this "substance"? At some point, Luther understood the *res.* At some point, something happened. "Gott lob, da ich die *res* verstunde." Something happened that allowed Luther to understand—but understand what? Here, one would expect to find the word *assensus*—if this were truly an irreversible sequence—but all we find is the liturgical act of praising God and the discovery of a *sweetness. Assensus* is absent. Instead, we find that Oberman inserts into the German text (and faithfully reproduced in the English translation) an exclamation mark: "Da ich erstlich im psalmen lass und sang[!]" Oberman should not be surprised that Luther would not only be reading but also singing the psalms—he was an Augustinian monk following the Liturgy of the Hours. I want to argue that the exclamation mark reveals Oberman's own surprise, embodied within the text, that the sequence is not irreversible—and, even more importantly, that the consequence of the assent is not a rational verification but the sweetness of the Psalter! The reading and the singing precede the assent! The confrontation with words precedes the living obedience of faith. Confrontation (and verification) with words and event is not a secondary (or even negative) experience; it is not a confrontation with "shadows" of the real but confrontation itself as assent, as prayer.

The confrontation or the dispute, the *auseinandersetzung,* was perhaps not primarily conceived linguistically even if Luther expresses the struggle as a struggle with words, with grammar. The words *iustitia Dei* confronted Luther in a place of prayer—in reading and singing. Confrontation with words was like a liturgical act. While Luther was struggling with the words, he was also writing his second Psalm commentary, *Operationes in Psalmos*.[47] In this commentary, prayer or meditation are defined as confrontation. Meditation is to be caught in a dispute with words, in a verbal exercise.[48]

This reflection on words, this dispute or discussion, this "setting out of words," even this scattering of words: this exercise with words characterizes prayer. Prayer then as *sermocinari*, as discussion, is prayer as confrontation with God's word. This confrontation occurs because "meaning" itself is being redefined: meaning, substance, is not to be discovered lurking behind words as the hidden, spiritual, and eternally true signification. The only definition of meaning provided by Luther in this passage is the experience of sweetness. Something escapes words; something is perhaps scattered by words; something is hidden in *res*— not behind, not underneath, as if the *res* were just a covering or a shell (for that would take us back to the irreversible sequence) but something in *res* itself—the thing, the event, experience, which eludes capture, remains mysterious, confronts the reader and singer and establishes prayer.

But what is *res?* How does Luther understand *res?* The English of the Table Talk translates *res* with "substance" (once again translating a bilingual text into one language). Perhaps this anomaly of translation is justified by Oberman's own suggestion (in the German text) that this passage would indicate Luther's adherence more to the *via antiqua* than to nominalism. Oberman suggests that, on the surface, this text apparently implies that there is a hidden layer of meaning that was first revealed and then demanded to be uncovered in the text. He cites another passage from the Table Talks in which Luther writes: "Res sunt praeceptores. Qui non intelligit res, non potest ex verbis sensum elicere."[49] Again, the published English translation states: "Things are teachers. Anyone who does not understand the substance will be unable to tease meaning out of the words."[50] Understood as part of the *via antiqua,* this translation may stand, but understood in the context of Luther's struggle with words, with God's word, with *res*, must we not translate it as follows: "Things (or referents) are teachers. Whoever does not understand the thing (referent), cannot draw out the sense from the words." Understanding the *res* is understanding not its essential quality or property but its paradigmatic possibilities and *assenting* to the possibilities and what, perhaps, they *do not relate*.

Within the autobiographical text of the Table Talk, the "discovery," for Luther, consists in the realization—in the assent (as the unnamed act)—to *iustitia Dei* as *iustitia in Christo Ihesu,* an assent to justice as gift, an assent to gift, assent *as* gift. The justice of God is known as God's mercy—mercy experienced, mercy revealed, mercy as Gospel. Luther realizes what amounts to a grammatical experience: the *"res"* to which the words referred was not eternally established in some mystical foundation. Luther is radically rewriting the word *res,* putting incredible pressure on its definition as "thing." In his move from the active understanding of God's justice to the passive understanding of God's justice (justice imputed to us through Christ), Luther moves from an understanding of experience as an act of the will (seeking verification in text, word, and so forth) to an understanding of experience as something through which God confronts the believer, experience as a place of presence and absence (a place of struggle). Experience and meaning are inextricably entwined and not on separate extremes of an irreversible sequence. Meaning is no longer eternally established and valid to be ferreted out from behind or within words, and therefore words themselves could be cut off from their ostensive definitions, their referents. Words are freed from acquired meanings. The struggle with words, the confrontation with the *res,* the freedom won from acquired, so-called eternal meaning allowed Luther to discover the sweetness of the words, of the Psalter, the sweetness of the *res* as free acts, event, things, in the world through which God, the Holy Spirit, reveals something about God. The sweetness is, of course, the discovery of the gospel in the midst of this confrontation with words. The sweetness is the Holy Spirit assenting to experience. It is incarnational. This is the location of the third *da,* which the English sequentially translates as "that"—"that I understood."

"There," however, Luther made the gargantuan linguistic and theological shift to the grammar of the Gospel, to the grammar of God's word.

A Liturgical Cry

The act of assent is absent in this text. I hope that, by now, this is not surprising. What is surprising, however, is the appearance of a different dynamic, something that, in a way, God is called upon. God makes an entry into the text not as object of study but as subject of praise and prayer. A liturgical appeal replaces assent. The appeal to God in the text, the entry of God into the text, happens at the moment of understanding the *res* of God's justice. The third *da* announces an advent; it opens up a space, or writes something absent, something for which God can only be praised, something that does not fit into an irreversible sequence. As something absent (even unwritten), this third *da* disturbs the notion of irreversible sequence. What Luther understood and knew *(verstunde und wiste)* was that the event of God's justice could not be captured linguistically, conceptually, systematically, philosophically, even theologically in the world, by the world. The event of God's justice—the *grammar* of God's justice—witnesses to something absent, something that cannot be contained, something that turns the believer to prayer, something that is apprehended only by faith.

The confrontation with words, the dispute, the discussion, the prayer brought Luther to the understanding that the grammar of event (in this particular Table Talk, we could even say the *grammatica* of the *res*) would not lead to speculative conclusions about, for example, God's active justice in the world (a justice that condemned all people for all are sinners). These speculative conclusions simply made God and God's justice part of human knowledge and human will. Rather, the grammar of event pointed to that which the words could not contain, that which thought could not systematize, that which continually irrupted, unexpectedly. The *grammatica theologica* confronts the reader with the *re absente*. *"Verba enim spiritus sunt annunciata de re absente et non apparente, per fidem apprehendenenda."*[51] The words of the spirit announce an absent thing, not to be seen (disruption of the senses) but apprehended by faith. The *grammatica* that Luther claims to have discovered—the grammar of event—was nothing less than the *re absente* (the absent thing) inscribed within event (in this case, within writing)—an absence that continually irrupts and confronts the subject, rendering human faculties passive and receptive because this absence is nothing less than the work of the Holy Spirit. It is of God. The *res absens* is inscribed in the events of human life, written in human hearts, and witnessed as disruption. The *res* of God's justice, for example, is that *iustitia, qua nos iustificat per donatam iustitiam in Christo Ihesu:* that justice by which we are justified through the lived justice of Jesus Christ. It is a justice that is given, inscribed, written, and to which we are called to witness (not create). This is the justice revealed in the gospel (Rom. 1:17). And this is the grammar of event, the grammar of Scripture—*grammatica theologica*.

Within that confrontation, within that event (of writing), within that something for which God is praised, within that liturgical act, Luther finally understood the grammar of the gospel, the confluence of words. "Da verstunde ich die *grammatica* . . ." *Da* (the fourth *da*)—"there," not "then," not after the event, not after understanding the *res* of God's justice as if understanding sequentially followed the event but *in* the event, Luther understood the grammar. The *grammatica* and the *res* are intimately connected. The *da* includes both the situation that is closed in on itself, shut up, blocked (the confrontation—the active situation) and the situation in which something is unblocked (the passive situation). The *da* encompasses both the restlessness of a desire (the desire to know a beginning that cannot be known) and the "coming back," the return to a place of rest. The discovery Luther "makes" or the insight he "has" occurs within the *da*—not beyond the da in some heavenly realm but in the situation of confrontation. It occurs within the *grammar* of Scripture.

If "assent" is at all present, it is in Luther's realization, in his assent to the impossibility of moving beyond the *da,* the impossibility of moving beyond the entanglement of history, grammar, event. The *"da"* is itself witness to this impossibility. In this particular Table Talk, Luther expresses his relation to a text—the Psalter read and sung, a text both written and oral—a relation that shifted from finding the words hateful to finding them sweet. What happened in that shift was not an irreversible sequence but a struggle with *res* understood as event, thing, words. In this struggle, in this experience, a theological grammar emerges that is no longer allegory (theology striving to uncover the veil to reveal hiding meaning) but a grammar that points continually to something absent. In that confrontation and in that discovery, the Psalter became sweet again. This discovery is described not as an "understanding" of the Psalter but as the discovery of a sweetness. It is the discovery not of a content or substance or meaning but of something that cannot be possessed, the discovery of a *res absens*, the discovery of something absent within event, word, thing.

This new grammar of God's word, this new theological grammar, points continually to something absent. Luther abandons the "hidden" meaning of words (as if grammar took us ever deeper into some type of spiritual and more "true" reality) and rests in a grammar of event that is continually disruptive. In this grammar, Luther discovers not a substance, not an eternal truth, not God in the highest heavens, but a sweetness. And here, in this sweetness, in this something that remains inaccessible—there!, *da!*—a gospel grammar reverses the irreversible sequence.

Chapter 2

Writing Life

Letter and Spirit

IN HIS STRUGGLE WITH THINGS, IN HIS "EXPERIENCE," Luther rewrites the way meaning is accessed. Language itself becomes event that confronts the reader ("I hated the words . . ."). Language is not simply a tool or an instrument that reveals or communicates eternal truth. Language, in its corporeality, in its "written-ness," events meaning through a particular context—associated and dissociated from previous "meaning." Language is liberated from a meta-system of meaning. Two temptations are continually present, however. The first temptation, of course, is to maintain a distinction between language and event, to keep "event" (or experience) and language separate, relegating language to a secondary role. The second temptation seeks to control event (or experience) through language, by giving event a particular meaning or name. This temptation lies in the desire to resystematize event through language.

Both of these temptations witness to what may be called an ideological desire: the desire to put the known in a continuum with the unknown, with that which is only anticipated or believed—God, for example, or any ultimate explanation. Ideological desire wishes to name God. This desire refuses to acknowledge the incapacity, the ultimate failure, of "ideas" to grasp experience. It refuses to acknowledge that there might be something in experience, in event, that escapes systematization or cannot be fit into a continuum. This desire does not recognize that there is an "absent thing" is every event, in every form of speech, that eludes yet influences the participant, the reader. This point needs to be underscored: this absent thing is witnessed already in event and not just in language, as if language were only secondary to event. Language reflects an absence already existent in event.

But language is not event

*Though it may appear that language as event does collapse the difference between event and words, language is never simply a representation of event. Language has event inscribed within it. It is a new event itself in the telling of event. Language (words) are not just a shell or instrument channeling meaning, nor are they pure meaning in themselves. Language (event, experience) confronts us with a grammar that directs toward an absent thing, a hole, an abyss, a need, toward something that cannot be captured. Language confronts us with a grammar that implicitly questions theory or the hegemonic use of words.

This questioning of theory, this questioning of the captivity of words within a pre-established system, is a resistance within language to itself. Michel de Certeau calls this situation of resistance a testimony of negation.[1] Language works against itself and its own captivity. It is a protestation. This testimony cannot be equated with power. It does not present a program or have an agenda. This testimony is always a negation of power throwing us into a struggle for meaning though it is not— and this is critical—itself a negation of meaning. Yet it is this negation that also allows or provides the space for the unexpected to emerge, for something to return, for an absence perhaps to speak. A testimony of negation reframes the quest for meaning in a wider horizon than conceptual knowing.

Luther's struggle with the reframing of experience and its relation to meaning, with the freeing of language, is evidenced in his wonderfully entitled treatise "Answer to the HyperChristian, Hyperspiritual and Hyperlearned Book by Goat Emser in Leipzig—Including Some Thoughts Regarding His Companion, the Fool Murner, 1521."[2] In this treatise, Luther engages Emser in a debate about scriptural exegesis (among many issues), about the interpretation of words and how meaning arises. Luther strongly rejects the systematization implicit in the classic fourfold interpretation of Scripture (though he will still use it occasionally in his own exegetical work)—a systematization that he rejects under the broad heading of allegory.[3] The allegorical interpretation, he writes, is an "infection" originating in Origen. This infection spreads the germs of personal interpretation and all the whims associated with personal interpretation; the interpreter can too easily invent "mysteries on his own" that have no actual basis in the text itself.[4] Creating mysteries on one's own, of course, is simply another way of creating the illusion of a presence of meaning. There can be, however, no certainty (or "presence") based on whims because the reader is denied the confrontation, the struggle, the experience of the text.

The passage in question in this treatise is Paul's text in 2 Cor. 3:6: "for the letter kills but the Spirit gives life." In his exegesis, Luther points out that, for Paul, the letter as law cannot be simply distinguished from the spirit. The letter, as divine law, is also spiritual. Therefore, it is not possible to argue for a "deeper" spiritual meaning because the letter itself may contain or reveal such a meaning. In other words, the distinction between letter and spirit cannot be made on the grounds of a predetermined sequence that moves from the grammatical (literal) to the hidden spiritual meaning as if the grammatical, or the letter, were only a shadow or shell for the spiritual meaning. If this movement from surface to reality, from letter to spirit, is shaken, a question arises: How are we to understand the distinction that Paul is apparently making in this passage?

For Luther, both the literal and the spiritual can be law—that is, both can kill. The spiritual is not simply equated with something "life-giving."

> [Y]ou [Emser] say, "The spiritual meaning gives life." Start whistling . . . which is the literal and which is the spiritual meaning in this commandment? You certainly cannot deny that no other meaning can be understood here but the one given by the letters themselves. . . . St. Paul still calls the law spiritual and says it kills.[5]

The meaning that we can know or experience is one given by the letters themselves, by the literal meaning. The work of the Spirit is to be found in that sense, in the literal meaning. Luther is using a classic distinction (letter/spirit) in order to make another distinction (law/gospel), and in so doing he destabilizes the usual binary distinction between letter (body) and meaning (spirit). The letter can be spirit, and in that work it kills—that is, it disrupts the frames of reference, the frames of meaning, within which we wish to hold it. The letter is not simply a signpost that directs us to deeper meaning. Luther blurs the line between the literal sense and the hidden meaning. In this blurring, he does not create a hierarchy in which one (the gospel) is more valuable than the other (the law); rather, he pushes the reader/interpreter to consider the fact of the distinction. The distinction, if you will, becomes more important than the qualitative nature of the distinction.

"From this it is now clear that the words of the apostle, 'The letter kills, but the Spirit gives life,' could be said in other words: 'The law kills, but the grace of God gives life.'"[6] The letter that kills is not the letter, the events, the history, the *res* as such (as if these were of no worth and required moving beyond them), but, more precisely, the letter that kills is these things understood as "spiritual" law.[7] In other words, the letter that kills is the Spirit working in and through the letter, in and through word, event, thing revealing an impossibility, permitting something unexpected to emerge that cannot be contained. The letter that kills is not just a shadow, not even a shadow of divine judgment. It is, in a certain sense, an experience of God in God's nakedness, a nakedness that we cannot behold, a nakedness that kills. "The true presence of the Spirit, when the law is his [*sic*] instrument, means that *Deus nudus* is face to face with the sinner. From this experience, no one can go further."[8]

To avoid the confusion between "letter" and "spirit"—as if these were opposed—Luther suggests that the "'literal meaning" is not a good term because Paul interprets the letter quite differently. Those who call it "grammatical, historical meaning" do much better, Luther writes.[9] The confrontation with the words—the reading and the singing and the praying—is a struggle with the grammatical, historical meaning. It is a struggle with event, with *res,* as it has been recorded in words. It is a struggle with the event of language, with a grammar of absence.

And it is, strangely, a struggle with death. Luther writes: "The Apostle [Paul] does not want us to avoid the letter or to escape its death." We escape this death when we look for a hidden, spiritual (allegorical) meaning. There was a veil over Moses' face so that the people failed to see "the letter, its death or its brilliance."[10] The spiritual meaning, for Luther, is embedded in the letter and in some way, in its death, its brilliance or sweetness is discovered. The record keeping—the literal sense—is not a shell of the event directing the reader to some mythic origin. The record keeping (the writing) witnesses to event, to the *res* in its multiple dimensions. The writing witnesses to both death and life in the present moment.

Luther could not have said it more clearly than he does in his commentary on several chapters in the "second book of Moses" preached in the years 1524–26. In a section entitled "Allegory or Spiritual Meaning of the First Chapter," Luther writes: "I pray that you hold to the kernel, the good treasure, the worthiest *hauptstuck* in Holy Scripture, namely, that you learn Holy Scripture according to historical way."[11] The kernel of scripture is not the so-called spiritual meaning according to Origen, Gregory, Jerome, or Cyprian but what these writers call the shell *(Schale)*. A few lines before this passage, Luther writes to "turn it around" *(wende es umb)*[12] and look for the best—that is, look for the historical, the event, as it is inscribed in the text. Can we say "look for the best," for that absent thing of the Spirit that is embedded in the grammatical, the historical, as it is embedded in "event"?

The move that Luther makes toward the *res,* toward thing or event, is significant because it is precisely a move away from positing an absolute origin. The so-called literal meaning of words does not open the door to some hidden mystery of meaning, some hidden origin where all meaning will become clear and definitive. Such an origin, such an understanding of meaning, is not within the grasp of history or experience. Rather, words—language as event—confront us with a meaning, both present and absent, in their testimony, in their immediate witness.

In a certain sense, we can say that all we have is the letter. And the Spirit manifests itself in and through the letter, though the Spirit always remains more evasive than the letter. Luther writes: "This Spirit can never be contained in any letter. It cannot be written, like the law, with ink, on stone or in books. Instead, it is inscribed only in the heart, and it is a living writing of the Holy Spirit, without [the aid of] any means. That is why St. Paul calls it Christ's letter and not Moses' tablets."[13] This Spirit cannot be contained. The metaphor of container suggests something controllable, something boxed in. Yet, this is precisely what we cannot do with the work of the Spirit. In the work of the Spirit, there is something that we cannot pinpoint or limit. The event of writing witnesses to this inability to capture an illusory "essence" of event. This impossibility is what we have previously called the grammar of God's word, a theological grammar. The event of writing, the event of language, as with any historical event itself, is always confronted with a failure—the failure of language, the failure of an accessible origin, the failure of event to be perfectly delineated or contained in a knowable context. Language has this failure inscribed on it, and yet it is precisely in this failure that language speaks.

Emser is afraid that meaning might be lost. He is afraid that, without a hidden origin, without a metaphysics, "anything will go." In his unwillingness to acknowledge the failure of meaning, he accomplishes that which he fears the most: the destruction of words and, therefore, meaning. Emser gives words different meanings, different signification, and in that move renders words meaningless. Luther, on the other hand, through hyperbole, through exaggeration, throws words back into the ring, so to speak. He puts them on center stage. Words, even the words in title and tone of this treatise (that is not a personal vendetta against Emser—if it were there would be little to laud in it), the exaggerated insistence on Emser's metaphors, place the debate within the realm of language. The important word of the title, for example, is not "Christian, spiritual or learned" but "hyper." Luther exaggerates his point so that there can be no other (hidden) meaning than only the words, no other meaning than the bare-naked literal sense that confronts and disrupts. Luther is fighting not a personal battle but a battle about speech and the way in which language can mean something here and now. Language can mean something only when it is recognized that language/speech is always failed language.

Luther attempts to move us beyond a simple letter/spirit, body/spirit, evil/good dichotomy. And so he argues that it is not just "letter versus spirit" or "surface reality versus deeper, spiritual reality." Of course, that is the dichotomy that we too easily fall into when classifying things in the world. This approach has a long and illustrious history in the Western world. Luther breaks down this dichotomy not through philosophical speculation but by an appeal to an absence that is witnessed in event and in language. The "letter" for Luther is the simple phenomena of the world. The phenomena of the world—things, events, words—are not to be systematically denigrated as simply superficial. They are not to be simply dismissed as insignificant or as if they were only a shadow of a deeper meaning. The things of the world are to be taken at face value, and in the seriousness of that encounter, we are often confronted with meaninglessness—that is, they contradict the meanings we have tried to construe. In that confrontation, they actually take on the character of "law"; they are like a naked God.

As such, as "law," they confront and "kill" us—that is, they disrupt the contexts, the subjects, we want to create, the boxes we build in order to live in the world. As such, as "law," they are God's work—but what Luther calls "God's alien work" or strange work. This is a work that is not proper to God but that pushes toward God. Suffering is an example.

Suffering, more than any other phenomenon in this world, confronts our logic, confronts our theodicies and theologies. Suffering is not a proper work of God.

In the confrontation, in the midst of struggle with "things" in the world, however, something does or can come to us; something continually returns to us. The same "thing" that kills us, the "thing" that is law, can also, through the Spirit, be "sweet" and life giving. However, that sweetness is found, paradoxically, by stepping into the suffering, by stepping into event, into experience, into the contradictions and failure of meaning. That which gives life is, then, not simply a remedy that gets administered, a hidden meaning that gets "discovered," but something like a confrontation and a call heard in the midst of confrontation, the struggle with an absence (even the absence of meaning), a submission.

A New Narrative

Where does this discussion of meaning lead? If meaning arises within the messiness of event rather than being imposed through constructed, invented systems, it will continually emerge as something perhaps unexpected. Words are freed of preexistent meaning, allowing for the emergence of both meaning and its negation, its failure. The words, the old words of a system or culture, are reinvented, but in that reinvention they point not toward an infallible source or first cause but toward their own failure in the present moment. A temptation consists in turning the reinvented words into another system that denies its own failing. A temptation occurs when the reinvention itself becomes like a mystical foundation.

The failure of language, the failure of event itself, points toward the impossibility of knowing and, more specifically, toward the impossibility of knowing beginnings or origin. Knowing an origin only reinforces the illusion of a continuum between source and event, between event and language, between unknown and known, and it holds us in the temptation of ideology. In the case of Lutheran scholarship, the narrative designation of a "moment," an "origin," the "turning point" in Luther's itinerary, shifted from the tower experience (*Turmerlebnis*) to the Reformation breakthrough. This shift in designation is important for it reveals another shift—a shift in scholarship away from localization to the significantly more nuanced view that the "beginning" happened not at one particular instance (in a tower) but progressively as Luther sought to understand more fully the meaning of God's justice and its relation to faith. As we saw in the writings of Heiko Oberman (discussed in chapter 1), this shift in scholarship does not preclude the "break-through" from occurring—it simply happens as an essential verification (the result of an irreversible sequence). It happens not in a tower but in Luther's conscience, in Luther as subject.

But behind the search for Luther's *Turmerlebnis,* or the Reformation breakthrough, hides the imposition of a law or truth—the truth that a beginning can be localized in time, place, and subject. The search veils its own desire for a clearly marked, designated, originary moment upon which to build a system, a work, a tower. Oberman argues for a development and an irreversible discovery that happens in and transfigures Luther's conscience. But, as we have seen, the text Oberman cites questions the irreversibility of the sequence by questioning the component parts (*res/substance* and *grammatica*) of that sequence. Luther's text questions the possibility of a pure beginning by dissociating "beginning" from a divine illumination or revelatory moment. For Luther, the "beginning"—if we can even use that term—resides not in a particular event or context or even in himself as subject but in a strange confrontation with the grammar of words, a theological grammar that disrupts meaning, that disrupts human control of event, context, and language. Beginning resides in death. Luther's confrontation with words was a confrontation in study and in prayer. Attempting to narrate this confrontation, turning it into a "breakthrough," reveals only the power of (and our attachment to) a metaphysical construction of meaning in which words merely represent a hidden reality. The event of Luther's writing reveals a contrary move: a move to maintain the continual disruption of meaning.

Perhaps the desire to localize a breakthrough persists because Luther's own writing witnesses to the complexity of defining a "begin-ning." Scholars are simply repeating a quest that haunted Luther himself. The *Preface to the Complete Edition of Luther's Latin Writings* (here-inafter cited as the *Præfatio*) draws the reader into Luther's struggle.[14] In the *Præfatio,* Luther outlines in considerable autobiographical detail the chronological order of happenings in the years preceding 1520–21. Curiously, the relation between these happenings and a Reformation "discovery" remains undefined. This account of happenings is written because Luther is "prevailed" upon, much as the happenings themselves (as we shall see) prevailed upon his life. Luther writes: "For I got into these turmoils by accident and not by will or intention. I call upon God himself [*sic*] as witness."[15] And later again: "Having been drawn into these disturbances by force and driven by necessity, I had done all I did: the guilt was not mine."[16]

In the midst of telling his story, Luther indicates what might be considered a "beginning" or breakthrough. He interjects that he had "acquired the beginning [*sic*] of the knowledge (*primitias cognitionis*) of Christ and faith in him, that is, not by works but by faith in Christ are we made righteous and saved."[17] The desire for a breakthrough moment, however, the desire to pinpoint a particular "beginning," seduces the translator into using the singular rather than the plural ("I had also acquired the beginning of the knowledge of Christ"). Luther's Latin text, however, employs not the singular but, rather, the plural *primitias cognitionis*—the first-fruits of knowledge, the beginnings (possibly) of knowledge as if this knowledge of Christ had multiple beginnings or, perhaps more suggestively, indeterminate beginnings. The indeterminate beginnings of faith or knowledge of Christ are indeterminate precisely because they do ✳ not belong within the framework of reason or within the construct of any metanarrative. They are not part of a continuum that bridges the outside of God to the inside of time. The *primitias cognitionis*—the first-fruits of a theological grammar—are harvested, if you will, within the chaos of events, as an irruption within experience that defies any chronology.

Primitias is also the word used by the Vulgate to translate Paul's ἀπαρχὴ in 1 Cor. 15:20: "But in fact Christ has been raised from the dead, the first-fruits of those who have fallen asleep." By using *primitias*, Luther connects the narrative of his own struggle with the resurrection from the dead, with *something* (an event) that breaks open the notion of time, that disrupts an easy chronology or continuum. As such, *primitias*, or first-fruits, is linguistically more accurate than "beginnings" (and certainly far more accurate than "beginning"). The term *first-fruits* suggests something that one receives rather than something that one has begun. The use of *primitias* raises, once again, the dilemma of naming beginnings in time.

But the plural *primitias* has other, grammatical implications. Only the first-fruits of the knowledge of Christ surface at this stage for Luther because, as he acknowledges, he was still submerged in errors confirmed by long habit.[18] The plural *primitias* scatters localization whether chronological or spatial. The "one" point or the "one" beginning is not only plural but also disseminated as if to say, there is not one beginning, one insight, one meaning, one substance that is understood. The "beginnings" are continually repeated in the events of Luther's life and in the event that is the writing of the *Præfatio*. Luther continually returns, ever anew, to interpret these *primitias*, which cannot be simply temporalized. He is constantly beginning over again in what might be called a dynamic of beginnings, a dynamic of first-fruits, a dynamic of the provisional.[19]

Near the end of the *Præfatio*, Luther interrupts the detailed chronology (once again) with an *Interim* ("meanwhile").[20] In the midst of these happenings (beginnings), Luther had already "returned to interpret the Psalter anew"*(redieram ad Psalteriun denuo interpretandum)*.[21] In the context of this interim, Luther introduces his explanation of the troublesome verse: "For in it [the gospel] the righteousness of God is revealed through faith for faith; as it is written, 'The one who is righteous will live by faith'" (Rom. 1:17).[22] Through meditation night and day, Luther finally gives "heed to the context" of the words, and there *(eam,* or in German, *da!),* in their context, he "begins to understand" *(coepi intelligere eam)* the passive righteousness of God (gospel) that the sinner receives as gift. This righteousness moves Luther from hatred and anger against God to love of this the "sweetest" of words. The beginnings happen in the midst of meditation, as Luther gives heed, literally "attends," to the context of the words, of language.

At the same time, however, he is also compelled to verify, in some way, these beginnings with tradition. Even at the end of his life, Luther does not claim—as he might have—a unique intuition. Rather, looking back, he is glad to find verification in Augustine's *de spiritu et litera.*[23] Only then, at least in the text of the *Præfatio*, does Luther return a "second time" to the interpretation of the Psalter.[24] Finally, Luther's narration is interrupted once again. This time he is "compelled" to leave his work. Emperor Charles V convened the Diet of Worms (1521). This event prevents Luther from completing the commentary, to complete the beginnings.

Luther is prevailed upon and caught up in the turmoil of events; not by will or conscience, he is compelled by the happenings to interrupt his work. In a confessional moment at the end of the *Præfatio*, Luther explains that these interruptions, this situation of force and necessity, all point to the realization that he is "not one of those who from nothing suddenly become the topmost" *(non ex illis, qui de nihilio repente fiunt summi)*.[25] There is no sudden, definitive intuition. There is only a working through the interruptions, only this attempt to understand the different situations—the manifold and many *da*. The intuition (the first-fruits) was not a sudden revelation. The unique intuition, the "one look" in which the spirit of the whole of Scripture is illuminated, is not part of Luther's way.

Luther, in writing the *Præfatio*—a writing intended to introduce his writing—returns not to the writings themselves, but to the force of events that interrupted his writing. In this particular event of writing that is the *Præfatio*, Luther once again experiences the continual disruption of his writing. Not even in this writing is Luther fully in control. The force of events irrupts even as he acknowledges, in this text, that he did not experience a sudden, originary intuition. The story, the events, continually interrupt the intuition; in the years 1520–21, the "indulgence matters proceeded" all else.[26]

As we have seen, the text of the *Præfatio* is itself a continually interrupted text. Besides these interruptions, how are irruption, confrontation, disruption, and awakening witnessed in the writing? Luther's use of liturgical language, I believe, provides a key to understanding this witness in his writing. The entire *Præfatio* is bracketed by two confessions (or perhaps it is but one confession repeated differently).

Luther had been asked—so he tells us at the beginning of the *Præfatio*—to write a preface to his Latin works to avoid further confusion concerning the chronology of his early writings. There is also an unstated demand: he should provide insight into the moment of his monumental break from the "evil" papist system. Luther is unsure of his ability to accomplish either task. He responds to the first by admitting that he finds it hard to arrange *(digerere)* the chaos of events.[27] To the second, unspoken expectation, he confesses to the "sincere reader" that he continued to be an "enthusiastic papist" for sometime ("I was so drunk"). In fact, he confesses himself to be a more authentic papist than Johann Eck himself, for Eck defended the papacy (in the significant debate between them in Leipzig in 1519) only out of a concern for his belly whereas Luther did so out of a concern for his soul.[28]

The entire *Præfatio* witnesses to the chaos, the disturbance, the continual irruption of events, beginning in the first paragraph: "But my books, as it happened, yes, as the lack of order in which the events transpired made it necessary are accordingly crude and disordered chaos, which is now not easy to arrange even for me."[29] Luther is asked to arrange the chaos of events, to put them in order—a task, he confesses, that eludes him. The events as such carry a disorder that becomes more and more literal as Luther writes. What Luther does accomplish is witness to his own inability to arrange the events. The text of the *Præfatio* seems to be continually disrupted by the very chaos of events. The writing witnesses to a process of dissemination *(digerere)* occasioned through events.

In the last paragraphs, again, Luther addresses the reader. After several interpretations, after several "beginnings," Luther confesses his inability to establish the much-desired order. His attempt has only manifested his inability; in fact, it may have disseminated the highly sought after "moment" or sequence even further. He writes: "I was not one of those who from nothing suddenly become the topmost, though they are nothing, neither have labored, nor been tempted, nor become experienced, but have with one look *(unum intuitum)*[30] at Scripture exhausted their entire spirit."[31] The *unum intuitum,* that privileged connection with some hidden meaning or some absolute spiritual meaning behind the text, is not Luther's way. Luther's struggle with the *res* of God's justice and the subsequent "first-fruits" came about only through much labor, temptation, and *experience.* Just before disavowing the breakthrough of a unique intuition, Luther writes: "I relate these things, good reader, so that, if you are a reader of my puny works, you may keep in mind, that, as I said above, I was all alone and one of those who, as Augustine says of himself, have become proficient by writing and teaching."[32] The narration reveals Luther's indebtedness to much writing and teaching. The autobiographical text has moved from the confession of the difficulty in establishing an order to the events to a confession that a "breakthrough" (intuition) never really happened. There was only writing and teaching (and labor, temptation, and experience).

Luther concludes the *Præfatio* with an appeal to God: "May God confirm in us what he [*sic*] has accomplished and perfect his work which he began in us, to his glory. Amen."[33] Luther appeals to God to confirm this work of uncertain beginnings, this chaos of events. He appeals to God to confirm the work of labor, temptation, and experience.

Heiko Oberman had already destroyed the physical tower. Now, Luther's confession demolishes the tower of the self (conscience) and its relation to events. The confession demolishes the notion of the subject as receiving a special communication or even vocation. The confession does not interrogate and reprimand the self but puts the subject (and any inherent receptivity to divine insight that the subject might claim) into question. The confession disperses the subject—like a multitude of languages—over the land. The events (res) break in upon Luther and disturb his habit (literally, his way of life); they disturb his sense of self. The letter as spirit kills. The events, the writing, all witness to a dissemi-nation. *[margin note: disturb L's identity]*

As in the text of the Table Talk, so in the *Præfatio:* the writing of confrontation and disturbance is itself interrupted by an appeal to God. In the Table Talk, the moment of the first *da*—the state of confrontation and fear, and even hatred, of God's active justice—is juxtaposed by the third *da*, the liturgical act: "*Gott lob*" (God be praised). In the *Præfatio*, the impossibility to arrange the events (and pinpoint one intuition) is acknowledged by an appeal to God. The only witness, in fact, to this interim or "in between" state is God.[34]

God is witness—God sees and destroys the tower and dissemi-nates the languages across the earth. The experience and the break-through, the subject and the mission, the conscience and its intention, are, like the tower, disseminated. God's witnessing in some strange way justifies the chaos and dissemination. Luther can only acknowl-edge this witness and acknowledge his own life and writing as part of that dissemination. Not even his writing can control these events. The chaotic, the uncontrollable, the unexpected events—*res*—have only God as their legitimate witness. Not Luther's life, not Luther's writ-ing, not Luther as subject, as designated, as "called," as instrument of God, can legitimate the events; rather, all of these (subject and con-text) are disseminated in the witness.

Luther's struggles to find an expression for his involvement in the events, in the *res*. He finds an expression, a metaphor, in a liturgical act: baptism. I propose that a baptismal motif runs through the entire *Præfatio*, moving from chaos and submersion to rebirth. As we have already seen, Luther begins the *Præfatio* by acknowledging the confusion in which his writings were occasioned and which they somehow reflect. This acknowledgment is also a confession: Luther himself is probably incapable of putting the desired order back into the writings (back into the events). Parallel to the confusion of the writings and the events is a state of obscurity within Luther's life. Luther himself was drunk, swimming in papal dogmatism.[35] He begs the reader to read with commiseration and remember the state of submersion in which the writing occurred. This submersion was dogmatic submersion in which Luther could not see clearly or understand but struggled as one who "from the depth of my heart wanted to be saved."[36] This submersion was not simply a passing drunkenness but was colored with death itself. In the midst of submersion, Luther struggles as one filled with the dread of the last day. This is a matter of life and death.

The events continue to unfurl—orders to recant, summons to Rome, resistance to a papal bull, appearance at the Diet of Augsburg (1518), an appearance that happened "on the third day," Luther notes, after his arrival in Augsburg. (The conscientious editor, however, unwrites this autobiographical moment by pointing out that this appearance actually occurred four days later!) Also during this time, and closely linked, in the writing, to the beginnings of a resurrection from submersion, Philip Melanchthon was called to Wittenberg.[37] Melanchthon, the one who would be Luther's associate in the work of theology, the one who put order in the labor, is greeted in the narrative of the *Præfatio* as the one who made Satan and all his adherents mad. Luther reads Melanchthon's arrival—*haud dubie* (without doubt)—as God working to bring Luther out of the chaos. Luther reads his arrival as the first sign of emerging from chaos, from submersion, from the waters of death. The event of an arrival, this first sign of resurrection, has angered Satan.

Yet, Luther continues, how difficult it was to emerge from errors and long-standing habit.[38] Luther may have known the beginnings of a resurrection but he did not yet know the consequences or the conclusions to be drawn from those beginnings.[39] Nor did he know that, perhaps even more significantly, such beginnings happen over and over again, that resurrection, at least in this life, is a continual event. Recognizing even at this later date (1519) that he was still absorbed (*absorptus eram*)[40] by the title of the church and personal habit, recognizing that he was not totally pulled out of the waters of the papacy, out of the waters of death, recognizing the difficulty of such an emergence from intellectual error and spiritual habit, Luther does acknowledge the "beginnings" of the knowledge of Christ and faith in him. These "beginnings" (as noted above) are in the plural and are intimately connected to the resurrection—a recognition that happens only in the events rather than in a sudden insight or intuition that could be more easily subverted into a pure and precise beginning.

Only afterward does Luther recognize this submersion and the concessions he made in that submersion as constituting the worst of blasphemies and abomination.[41] He was incapable of freeing himself, of pulling himself out of the papal waters in which he was submerged. But as his friends and protectors urge him to write, yet another figure unexpectedly appears in the text to render witness to the submersion. This state of submersion, this inability, this unrecognized death known only as dread of the last day, is in itself forgivable—it has a way out. The unexpected witness upon whom Luther calls is God's self—*Deum ipsum testor*.[42]

The sequence of events—the posting of the Ninety-Five Theses, the German Sermon on Indulgences, the *Explanations*—these events and the suggestion in the *Explanations* that good works of love should replace indulgences brought the whole papacy against Luther. *Solus primo*[43]—at first Luther was alone and incapable of conducting such great affairs. Luther again appeals to last day imagery: these "events"—these publications—were demolishing heaven and consuming earth with fire ("Hoc erat coelum deturbasse et mundum incendio consumpsisse").[44] The turmoil Luther found himself in not by will or intention—not by conscience or as subject—and the event of writing the turmoil witness to the demolition of heaven and the consumption of earth by fire. The writing itself is like a baptism. This baptism by the Holy Spirit and fire (Matt. 3:11–12) is enacted in the unexpectedness (the fire) of these events, of this writing, in this life.[45] Baptism, as death, as submersion, as immersion into death, as immersion into the death of someone else, into the death of Jesus Christ, is the demolition of heaven. In baptism, God witnesses God's own death and the heavens are broken open, even demolished, and the earth is consumed by fire.

Baptism is now not the active adhesion to a belief system but a participation in death and life. Baptismal language allows Luther to rewrite the narrative of his so-called discovery of justification through faith alone. Luther does not understand himself as the hero-Reformer who instigates the events and the transformation of society. Rather, Luther understands the turmoil of events in which he participates as baptism: as immersion into first a demolition, a destruction, a dissemination of God into works of love. Baptismal language serves Luther to write the destruction of both earth and heaven, to write the demolition of the two spheres, the ordained and the absolute power of God, and to write the illusion of a knowing in the world as theological knowing. But then, who survives? Can God survive? Can human beings survive this destruction? This destruction, this demolition of earth and heaven, is not the negation of God or of human beings—God is, strangely, witness to this dissemination and consummation, God is witness to God's own death—and human beings participate in this death and in this strange witness (life) through God's witness, through the gift of faith alone.

Events themselves—the events of these years 1517–21 that Luther is attempting to put in order—reveal God as the witness and the judge. While all of these events are flooding the narrative of the *Præfatio*, while heaven is demolished and the earth consumed by fire—with God as witness—Luther returns to different beginnings: "Meanwhile I had already during that year returned to interpret the Psalter anew."[46] With God as witness and in the beginnings of knowledge of Jesus Christ present in event (or can we say, in other words, independent of the subject Martin Luther, independent of the self?), Luther returns to that one word that was a stumbling block, to that one hateful word in the Epistle to the Romans—the justice *of* God.[47] Luther hated the word *iustitia* because its philosophical grammar could only place the word within a system, within a tower that reduced both God and human beings to the dictates of an ontological hierarchy. Faith itself became a human work that God would judge.[48] In that hierarchy, God's justice could mean only one thing: God's active justice or righteousness (*formali seu activa*), by which God alone is ever righteous and by which God judges and punishes the sinner for a lack of faith.

Luther's emergence from this philosophical drunkenness, his awakening, is metaphorically described in terms similar to the act of baptism: the emergence from the waters of death, being "pulled out" of the waters. Luther emerges from the habit, emerges from the error, the drunkenness, the submersion of the papacy and his late medieval scholastic training. This is a passive act. The individual cannot accomplish it on her or his own merits. Here, *ibi, da*—Luther experiences rebirth. "Here I felt that I was altogether born again and had entered paradise itself through open gates."[49] This emergence is understood as the first-fruits of knowledge. This awakening is understood as a continual resurrection.

And then, immediately in the next paragraph, Luther repeats that this "place in Paul was for me truly the gate to paradise" (*ita mihi iste*

locus Pauli fuit vere porta paradisi).[50] The "place" in Paul—the locus—
was a place of writing, a text; it was the place of rebirth, of emergence,
of baptism, of first-fruits, of resurrection.

The baptismal imagery in the *Præfatio* suggests both submersion
and emergence within events, within history. Disruption in Luther and
awakening are intimately linked to experience, to understanding *res*—
understanding the connection between words and *res,* understanding a
theological grammar in which what is absent is experienced in event and
apprehended by faith. This disruption and emergence, for Luther, is a
continual process; baptism is never completed until death.[51] The beginnings, never completed, are repeated as if the believer is continually
baptized by fire, by *res*, by events.

The writing of the *Præfatio* as an attempt to put order into chaos
(and, in a certain sense, to remember) witnesses to the impossibility
of a narrative ordering (a metanarrative, if you will) founded upon
Luther as subject. Luther's turn to baptismal language is a witness of
this failure, of Luther's own failure to constitute himself as subject. This
failure, however, also points toward another impossibility. The turn to
baptismal language points to the impossibility of remembering event
(as cognitively, rationally accessible)—event, context, and subject are
disrupted, and it is through liturgical language that Luther is able to
write this disruption.

Confronted with the *res absens*, confronted with what is not known
in every event, in every context, confronted with something event could
not make accessible or communicate, in that confrontation Luther was
able to connect, to make a grammatical move, to connect the words—
connexionem verborum attenderem . . .[52] "There I began to understand
that the righteousness of God is that by which the righteous lives by a
gift of God, namely by faith."[53] The baptismal imagery in the *Præfatio*
suggests both submersion and emergence within events, within experience, within history. Disruption and emergence in Luther are intimately linked to living in *res*—understanding the connection between
words and *res*, understanding a theological grammar in which what
is absent is experienced in event and apprehended by faith. The only
witness to this confrontation, to this baptism—the only witness with
access to event—is God. And the only apprehension of these events
for the human being is through the gift of faith alone, through faith
standing alone.

Scattering of Words, Subject, Context

The Reformation breakthrough, the *Turmerlebnis*, like all towers, is destroyed by God who sees, who witnesses. The one tower, the tower of one language, the tower of one philosophical and theological system, the tower of human work, calls for its own destruction. The destruction of the tower—the dissemination of people and language—fulfills God's work.

This demolition is witnessed as well in Luther's autobiographical preface. The writing as event is inscribed with a demolition, with the impossibility of pinpointing an origin, a specific beginning. Rather, "beginnings" is rewritten as resurrection, as a continual dying and rising. Meaning—the meaning of words, things, events—is also reoriented. Meaning is now not of a "system" but of the Spirit. Meaning is something that continually irrupts unexpectedly. Language itself becomes like a ritual, pointing to something that it cannot contain, pointing toward an absence. The grammar of the "absent thing" is the grammar of the gospel that disrupts and pushes towards rewriting.

I have called this grammar by various titles—grammar of the gospel, grammar of God's word, grammar of absence, a theological grammar; we could also call it a baptismal grammar. What Luther sets up as a young man—the permeability of every context, the absent thing in every event, in every word—becomes for the older Luther, who is seeking order in the chaos, an impossible task that can be understood only metaphorically through baptismal language. Luther understood that any context that human beings create for themselves can never negate or surpass that first baptismal claim.

However, we do not care for drowning or for unexpected awakening. We prefer a knowable beginning and established origins. The *res* of God's justice, the thing that is God's justice, is easily equated or conceptualized with an eternal truth. Conceptualized truth always appears more durable than concrete truth. Perhaps even Luther sought something of that comfort in his attempt to write about his own beginning, but, as we saw in the *Præfatio*, that comfort, the assurance of positive origin, was denied to him. It was continually interrupted, disrupted by event. The writing that is the *Præfatio* reveals to us a Luther who immerses himself within the biblical text, within the words, within experience, within history. A presumed "substance," or a meaning hidden or concealed by the words, is cut off from consideration.

However, the confrontation with words, the struggle between words and what they refer to, and this struggle understood, yes, as theological grammar but, even more, as prayer, engages Luther in a work of dissemination radically affecting language and, therefore, both theological and philosophical concepts. The scattering or freeing of word and concept requires a new definition of *res*. I want to argue that, for Luther, the *res* of God (whether it be justice or mercy or forgiveness or any other divine reality), those things that we are tempted to consider "eternal truths," remain *res absens*—as that which is absent in event, that which cannot be grasped or known but can be apprehended by faith alone. The apprehension is not of eternal concepts or ideas but of God active in event, in history. The *res absens* continually disrupts event, context, and subject. The first-fruits of a knowledge of Jesus Christ is perhaps this first apprehension of an absence: the beginnings of a resurrection that is a continual disruption. In this disruption, strangely, faith awakens.

The scattering of words, subject, context—the event of dissemination within Luther's writing—points toward an impossibility: Luther's own inability to situate his life. Luther was unable to make that extraordinary transcendental move in which the self is separated from history and from a unique inner/outer perspective that observes life, history—events—even God. Luther, indebted as we make him to the origin of his order, the Augustinian Hermits, indebted as he makes himself to several of Augustine's writings, was unable to concede that core Augustinian invention and legacy to Western thought: the ego. Liturgical metaphors do not help Luther situate his self or define his context as if the liturgy created a new context. This was particularly clear from the use of baptismal language—baptism is not the adhesion to a new set of rules, to a new way of life in which the believer "has" Jesus. Through baptismal language, Luther was able to write the disruption of event and the impossibility of remembrance. Liturgical metaphors provide Luther with a language through which something that cannot be grasped or controlled in event (something absent in every event) can irrupt anew in every context.

Chapter 3

Writing the Other

An Impossible Repetition

AT THIS POINT, WE NEED TO ASK WHETHER THE NOTION of event as such can be isolated and defined. An initial distinction was already made between event occurring in space and time and event as something irrupting in and through writing. And Luther's turn to liturgical language has also pointed out that something in the so-called historical event irrupts in writing, something that cannot be controlled or grasped. The writing of Lutheran and Reformation scholarship, however, has moved in precisely the opposite direction: it has attempted to master that which cannot be grasped or known. The difficulty of pinpointing the tower experience has highlighted this desire (particularly the desire of the "reader," or scholar) to invent an origin, a source, an event that sustains the subject as autonomous actor in a knowable context (despite Luther's resistance to such invention).

Focusing on the writing of Lutheran scholars who have attempted to define this breakthrough, we discovered, as we did in the writing of Heiko Oberman, that the struggle centers on the *nature* of the initial Reformation insight. What exactly constituted the breakthrough? was the question that preoccupied historians and theologians alike. When did the illuminating insight occur, and in what context did it happen? I believe that behind all these questions lies another motivation: the desire not only to know what constituted the Reformation breakthrough but to somehow claim that breakthrough back into a philosophical and theological framework—in other words, to know the "what" of the event is in some way to control that event and perhaps even self-justify (and thereby avoid a similar reformation?). Laying claim on that "event" within a particular theological and cultural framework has been one of the most powerful tendencies within the Lutheran family.

This desire to know what constitutes event will serve as a frame—even context—for the following methodological discussion. Just as the question of the Reformation breakthrough, the tower experience, haunts scholarly writing (even the writing of those who have denied the possibility of pinpointing the precise moment), so the question "What does it mean?" haunts our own endeavors to read the continual dissemination of subject and event inscribed within Luther's writing. The question we should more appropriately ask is this: How does writing of event translate something of the event, or how does the writing of event become itself an event of writing?

Yes! This question about writing connects the present study with literary theory. This connection to literary theory for a theological study need not be done bashfully, as if theological writing were not writing. We have already seen in the first chapter the extent to which theologians have either created narratives to explain a theological insight or sought desperately to justify the narrative of a heroic beginning. The narrative itself has proven to be elusive—for both scholars and for Luther, though in different ways. We will now pursue narrative as a literary question and as it functions in Luther's writing.

The turn to literary theory is an appropriate turn. Its appropriateness lies in that characteristic of literature that attempts at one and the same time to refer to event, subject, and context while also questioning the referents used to write. We have already uncovered Luther questioning and resituating the referents used to narrate the events of his own life. We have discovered a Luther who is engaged, albeit indirectly, in elaborating a theory of narrative through his biblical exegesis and his search, in the midst of chaos, for the ways in which words and events can still refer, especially when they have been denied any special access to a "hidden" meaning.

Several topics are now on the table: How does a narrative relate to the question of historical accuracy? Can the two coexist? Or, stated slightly differently, how does a narrative refer to such things as event, context, and subject? The current chapter does not intend to resolve the issue of referents in literary theory, but it will begin by examining the question and then attempting to apply it to Luther's writing. Several contemporary theorists will be invoked to approach these questions, not only to understand Luther's writing but also to outline the beginnings of a rewriting of the classical theological loci.

The beginnings of a response will involve a reading of the notion of event, of context, of singularity and iterability, primarily through the writing of Jacques Derrida and secondarily through the work of Maurice Blanchot. This appeal to contemporary French philosophers may appear incongruent with a study of Luther. I would, however, propose that a curious connection exists between Luther and postmodern French literary theory—a connection that takes places through the reading and writing of Nietzsche. Nietzsche was a fine reader of Luther, invoking the disruptions of the Reformer and even rehearsing, at moments, Luther's literary style. Jacques Derrida and Maurice Blanchot were fine readers of Nietzsche. I would even suggest—without falling into the trap of defining origins!—that Luther was an important thinker of poststructuralist literary theory and postmodern deconstruction. This resituating of Luther will become more evident in the final section of this chapter, when we will read Luther on the subject of a particular context and a particular iterable mark: the monastic life and vows.

The concern to define event preoccupies the writing of Derrida and the meaning of literature, and to a different degree, the writing of Blanchot. Both of these authors are struggling with a question— the "what" question—brought to the center of literary discussion by Jean-Paul Sartre. The question "what" was the title of one of Jean-Paul Sartre's early theoretical works: "What Is Literature?" (*Qu'est-ce que la littérature?*).[1] The "*qu'est-ce que . . .?*"—the "what is this?" question— demands, pushes, even asserts the need for a definitive response, one that will "hold good" through time. The question imposes a reification of the language employed to answer it. The response, whether oral or written, must be—or at least must indicate—that which is not held by a particular context (that which is beyond time). The response would define the essence or substance of some thing, an essence or substance that would be unchanging, permanent, and necessitating the establishment of a homogeneous space, a continuum between author and reader, between past event and present perception. The response could be understood, perhaps even intuited in a moment of illumination, and then imposed through space and time (through any particular context, in any particular event, by any particular subject).

However, Sartre, in asking the "what" question, points the reader already to the demise or deconstruction of the question in its own response. There is a resistance to the question from within itself. Sartre proposes the literary work as "gift" (*don*) and in "freedom" (*liberté*). The literary text is a gift of generosity given to the freedom of the reader. Sartre writes: "Thus reading is an exercise in generosity, and what the writer requires of the reader is not the application of an abstract freedom but the gift of his whole person."[2] Of course, this gift has the intention of the author inscribed upon it. The gift is controlled. It is a secure gift in that the reader knows in advance that where the book goes the author has already gone. At the same time, however, Sartre is aware of contaminated structures, of contaminated words. A word—a sign—is always a thing. There is never a pure sound, a pure word. And, therefore, words need to be healed. The reader is called upon by the writing. But this calling of the reader, this demand for a response out of human liberty,[3] opens a space for a multiplicity of responses; it opens the possibility that the direct intention of the author will be relegated to an inferior place or maybe even ignored. Freedom and gift, generosity, open to the possibility of an excess in reading. This excess gives rise to unique, supplemented, novel readings/answers. At the same time, this excess offers a resistance to the initial question; it negates to a certain degree the possibility of an answer, at least an answer to a question such as "*qu'est-ce que?*"

Both Maurice Blanchot and Jacques Derrida have attempted a response, if not to the "what" question then at least to the questions delineated by Sartre. Jacques Derrida, first of all, in "Signature Event Context," asks about the possibility of knowing a singular event.[4] This question is coupled with the recognition of the nonsaturable aspect of every context and, therefore, the impossibility of the classical understanding of communication that presupposes an absolute time-space continuum. Derrida concludes with further reflections on the possibility of absolute performatives, such as vows—both oral vows (for example, the "I do" of the marriage vow) and written vows (for example, the signature). My own reading of Derrida's "communication" will highlight the terms of event and iterability, of context and singularity.

Maurice Blanchot's untiring dismantling of the person of the writer and the writer's intention as "communicable," his unceasing attempt to write the death of the author in "Literature and the Right to Death," focuses, for one part at least, on the term *excess*.[5] It is the excess in writing, that which cannot be contained, which will complement Derrida's understanding of dissemination as a form of communication. Again, the reading of this "excess" may be redefined, even totally transformed but it serves as witness to the continually deferring quality of a written text (whatever form that written text takes) and to the question Derrida poses: How is the event communicated?

The response of both authors to the initial question—"what is it?"—raises other questions as well or at least seems to require the intervention of a definition. Does not the "what" question continually intervene and, in a sense, disrupt communication? Is not every attempt to answer the "what" question—that is, to locate the essence or substance or insight—a restriction of "meaning" that makes "meaning" something immediately communicable? Stated theologically, does it not restrict the *res* of God? The tensions created by the "what" question—tensions of closure, definition, abstraction—open the door (surprisingly) to what is also indefinable and irreducible in our interrogation of event, its singularity, its iterability, and its code. The desire to understand the relationship among event, singularity, and iterability shifts the focus of the question from the event itself to the witness (even the far-distant witness or "receiver" of the event—for example, the reader). The focus shifts from the event itself to the possibility of communicating the event and, therefore, to the question of what is meant by "communication." The "what" question now surfaces as the implicit desire to be in some form of relationship (communication) to the event.

The Displacement of Repetition or the Iteration of an Absence

In *Signature Event Context*, Jacques Derrida begins by posing the question of communication. Behind a classical understanding of communication (metaphorically understood as transmission of a meaning, and, in particular, one single meaning, or *sens*) lies the problematic term *context*. For the classical (metaphorical) understanding of "communication" to function, a homogeneous context is presupposed. The meaning "communicated" depends on an unbroken line established between the context of the sender and the context of the receiver. Communication depends on the compatibility of context, but does this not harbor, as Derrida asks, certain determinable (definable) philosophical presuppositions?[26] Is not the "what" question lurking in the background? In the classical perspective, to define the "what" of meaning or communication or context presupposes a profound compatibility between sender and receiver through both time and space.

One of the issues raised by the "what" question is the possibility of homogeneous presence. By asking, "what is it?" the interrogator assumes the possibility that one meaning (or even several meanings) can be constituted as valid, that is, functioning equally in all contexts. Meaning, in this understanding, transcends context. Meaning is in some fashion related to something stable—an eternal presence, for example—which is at the origin or beginning of all meaning. In fact, it demands an origin to which everything can be related and then defined or explained. The question assumes an originary presence that, despite transmutations and often deformations, is still recognizable or attainable. Transmutations occur within a homogeneous field (context), and deformations develop either through inherent flaws in the originary system or from mythical (quasi demonic) interventions from outside the system.

The inherent flaws or the mythical/demonic intervention, however, becomes a point of tension always threatening the system and significantly compromising the hegemonic control of presence. As Derrida points out, in order to integrate the flaw into the system, the flaw itself becomes quasi fundamental or foundational. A dependence is created out of the unexplainable flaw, and its intervention simultaneously creates a continually burning and unexplainable holocaust that is, in one word (or a singular event), the demise of presence, promise, and communication. A flaw, such as death for example, negates presence. But that which is negated can be any form of "first cause"; it does not need to be defined as presence. It could be an originary, singular event. The extension of presence (of a singular event, for example) in time and space through writing (classically understood as communication and promise) is broken by the flaw or unexplainable intervention of the writer and the reader. In any system, origin cannot be located or pinpointed as origin; a tower is known only as a destroyed tower, a tower of dissemination, a tower of Babel.

The unexpected and unexplainable—something that cannot be known or captured—breaks the hegemony of presence, breaks the possibility of simple, direct, perceptual communication. This breaking, in turn, questions the role of witness: What does it mean to see or remember or witness an "event" when knowing can no longer be equated with simply seeing or experiencing? What does it mean when seeing and

experiencing are not confined to the representational and when one cannot reach back through a homogeneous context to the event? In other
words, what does it mean to witness or remember an event when the
truth of the event cannot be represented? Of course, it will be objected
that "meaning" is not only a matter of seeing. But as soon as we refer to
meaning as existing outside of context, are we not reestablishing, epistemologically at least, a hierarchy that depends on vision—whether vision
is of the immediate, shadowy realm or of the deeper mystical variety?
There are simply different prerequisites for various penetrations of sight.
And is not theory, then, always some form of perception?

As resistance to the representational, as resistance to a hierarchical epistemology, Derrida proposes something he calls the "eventhood"
of event. For Derrida, the eventhood of event—*l'événementialité*—is
something "produced" by the event. It is the mark or code of event that
has a repetitive or citational structure[7] and that is constituted precisely
by an absence of both the original referent and authorial intent. It is an
orphan, if you will. Derrida quickly points out, however, that repetition
and citation may lead to confusion: he therefore prefers the word *iterable*.[8] We will return to this possible confusion in a moment.

It appears, then, that the relation between the singularity of an event
and its eventhood, which supposes, according to Derrida, the intervention of an utterance (necessarily iterable), cannot be understood in terms
of "communication" as transmission or transportation of a meaning or
intention through a homogeneous context. The utterance itself intervenes as event. The writing about event, for example, intervenes but
cannot "communicate" an absolute representation. This does not mean
that the writing, the utterance, is secondary communication. Rather, the
writing itself is marked by the event and iterates the event, the eventhood, through a form of code. The consequences of this reformulated
communication between event and its iterable code are witnessed in
writing that can no longer be understood as the communication of authorial intent or the "real" meaning but simply as the possibility of iteration,
as that which bears the mark of event, as that which has event inscribed
within it,[9] as that which, in Blanchot's terms, witnesses to an excess.

We are still left with the question of why Derrida uses here the word
intervention. Who or what intervenes? Who or what produces the utterance? The author of a text? A person repeating an event through a vow?
These questions point to something left open in Derrida's own text—and

to a danger. If "meaning" or "intention" (particularly authorial intent) remains inaccessible—if writing, therefore, is the dissemination of the subject and we have only the singularity of event (in this case, the event of writing)—how do we avoid turning "event" into a new mystical "origin"? The dissemination of the subject must also be simultaneously a dissemination of event, yet by attributing to event certain qualifiers (unexpected, singular, unpredictable, and so forth) do we not risk enthroning event on the very pedestal from which metaphysically established truths have just been ejected? How can we approach event through writing when, through writing, as we saw in Luther's attempt at an autobiography, event itself is continually disseminated?

Another objection could be raised: Does not a homogeneous space remain operative whenever iterability becomes a possibility? Does not writing the singularity of an event as iterable encompass the singular in the domain of code and not break from the question of context? Is there a difference between something that is repeatable and something that is iterated?[10] Though Derrida warns us about the possible confusion between repeatability and iterability, this confusion is sometimes operative in his own text: "This implies that there is no such thing as a code—organon of iterability—which could be structurally secret. The possibility of repeating and thus of identifying the marks is implicit in every code, making it into a network [une grille] that is communicable, transmittable, decipherable, iterable for a third, and hence for every possible user in general."[11]

For Derrida, a constitutive element of code is its iterability as a mark that functions even in the author's absence, and even in the author's radical absence (death). This functioning in the author's "absence," however, is not the possibility of a code (or writing) to communicate the author's "idea" or "intention" through time; it is, in fact, the renunciation of the author's intention (and therefore context). Writing continues to function even when the author can no longer respond, that is, even when the author can no longer be responsible for what has been written.[12] A code continues to function as a measure or rule ensuring not the possibility of communication (the simple transmission of an idea/meaning) but the impossibility of transmission or communication. The code as such witnesses to the impossibility of the transmission of the author's intent or meaning; it witnesses to the breakdown of context or the nonsaturability of context. Stated in more positive terms, code is the structuring of inaccessibility, even the structuring of death. Death itself becomes part of the iterable structure because it has lost the power of finality. The code still functions despite the death of the author and intent.

Do we then have, in the negation of a singular context, the imposition of a super-context through an iterable code? A code, Derrida points out, is not secret. It will always function (that is, be iterable) even in the absence (death) of both sender and receiver. Even the most idiomatic code will always function because code is not dependent on the intention or meaning of even the most private and secretive idiom. If code is the mark of event, then iterability is the mark of the code.

Despite this power of code, though, it does not create a super-context because the code does not simply "repeat" (that is, copy) but, rather, knows itself as continual disruption through the intervention of an utterance. There is a break in context through this intervention. And this break with context and intent is always brought about by the advent of the "other." Iterability is, in this sense, necessarily linked to the "other" because it always moves beyond a particular context or intention.[13] Not only does it move beyond a particular context, but it does so only through the intervention of an "other," through an utterance from without, thereby preventing the establishment of a super-context (since there can be any number of interventions).

Iterability is, then, a condition of possibility of any code whether that code is enacted or not. It witnesses to the impossibility of transmission of any "original" intention/meaning. It is the departure from the singular event—one step beyond, one step removed, one interruption, *une force de rupture*—a departure, if you will, that constitutes the code. Iterability is therefore linked, first of all, to absence; it witnesses to the impossibility of a return (to the singular event, to the author's intent), to a radical loss of presence. Iterability is witness to what is unreadable and yet codified.

This confronts us, however, with a serious question: Is not the code—any code—undoing the work of iterability? Is not the code merely a resystematization now not of presence but of absence? Is not death now reinserted into a repeatable system, a continuum of presence? Derrida is correct in bringing back "absence" or "death" from the periphery, where it had been exiled by metaphysical thinking, but in what way does this reinserted absence and death continually confront and disrupt thinking and writing? How is death maintained within a code yet not of a code? How is renunciation of theory part of theory? How is theory written without rewriting theory? (How does Luther write the Reformation event without destroying the event, that is, without resituating it in a metaphysical history?)

Iterability itself—as impossible return, as radical loss of presence—cannot be codified. It can only be witnessed as inscription, as mark, or heard as a voice intervening, calling. Because iterability cannot be codified, it confronts or disrupts the reader. In this sense, iterability is the negation of repetition. Iterability defies itself: it is that which cannot be repeated yet opens up the possibility of the breaking in—the intervention—of the other and therefore the possibility of an iteration. But this is what Derrida perhaps "intends" by his notion of code—it is a mark, an inscription that continually demands a nonrepetitive rehearsal; it is a mark that witnesses to something that cannot be repeated and yet is iterated. Like Derrida's own signature at the end of this *"propos très sec,"*[14] Derrida suggests that his writing, the writing of this *propos*, is itself a singular, event, context *(sec)* whose intention remains inaccessible though the possibility of its iteration remains actively pursued—already in this, my own, writing. The *"force de rupture"* (of the other within the writing) is its essential iterability.[15]

> But let us explore awhile longer this notion of intervention.
> We should first be clear on what constitutes the status of "occurrence" or the eventhood of an event that entails in its allegedly present and singular emergence the intervention of an utterance that in itself can be only repetitive or citational in its structure, or rather, since those two words may lead to confusion: iterable.[16]

What is the relation between the possibility of intervention and the eventhood of event? The possibility of intervention—not the intervention of an utterance itself but simply the possibility of such an intervention—is itself a singular possibility. It would appear that the intervening of an utterance, the breaking in of an utterance, does not "repeat" an originary, singular event but, on the contrary, witnesses to an impossibility of such a repetition. The singularity of the event—the unexpected act, the surprise that cannot be prepared or contained—is experienced only through its essential iterability, in the force of a rupture, and then through the intervention of an other, as if, belatedly, in a moment afterward. The possibility of intervention, as code, is necessarily iterable, but the intervention itself, the breaking in, is not a repeatable gesture, act, word (here, "repeatable" is understood negatively as the dilution of the singular or the compromising of the singular). The intervention itself, the utterance, is a rupture that is event itself, a rupture as singularity. The utterance preserves the singularity of both event *and* curiously the possibility of intervention in and through time and space or, perhaps we should say, in and out of context.

The continued possibility of intervention (its iterability) witnesses to an absence within the singularity of the event. This absence calls upon iterability. This absence is the very condition of singularity. This absence as the condition for singularity is also the very possibility of death (as law) inscribed in every event. (The assertion that the singularity of an event remains intact or present through its iterable mark—as if death held no sway—is perhaps nothing else than the expression of an illicit desire of naive historians or overly zealous theologians.)

How is this absence—the ultimate condition of the possibility of writing, a condition that is inscribed within the iterability of the mark itself—defined? Or, to repeat the question differently, how does the mark account for the singularity (the force) of the event? The event is "known" only paradoxically, in what cannot be known about it. It is "known" only through its absence; the iterability of intervention points to that which is absent in event. When the utterance (*énoncé*) intervenes (that is, when the other steps in), the homogeneity of context (present past and present and even future present) is scattered.

As noted above, "intervention" suggests something unique, something singular, irrupting within the context of the event. But the possibility of this intervention is also iterable—the utterance spoken, the vows pronounced, for example, can be pronounced many times by different people in different contexts. The iterable structure witnesses to a singularity that is not repeatable but is known as the singular breaking in of an utterance, of the other. The focus on utterance as singular (rather than on some originary, singular event) points toward that which cannot be contained within the iterable code or mark, that which breaks from repetition as well as from context.

Let me begin once again with the question of the singular event. At the end of *Signature Event Context*, Derrida writes: "Rather than oppose citation or iteration to the noniteration of an event, one ought to construct a differential typology of forms of iteration, assuming that such a project is tenable and can result in an exhaustive program, a question I hold in abeyance here."[17] Derrida suggests that iterability itself must be preserved from becoming the tool or instrument of a metaphysical opposition of cause and effect or origin and derivation. He does not want to maintain an opposition between the citational event (as defined by Austin) and the singular (originary/performative) event but, rather, wishes to point toward a "chains of differential marks" (*chaînes de marques itérables*).[18]

Derrida has argued for the unsaturability of context: context cannot be certain or saturated, that is, contained within a homogeneous space-time continuum.[19] He has also pointed out the difficulties involved in the notion of a homogeneous space or presence as if the field of communication lies unbroken behind and before us.[20] He has argued repeatedly for the necessary iterability of a mark (or code) particularly in the absence and the absolute absence of receiver or sender.[21] There is a rupture in presence.[22] The rupture questions the presumed "pure presence" of every experience,[23] and therefore the force of writing is linked to mortality. For the iterability of a mark to function, it depends on the absolute absence—we could say that it depends even on the death—of its singular context. This death ruptures presence, homogeneity, certainty. This death—or absolute absence—is the rupture continually iterated. This iteration does not simply repeat an absence; rather, it witnesses, as singular event, as singular intervention, to an absence, but an absence that itself continually calls upon utterance, upon us, upon an attentiveness, even a responsibility to this absence and, therefore, to the one who is never fully embraced.

The rupture of presence, as pointed out above, is the disruption caused by another. It calls upon the other. This rupture of presence is not the metaphysical patricide that assumes a presence but then renders it absent (by murdering it). Rather this rupture—the intervention as event—is a continual confrontation by the other (in all of its forms—event, thing, word, person). The intervention stems from that which is constitutively absent in the thing—or the "other" already present in every event. This would suggest that it is not so much "death" that is the condition of possibility of iteration, but the other, and in particular, the other as neighbor, as the one different from me, who calls upon me. This does not mean that death is banished from the system or newly relegated to a peripheral role. The "other"—the call of the other—can always imply my own continual death. Perhaps death then becomes an even more integral part of life, not simply as a condition of life's possibility but as an exercise of life itself—dare I say, as a baptismal exercise?

Suspending the "What" Question

The noncommunicability of context or the nonsaturated aspect of context defers or displaces any particular meaning or control that the subject, as autonomous entity, wishes to exert. This deferral of context and, necessarily, event is subsequently a deferral of the subject. This deferral, of course, has been the subject of intense debate, particularly among the detractors of the writings of Derrida. "Transcendence" is still maintained as a necessary safeguard for meaning as if meaning and reference in the world would not be possible without some source or origin that is eternally present. If we reformulate this argument for a necessary transcendence, we read Catherine Pickstock's fear: should the source (of meaning, for example) be found within the text, should it be "immanent," a spatial reality results that has no depth, and a history is created that does not know time. Only the transcendent, according to Pickstock, allows us to see the "incipient structures of the immanentist city" (the city Derrida supposedly constructs) for what they are: pure sophistry.[24] Only the appeal to something transcendent allows us to see the complex relationship that must be maintained between space and time if we are to avoid the sophistic world. In other words, we need to "look" from without, from a certain vantage point over and above what is happening in this world, over and above things, events, words. The fear, of course, is that "meaning" becomes unattainable if "we" (writer/reader) remain confined within an ahistorical realm. It is the fear that the human ability to refer (and therefore to know and remember) has been denied. This anxiety is created, I believe, by a perceived (or not perceived) inability to capture or control the event—the disruptive event. It therefore reveals itself as the fear of something unexpected, something always returning, always haunting, that will continue to disrupt our memories, our contexts, our systems, our rituals.

For Derrida, however, the "source" is not within the writing, whatever form that writing may take: letter, autobiographical text, academic text, literature. The writing is a constant dissemination of any source that departs in a series of deferrals—a dissemination that, as we have seen, disrupts event and subject. The series of deferrals, or "chains of differential marks," disseminate context as well. We can no longer point to one, hermetically enclosed, hermeneutically definable "moment." In other words, we cannot capture the event or even the utterance that intervenes in the moment of event. The corollary risk is a transcendentalizing of context (super-context) that would simply be the reestablishment of a homogeneous presence through time: we have access to any event, any writing (whether Plato, Luther, or Derrida) simply because the value of contextual limits has been broken down. This is summed up in the popular dictum concerning postmodern thought: anything goes.

Those who subscribe to such a view are, not surprisingly, still seeking to impose a meaning on writing as if meaning (any meaning) could be positively discernible within a text. They are still answering the "what" question and believing that they can answer it without regard to limits. Derrida, on the other hand, never ceases to point out the limits of an indefinable context.[25] The situation that allows us to cite a text or person, the situation that allows us to put words within quotation marks, suggests not that the citation is valid in absolutely every context but simply that the context from which the citation was taken does not have an absolutely definable center.[26] In other words, the iterable utterance, the possibility of citation, breaks open the centrifugal force of context that initially we thought it created and maintained. The striving of "chains of differential marks," the continual deferral understood as striving, the striving of language, of writing, moves, then, not toward some transcendental "good" but toward a confrontation with limit, a demolition of fictitious limits defined as absolutes, the destruction of a tower and a dissemination into noncommunication—toward absence. This striving toward a limit avoids the danger of transforming any acquired meaning, any possible reference into a "prototype" such as "the good." But is not this also the striving of life—a striving toward the recognition of limits, a striving toward an understanding of death?

Derrida obviously avoids the danger of absolutizing the notion of context, which would make it either so restrictive or so permeable that any meaning would be possible and therefore meaning itself would be eliminated. I want to suggest that this risk can be further avoided by paying closer attention to two notions: (1) the problematic question of value, that is, the distinction between true and not true, or between valid and invalid,[27] and (2) the idea of excess as developed by Maurice Blanchot.

Underlying the question of value is, of course, the notion of validity. I will not attempt in this writing to debate the multiple facets of the problem of value or ethics (for example, defining good and evil) but simply to ask in what ways ethics (or value) and event (context, writing) may be interrelated and how this interrelation avoids a relativizing and absolutizing of event. In Derrida's text, the context itself is not considered as valid or invalid, as appropriate or inappropriate, as right or wrong. The fact that an iterable mark or code can function in different ways in several contexts suggests that value itself is in the deferral of meaning. If a mark or code were eternally valid and functioned equally in every context and for every subject, we would be in possession of an utterance or event that would break or render irrelevant any context. Context would be only a support, a shell for something "more" valid. Language would be only a tool or an instrument communicating a preestablished meaning. On the contrary, context—and what cannot be totally understood of context—establishes the possibility of an iterable mark that may or may not be valid. But this is also wrong: it is neither context nor mark (code) that ensures validity (truth or value), for, in the end, this is not their goal. Neither context nor code has a teleological subtext, as if they presupposed or existed for a particular goal. The striving, which I have underlined above, is not so much a striving toward a goal as such as it is a striving toward that which is absent within the event itself.

The "validity" of either mark or code resides in the possibility of awakening to that which is absent, that which is inaccessible in event. This is, then, not an ethics of "end times"—a capitalist ethic, for example, that strives toward profit (in the now or the hereafter)—but an ethic of the other as the other irrupts and disrupts context and event. It is an ethic that finds its language through the necessity of responding to the other, to that which exceeds a given context or writing, to a singular utterance. Writing itself is, then, an ethical response—not an attempt to contain or represent or simply communicate but a witness to something within itself and within event that cannot be contained by either the event or the writing.

Maurice Blanchot attempts, in his own writing, to highlight this characteristic of writing—we could say of writing always resisting the act of writing? In the chapter "Literature and the Right to Death," Blanchot notes—"*with surprise*"—that the question "*Qu'est-ce que la littérature?*" has received only insignificant answers.[28] Blanchot describes this question as an imposition. When this question is addressed to literature, when reflection imposes itself in this way, literature itself revolts; it becomes a caustic force capable of destroying the reflection and its imposition.[29] On the other hand, if this imposition is rejected, literature can become something more important than philosophy and religion and even more important than life in this world.[30] Literature without the imposition of the question *"qu'est-ce que?"* makes space for an excess that is fundamentally more vital than any system that we might call "life."

Blanchot appears to focus on what escapes from writing and from reading. Is there a failure in both writing and reading? There is perhaps a failure, but literature does not remain in that failure. Blanchot describes two slopes *(deux versants)*: "One side of literature is turned toward the movement of negation by which things are separated from themselves and destroyed in order to be known, subjugated, communicated."[31] The first "slope" realizes that something is not being said when a "thing" is put into words, when a "thing" is negated or conceptualized. The recognition of this failure—not of negation but of the possibility of loss—brings the reader to the second slope: "Literature is a concern for the reality of things, for their unknown, free, and silence existence; literature is their innocence and their forbidden presence, it is the being which protests against revelation, it is the defiance of what does not want to take place outside."[32] This citation, taken out of context, appears to reintroduce words that I have avoided—the reality of things, innocence, presence, being, and so forth. Literature, however, in this text takes over a role that was traditionally (at least in Western thought) restricted to the metaphysical philosophers and mystics: literature has an awareness of an "unknown existence" of things that perhaps constitutes their reality. To account for this unknown, literature calls on writing, on words. However, in the strange incapacity of words to contain any "form" *(content without form)*,[33] they actually reveal or confront the reader with the differential aspects of things. Through a metamorphosis, words indicate an *elusive existence*.[34] Through words—for Blanchot, the writing that is literature—the reader is confronted by something that is not known, something that is strangely absent. Though it is legitimate to ask whether Blanchot, in the end, does not turn back to the "what" question (Is not the "unknown existence" that he posits also the secret response to the question *"qu'est-ce que la littérature"*? Does not this "unknown existence" secretly cling to the question, turning it into "true" question even if its answer is "unknown"?), he nonetheless pushes the question beyond its classical boundary.

Jacques Derrida, in his own way too, suspends the question. He suspends the question in order to avoid that necessary imposition that the question supposes—the imposition of a source. The question posits an origin (whether in the intention of the author or elsewhere), and for Derrida there is nothing outside the text.[35] The text itself, the utterance, is established as the limit—not authorial intent or context. But writing is, then, also a series of signifiers whose origin or end cannot be positively defined. There is really nowhere to escape from this negative differentiality that constitutes the excess in writing. This does not mean, of course, that a series of signifiers can propagate themselves in any direction (as some critics wrongly hypothesize!). The text—writing—does establish a certain limit but within the writing of the text itself, within the event, that is the writing. The writing (text) sets its own limit. The "intent" of writing—that which is to be "communicated"—is not in this sense outside or elsewhere, for example, in the author's mind eternally established in time/space and discernible through sophisticated exegetical tools. Rather, that which is to be "communicated" is precisely that which is absent in intent, in event, and yet marked in the utterance, in writing. The text witnesses to that which is absent and which is inscribed in writing.

Writing cannot respond to this question—the "what" question—because writing itself, as witness to something inaccessible, is always writing a resistance to substance, essence, source, origin, father. Writing writes, but something in writing also cries out, caught in a life-and-death struggle. Writing writes the inaccessibility, even the absence, of origin, it writes the non-authority of the father, and it writes the disruption of an imagined eternal, ever-present context and the supremely conscious self. It, therefore, writes the impossibility of perfectly repeatable (and audible) citation. It writes the disruption of ritual.

A Strange Addition

Derrida's questions about the validity of context as communicable and Blanchot's insistence on an excess in writing that resists event, context, subject, and even writing itself are both, I believe, encountered in the writing of Luther that we have already cited. Perhaps they make it possible for us now to understand the radical break Luther made through writing—his resistance to a form of epistemological "seeing" or representation. Luther, in his biblical exegesis, in his insistence on that which is absent in things, witnesses to something in writing (and event) that cannot be controlled or systematized, something in excess.

This is clearly stated by Luther as he reformulates the classical epistemology and spirituality of his day. A typical medieval epistemological and spiritual progression advanced from *lectio* to *meditatio* to *oratio* and culminated in *illuminatio;* it culminated in a special form of seeing, even negative "seeing." Luther, however, breaks this metaphor of sight (and in so doing also breaks the irreversible sequence) by replacing the final term (illumination). For Luther, the movement is from *oratio* to *meditatio* to *tentatio* (which Luther translates as *Anfechtung*).[36] Once again, *oratio* and *meditatio* are characterized by a confrontation with things—with words, events. This confrontation itself leads to *tentatio*. In stating that "meaning" is not something hidden behind the surface, as if there were a spiritual, life-giving meaning independent of the letter, or surface, Luther continually points to the surface or shell (experience) and states that here is the most precious kernel. Confronted by the text, confronted by "something" in the text that we cannot capture or control, we are freed of the burden of our selves; we are freed of our own reason, our own imagination, our own theories and interpretations. The reader, the participant, is left to struggle with the structure or, in Derrida's terminology, the "eventhood" of the event. This struggle or disruption, however, is sweet, loving, mighty, and comforting.

The reader is confronted by what the writing disseminates, by what it retains as inaccessible. The inaccessible in event is both scattering classic reference and scattered itself in the process. The reader of the *Præfatio* to Luther's Latin writing is confronted by the writing of the event—a writing that is nothing but a continual dissemination of the tower, of subject and event. Subject, tower and event itself are deconstructed and in that deconstruction, they are sown as seeds, scattered as fragments, disseminated towards other significations that are neither representational nor referential.[37]

In the writing, Luther was not seeking a relationship to the events; he was not seeking a homogeneous context in which the events could be understood as simple "objects of knowledge"[38] (and thereby eventually related to God as source of all homogeneity). Rather, Luther was writing the very dissemination that was happening around him during the early years of the Reformation—a dissemination, or otherwise said, a deconstruction and totally different re-construction—in which

Luther found himself through his writing. We need to ask, then, how this writing as dissemination is itself singularly inscribing event (inscription perhaps through resistance) and how singularity itself is disseminated through an iterable (though non-repetitive) structure—and all this *without* reference to a homogeneous context or absolutized event, without recourse to the "what" question, or to a definition.[39] We will discover that this writing is a dissemination not only of event and subject but of every context as well. The inscribed event (the written utterance) is the inscription of a continual dissemination; it is the law written as mark (or clothing) on the body, a letter, however, that always already resists the law.

To approach the question of dissemination of event, context, and subject, I will focus on just one short, strangely forgotten text—the preface to *De votis monasticis* (1521/22) and part of the treatise itself.[40] There is a close proximity between the writing of *De votis monasticis* and the sudden exodus of monks and nuns from the monasteries. The writing of the treatise and its preface, however, came as a belated and worried response to the departure of several monks from the Wittenberg monastery.[41] The writing was born out of the event of this exodus (and perhaps occasioned a much greater exodus—though we do not wish to fall, once again, into the trap of establishing origins!). Oberman describes the exodus in this way: "Just as St. Paul 'read' the mighty immigration of Gentiles into the Church, Luther is legitimized to 'read' the amazing *emigration* from the monastery—both are telling, liberating signs from God."[42] Luther responds to a movement by "reading" into it the freedom of a Christian—the liberating signs of God.

But Luther (who still lived in the monastery at Wittenberg and still wore his monk's cowl and tonsure—his habit) was not only late in his public response to this exodus but also late in his own private response. The second instance of "coming too late," of intervening after the fact, is noted by Oberman primarily in a footnote. We learn from one of the Table Talks that Prince Frederick (the elector and protector of Luther) was sent a copy of *De votis monasticis* and was dumbstruck for two days by its force.[43] He understood what this treatise meant not only for the church but also for Luther's appearance in the public forum and immediately sent Luther a fine piece of cloth for new clothes. Oberman notes: "For once the Elector thought faster than Luther could act."[44] But the astonishing piece in this history is not the writing of the treatise nor the elector's reaction but the fact that Luther was unable to put the new clothes on! In fact, he retained his monk's habit for another three years.

Luther gives two reasons for retaining the habit. First, he had a concern for the weak in faith (those for whom the events of the reforms were moving too fast). Of course, Luther himself, it has been noted, has to be included among those weak ones. Second, Luther retains the habit in order to spite and anger the pope. But what does it mean to spite the papacy by the maintenance of the monk's habit? Was it to state that a monk was accomplishing these reforms and not a heretic or apostate— though Luther well knew that many great heretics had been monks. We will not deny or refute or even explain these narrative reasons and their contexts. What remains significant for us is that Luther's writing in *De votis monasticis* itself disrupts all comprehensible contexts; it literally undresses the context Luther was attempting to retain. The event of his writing, in other words, offers the best witness to this disruption of context.

The Latin treatise *De votis monasticis* was prefaced by a letter from Luther to his father. The letter appears as the preface in the Weimar edition, though in the English translation it has been separated, or cut off from, the body of the text. The letter is a curious dialogue with the present yet absent father (the "receiver" or reader of the letter is absent or perhaps displaced by the current reader). The letter consists of a questioning that results in a submission, followed by a retraction, an acknowledgment, and then a denial, and then culminating in a different form of submission. Luther begins the letter by stating that he wants to recall what took place between his father and him. Luther then confesses his error: he disobeyed his father by taking the monastic vows, and thus he broke the fourth commandment ("You are to honor father and mother"). The monastic vow—a vow to God—was in fact a vow against God. Though he confesses his error, he also pulls his father into this ignorance—"this ignorance was common to both of us." [45]

Luther's father was as unaware as Luther of the paradoxical context. Throughout the years that Luther was a monk, he constantly remembered his father's words, his father's warning that the monastic life might be only an illusion. Luther again confesses: "In my heart I could not ignore your word." The recognition that the vow was an error, that it was of no value, rested on the recognition that, on the one hand, it had been taken against God (that is, against God's commandments) and that, on the other hand, it had not been taken voluntarily. The error itself, though, is recognized as part of God's will since the error allowed Luther to fully understand the monastic discipline and spirituality "by my own actual experience."

This recognition is followed by a passage where Luther appears to be tempting his father: "What do you think now? Will you still take me out of the monastery?" Luther, in the recognition of the error, is now able to be a monk voluntarily and in accord with God! It would seem that now Luther understood why he was a monk and that he is perhaps suggesting that his father should consent. The letter continues to deconstruct the medieval argument for celibacy through a contextual exegesis pointing out the way papal interpreters had dressed up the notion. And then again that haunting question: "But to come back to you, my Father; would you still take me out of the monastery?" But it is already too late for his father because God has already taken Luther out (though he is still wearing the monk's habit). The fact of clothing does not matter, for his "conscience" (conscientia) has been freed: "Therefore I am still a monk and yet not a monk."

But once again, there is a tempting of his father: "But am I not robbing you again of your right and authority? No, for your authority over me still remains, so far as the monastic life is concerned; but this is nothing to me anymore." God has taken Luther out of the monastery and given him a new ministry—the ministry of the Word. This has been *added* to his monastic profession. It has not replaced it. The letter ends with Luther submitting to God who gives him this ministry and has absolved him from his monastic vow. It is a submission that makes Luther servant of all, subject to none (that is, retracting the submission to his father with which the letter began). Now God is bishop, abbot, prior, lord, *father,* and teacher. After a farewell to his father, the letter is signed (as many of the texts from the safeguard of the Wartburg Castle): *ex eremo* (from the wilderness)[46]—or from the desert, the original monastic place.

This is the curiously circular letter that prefaces one of the most strident polemical treatises against monastic vows written within the Christian tradition. The main body of the treatise itself discusses under which conditions vows are possible—in other words, what constitutes valid vows or how the relationship between context and vow is to be understood. This question of the validity of vows is developed through opposition: vows are contrary (in this written order) to the word of God, faith, evangelical freedom, the commandments of God, and finally (and perhaps most surprisingly for those less familiar with Luther), reason. Vows are considered invalid when they oppose the Gospel, when they become a way to salvation or claim for themselves eternal value. Vows are invalid when, as utterance, they are imbued with absolute authority. However, vows, when voluntary, are not to be dismissed, for choosing to be a monk should be no different from choosing any other walk of life, be it as a married person, a farmer, or a worker.[47] The value distinction between different walks of life (secular or monastic primarily) is demolished; the value attributed to particular contexts is broken down.

In one gesture (the opposition of vows to the gospel), Luther has denied absolute validity both to the context in which vows may be enacted and to vows themselves. There is no vow that is absolutely free from a certain form of degeneration, and there is no context that can absolutely maintain the vow. Context cannot be considered eternally valid or absolutely communicable, and utterance cannot, as singular event, be codified. "Nothing has ever been instituted—no matter how godly and holy it was—that has not been perverted by distorted zeal and godless hypocrisy"[48]—or, we might translate, by absolutizing tendencies.

The intent behind the vow—the intent of the so-called subject, the absolute "yes" said to "Jesus," for example—that all-binding, absolutely conscious intent, is subject to disintegration within the very subject pronouncing the vow. In other words, or better said, in Derrida's words: the subject is never present to itself even in the moment of writing.[49] The intention of the author—in this case, the one speaking the vow—is never totally "present" to itself because every vow, every iterable performance of the same vow, is forcibly always a break with the very "present" of the context in which it is performed. The singular utterance (vow) that intervenes into a given context breaks that context, but at the same time it too is broken by the nonsaturability of the context. Luther himself in his writing struggles with this dissemination of context and utterance, with an absence in context that continually returns and haunts every utterance (vow).

Working through the vow as utterance is a temptation that attempts to define the context as originary. This force or striving behind the vow is once again the striving toward a teleological end, whether that end is defined as "the good," as salvation, and so forth. The attempt cloaked behind the "vow" (and of the subject performing the vow) is the attempt to absolutize context and thereby establish a repeatable utterance as vow. The vow as repeatable utterance, as something that can be cited and *is* cited over and over again ("I do"—"I will with the help of God"), maintains the desired absolute context that can be rehearsed infinitely. This vow, as repeated citation, is merely a copy that attempts to preserve an illusory context. "The holier a thing is the more it is assailed by the perverted copying of blasphemous hypocrites."[50]

The intervention of a singular utterance, on the other hand, always breaks open, always introduces a crack *(une brisure)* into, the desired absolute context. Derrida speaks of a dehiscence—the splitting open to let out seed. A tissue is broken, resulting in dissemination. A rupture (producing life) occurs. This dehiscence, this break, is nothing less than an essential break. Life itself cannot go on with this break. If the context were closed by the vow, if excess were denied, if value were absolutely defined by the vow as absolute utterance, then we would again fall into the original hypocrisy (because of our horror of death—*qui mortem vehementius horreant*)[51]: the belief that we can master death, that we can be like God. Then life itself is worshiped like a golden calf (Ex. 32).

The vow can be such a singular utterance. The vow can be a witness, as intervening utterance, to the impossibility of vow itself. "I speak this vow but I cannot accomplish it." Such a vow witnesses to a hole in every context, to an abyss that calls. The vow does not fill in the hole and make it hermetically impenetrable; rather, the vow itself is the breaking of hermeticity. The vow, rather than closing the gates of the monastery, breaks down its walls. Luther himself breaches the wall of an eternally defined context as if penetrating into the world—not, however, into a new world of perfect illumination but, rather, into one of ever great *tentatio, Anfechtung,* confrontation—with perhaps the greatest *tentatio* being the ever-present desire to reestablish the walls of an impermeable context.

Luther does not deny the possibility of a vow. His concern in the treatise is to discern the difference between valid and invalid vows (though at the same time he points out that even the most true vows—*vere vota*—can degenerate *[degenerasse]* into blasphemy). It is this degeneration, this sliding into hypocrisy and superstition, the constant possibility of such a degeneration, that destroys the imagined homogeneous space-time continuity; it is the possibility of this degeneration that dislodges the vow, that displaces the vow from its position as an eternally effective and repeatable absolute. For Luther, vows do not rest on, lean on, depend on the "Word of God"—*vota non niti verbo Deo, immo adversari verbo Dei*.[52] The utterance that is a vow appears to be much more a response to this impossibility—the impossibility of a saturated context, the impossibility of a hermetically sealed, eternally valid context. The vow is "dangerous" when it attempts to stop the leak, fill the gap, repair the impossibility, and make the nonsaturable "whole" again. (Is this not where the current debate about "marriage"—as only for a man and a woman—falters, at least when argued from a Christian perspective? When Luther clearly argues in *The Babylonian Captivity of the Church* that the only vow a human being need fulfill is his or her baptismal vow,[53] this does not open the door to a simple dismissal or relativizing of vows. The baptismal vow is first of all that call to dying and rising, a call to an impossible responsibility to God and neighbor lived out in the best form that is given each person—sexual orientation does not matter in this perspective.)

The mark, the utterance—the vow—is a witness to an impossibility that is continually iterated. It is a witness to what Derrida calls a missing center: "Cela ne suppose pas que la marque vaut hors contexte, mais au contraire qu'il n'y a que des contextes sans aucun centre d'ancrage absolu."[54] What is absent, what is broken, in every context calls for iteration; the hole, the missing center, curiously demands the vow. The breach strangely calls upon iteration, an intervention, an utterance. Luther is not able in the moment of breaching the wall to abandon the vow. The penetration of the world is not immediately completed.

This difficulty is perhaps most strongly witnessed in the letter/preface/dedication to *De votis monasticis*. As has been noted earlier, the purpose of the letter is to recall both what took place between his father and him and to outline the argument. The two are closely entwined. The themes of the letter itself are intricately enmeshed with the questioning of the father that serves as leitmotif. First, I will present Luther's metaphorical description of his "space," of his context, and then discuss the implications of this context (or demolition of context) with the haunting questioning of his father.

Luther describes his own state at this time as being "walled in (besieged, surrounded) by the terror and the agony of sudden death and forced by necessity to take the vow."[55] The imagery of wall, barrier, being surrounded, but also and related to these, clothing and mask are maintained throughout the letter. These walls are further sealed—something known to Luther by his "own actual experience" (*propria et certa experientia*)—by men "who are so ready to inflame other men's souls to lives that endanger their salvation" by "dressing up" virginity "in borrowed plumes."[56] This dressing up is, for Luther, a basic misreading of scripture, a misreading of a text, words, *res*. It is a masking that covers up the hole, the absence, the impossibility of salvation through human work. This dressing up creates "puppets and straw-men" (*puppas et pappos*),[57] toys that can be used to inflame an illusionary outlet for desire—the desire for life, the desire to control life (that is, eliminate death), the desire for salvation through works. The dressing up has turned many men and women who have taken monastic vows into masks and idols (*similes larvas et idola*) of the pope.[58] The "context" of this dressing up is the monastic life, which has now become itself this walled-in space. The monastic life is a walled-in space, a closed, saturated context, because of this systematic elimination of death. The context has degenerated into an evil, demonic mask (*larvas*) under the pretense of being from God, absolute, eternal. This illusion, this "towering" context (tower in the sense of being one unique construction reaching God) leads, however, not to life but to death.[59]

And in the midst of these reflections, Luther continually questions his father: "What do you think now? Will you still take me out of the monastery? You are still my father and I am still your son and all the vows are worthless."[60] "But to come back to you, my father, would you still take me out of the monastery?"[61] Luther had begun the letter by acknowledging that his monastic vow was taken against his father, against God's command. Luther places obedience to his father above the monastic vow, the written command of God above the humanly constructed context. At the same time, however, he pulls his father into his mistaken act.[62] The father did not understand his own authority and, in the end, allowed his son to abandon parental guidance and plan. The father, as figure of presence and authority, did not or could not call on his own position, his own power as presence. The father was incapable of intervening.

In the text, the father keeps reasserting his presence despite being cut off by the son. Though he is himself part of the same ignorance as Luther, the father's words, as memory, even if spoken under shared ignorance, continue to return and haunt this walled-in and dressed-up space: "Then you [father] said, 'Let us hope that it was not an illusion and a deception.' That word penetrated to the depths of my soul and stayed there."[63] And again: "In my heart I could not ignore your word."[64]

Even spoken in ignorance, the father's utterances haunt and interrogate. They express perhaps less a claim of the parent as they haunt Luther with the more general question of authority. Who has a claim on the context? On the vow? On the subject, Luther? Luther gives authority to his father and then takes it away again. Luther unmasks the authority of the monastic context and yet maintains it when voluntarily chosen (yet always subject to degeneration).

Finally, Luther acknowledges his own impotence. Despite what he has written—and now I wish to add an exclamation mark in my own text!—despite what Luther has written against monastic vows, despite having been absolved of his own vows by his spiritual father, Johnann von Staupitz, he cannot lay aside the monk's clothing, his identity (of sixteen years, as he points out). But then he quickly adds: "What difference does it make whether I retain or lay aside the cowl *(vestem)* and tonsure? Do [they] make the monk? 'All things are yours *(omnia vestra)*, and you are Christ's *(vos autem Christi)*,' says Paul. Shall I belong to the cowl or shall not the cowl rather belong to me?"[65] Luther belongs no longer to father or to self but to Christ. He is "a new creature . . . of Christ."[66] Despite the temptation in this particular place of writing to assert his own authority, Luther as subject finds himself immersed and reborn. Baptism once again is inscribed in the writing as the drowning of authority through the dissemination of the principal actor (subject).

And *res*—event, word, thing—is once again placed in the middle. The writing as response to the exodus from the monasteries, the haunting questions of the father (father in his plural manifestations as paternal father, spiritual father, textual father, God), the inability to undress—all of these are inscribed in the writing and point toward something that cannot be contained within one context, something that is inaccessible. The imagined knowable center is dispersed, and there are only chains of iterable marks, that is, a chain that witnesses not to continuity but to that which is absent in every context. These disruptive things, the surface, the shell, the experience become the kernel—nothing hiding them, and they hiding nothing.

This dissemination of subject and context within the writing, Luther as "new creature," is, however, continually haunted by his father. "But am I not robbing you of your right and authority?" Luther asks.[67] Luther has "robbed" his father of authority but finds a new source of authority not in himself as subject but himself still subject to a different authority—the authority or calling of an other, of Christ. Authority has been robbed, but a new authority—now defined as the ministry of the Word—has been added (*accessio*).[68] Luther is now subject to this ministry of the Word.

Vow and context have both been subsumed under this ministry, this calling, this witness to the Word. The relationship between this newly added ministry and vow is unclear. A vow is not needed to fulfill this ministry, nor is a vow needed to fulfill the other "callings" or walks of life Luther enumerates: farmer, worker, and so forth.[69] The ministry of the Word is like an utterance that breaks into Luther's context and that disperses all previous authority. The monk's habit could, then, perhaps be read as an expression of this new utterance, this singular utterance, and this new subjection—in fact, the monk's habit might be the iterable mark of that utterance. The Word itself is, then, like a large cowl covering subject and event, covering vow and context.

However, such a representation risks once again making the absolute "visible" or in some way attainable. The ministry of the Word would then become the absolutely valid vow. But what we have seen in Luther's objection to monastic vows is that God remains unattainable through context (monastic life) or vow (repeated citation). "God," on the contrary, can only break into context or vow as inaccessible and there lay a claim. Why "as inaccessible"? Nothing in the vow or in the context permitted a sighting of God. God remained absent. This absence breaks open context not as a place for eternally valid works but as a place of gift, of faith alone. God is the absence that faith alone, through the Holy Spirit, can apprehend.[70] The absence ruptures; it is a dehiscence that engenders life and calls for a witness (not for a vow!).

But this witness is not of a paradisiacal vision; it is not a sudden illumination. The witness does not replace vow as eternally valid. This witness is a written *Anfechtung*, an inscribed temptation: the continual dissemination, for example, of the authority of the father in Luther's letter written simply from a son to a lost and found and lost again father. It remains inscribed in the monk's habit that Luther continues to wear on his body. As noted earlier, we can read Luther's inability to leave the habit behind him in several ways, accepting Luther's own reasons (to avoid shocking the weak or to spite the pope). We could read the cowl as the mask of a vow still covering the body (Luther's heart and mind may have been in the Reformation, but his body still held the trace of a resistance, a resistance to event, to the disruption of his medieval world). Or we could even suggest (as I intuited above) that the clothing is the symbolic representation of a new vow (the ministry of the Word, which takes precedence over an older, invalid vow). But these would all be misinterpretations, misreadings. What interests us in the clothing is not the clothing but the realization that Luther could not, would not undress. Luther's body is a witness to a nonsaturable context. Luther's body is simply not "at home."[71] Keeping the cowl does not mean that Luther's body is clinging to a lost shadow (a metaphysical world) that Luther himself has destroyed; it is not the reconstruction of another tower, different from yet equally absolute. It is Luther's resistance to any further, any new, systematization. Inscribed on Luther's body, in the form of the monk's habit, was embodied Luther's own deep resistance to theory.

Finally, as if to underline his opposition to any new tower, the inscription, the resistance, comes to the reader from a displaced location. The letter (and, by implication, what follows) is written from and witness to a wilderness—a place where Luther felt out of context. The letter is signed in an empty, absent place—*ex eremo* ("from a wilderness"). The resistance is always in some ways a displacement.

Luther appeared for the first time in public without the cowl on October 9, 1524; he then undressed the cowl permanently one week later.[72] At the same time (throughout this time period and particularly from October 1524 onward), Luther was concerned with finding a spouse for Catherine of Bora, one of the nine nuns who had fled from their cloister in 1523.[73] The advent of an other, the intervention, in this case of a woman, perhaps brought Luther to a different form of resistance. The other now appears as a singular utterance that intervenes once again in Luther's context. Luther's attempts to find a spouse for Catherine of Bora are unsuccessful, and the two get married. Finally, it was the ethics of a relationship rather than the maintenance of a cowl that embodied his resistance to theory. Luther accepted another type of vow not to replace the previous vow, not as new systematization—marriage was not a sacrament that ensured such a systematic communication with God through an immutable context; rather, Luther turned to Catherine as his nearest neighbor, as the other who intervenes and disrupts context and subject. The vow is now not citation but the singular intervention of the neighbor. And event is this iterated disruption.

How does Luther qualify this intervention? This struggle with the cowl, the clothing, the mask is a struggle with naming, with identity, and finally with responsibility. The breaching of the monastic wall, the disruption of both context and vow, is justified or absolved *(Christus me absolverit a voto monastico . . .*[74]) not by a new vow or a new context but by an addition *(accessisset)*. The intervention is experienced as an *accessio*—an addition, an onset, a repeated approach, perhaps even an excess—not of God but of a ministry, a calling of the Word. The repeated approach, this repeated, intensifying onset, awakens Luther to a responsibility, to a ministry, to an ethic. It is the awakening from vow and context to an ever renewed—because ever singular—call of the other.

Chapter 4

Writing Trauma

The Christ Event and Resistance to Meaning

THE PRECEDING CHAPTERS HAVE FOCUSED on two moments of not knowing or inaccessibility. A close reading of Luther has revealed the elusiveness of the tower experience, or Reformation breakthrough, as event. The impossibility of writing the tower experience comes to expression in Luther's writing through the almost total inability to define or pinpoint the specific moment or to attribute an agent to it. Luther's own inability, however, to write the event produced an event of writing—the *Præfatio* to his Latin works. This work, which is just one among many of Luther's writings, bears the mark of an impossibility; it bears the mark of a not knowing and, in that witness, it points the reader to a different appropriation of event. Luther's inability to capture the event was precisely the singular event. Luther's attempt to define the breakthrough event, to bring order into chaos through the writing of the event, results in a writing (the *Præfatio*) that is not able to define the event and that becomes itself an event of writing marked by the inaccessibility of event. The writing witnesses to the force of *another event* continually irrupting and displacing Luther as author, as subject, as agent, as conscious enactor of the event. The writing becomes, like a baptismal moment, a passive witness of something emerging.

This other event, I want to suggest, is the Christ event. However, the Christ event is used here not as a sacred event nor simply as a historical event but as an event that breaks the divide between sacred and secular. Can the Christ event be known differently from other events? Does it not also fall into that typology of event outlined by Derrida? Does it hold special privilege as if different from all other events? What is perhaps surprising is that it does not hover above event, above history, as if in its own realm but, rather, is deeply embedded, more than any other event perhaps, in eventhood.

How is this singular event to be approached? What is its iterable code, if any? Derrida has guided our journey toward a perception of event through its iterable structure (rather than in itself). He has pointed out that there remains something inaccessible in event and in the context of event. But what language will we use to better approach this inaccessible character without reinserting it into known categories? I believe trauma theory gives us such a language. Reading event through trauma theory (both historically and theologically) will open a way for the impact of an iterated inaccessibility, perhaps even for an iterated remembering through ritual. Trauma theory specifically focuses on the not knowing, on the inaccessibility of event, that continually returns to haunt the trauma victim. It is this not knowing and this return that cannot be captured that will delineate this study.

In liturgical terms, we could already propose that repetition (liturgical repetition) does not repeat or capture the Christ event (life, death, and resurrection) but, paradoxically, repeats or iterates the impossibility of repeating that event. The writing of Luther bears witness to this paradox, to this impossibility, in that Luther cannot write the event. Or, to put it perhaps in more accessible terms, Luther needs to find an impossibly new language to write the event. I will argue that he finds that language in the liturgy—a language of word, image, and gesture that reveals the failure of language to capture the event.

What Luther sets up as a young man—the permeability of every context, the absent thing in every event and in every word—becomes for the older Luther, seeking to find order in the chaos, an impossible task that can be understood only metaphorically through baptismal language. We began this study by pointing out the impossibility of defining event (specifically the Reformation breakthrough both in Luther and in Lutheran scholarship). We then moved to a corollary realization: the disruption of context. This disruption of context is intimately connected to the accessibility of event and therefore to our memory of (and the possibility of repeating) event. We now need to ask how the confrontation with the inaccessibility of event (with an apparent inherent absence in every event, context, thing), with the inability to capture event, is to be understood (where "understanding" is an act that always succeeds by failing). The question is not, what does it mean? Rather, it is, how does the loss of verifiable "meaning" find expression without becoming once again newly systematized or encoded? How is the inaccessible event itself remembered and enacted?

I believe this question is at the heart of Luther's rewriting of theological discourse. If "meaning" is not to be attained by climbing the metaphysical ladder to an ever more profound knowledge of God, if it is not reached through a mystical exercise that peels off the layers of visible existence to uncover the true, invisible reality, if "meaning" is not hidden somewhere behind the words only to be deciphered through intense allegorical work, then how do we even speak about meaning? What words can we use without falling again into abstract theoretization? We have already witnessed in Luther's writing his intense struggle with words, in particular with liturgical words (the reading and singing of the psalms in the Liturgy of the Hours, for example).

Luther defined prayer as a confrontation with words. But this confrontation, as we saw in the *Præfatio*, was also a confrontation with events that could not be ordered but that apparently pushed Luther, despite himself, in a particular direction. Two realizations require highlighting from this reading of the *Præfatio*. Luther's writing registers his surprise that somehow he actually survived all the disturbances of the early Reformation period and that he could give witness to this disturbance, this demolition *(deturbasse)*, this departure. The writing itself bears the marks of this disturbance in Luther's turn to liturgical language to translate his survival. "Meaning," then, is rewritten. It is no longer "hidden" but is a continual confrontation with the failure of meaning, with an absence in everything. And since "meaning" is in the process of being rewritten by Luther, so is theory also rewritten. The only "theory" Luther finds that is appropriate to express the inaccessible in event, a theory that maintains the confrontation, is found in the language of the liturgy.

A preliminary assessment of Luther's situation could lead to an obvious conclusion: Luther struggled with the fact of survival—he survived the posting of the Ninety-Five Theses, he survived the debates, and he survived the Diet of Worms. He had not been burned at the stake, like Jan Hus before him. He survived as a monk, still wearing the cowl. Luther's own inability to define the exact turning point could be attributed to the fact that he was surprised he survived. This form of survival, however, would be a conscious act—Luther would be consciously aware of his survival as subject. And though I do not deny the possibility that this conscious surprise may have been present in Luther (for who would not be amazed that he or she were still alive after such protestation!), it is not this form of survival that interests me here. The idea of the survival of a supremely conscious subject correlates neither with what we discovered in the *Præfatio* nor with the reversible sequence (in fact, inverted sequence) nor with what we discovered in Luther's letter to his father. Luther's description in the *Præfatio* of his life's itinerary points not to a conscious survival against all odds, as if the subject were claiming life, but, rather, to the astonishment that somehow he had been pulled out of death; that, despite the demolition of both earth and heaven, the gates of life had been opened; and that somehow, despite the demolition of every context, in that very departure—for was this not a departure from the strictly controlled world of metaphysics and piety?—history still bore the mark of an event, the mark of a life-giving irruption in history, the Christ event.

In the letter to his father, Luther describes this life-giving quality in the midst of departure by the word *accessio:* an addition was made. In departing from the monastery, something was added: Luther was clothed in the ministry of the Word; Luther received new clothes. This "addition," as we will see, has peculiar traits. As the consequence of a departure, the addition is strangely the continued possibilities of an intervention, of an utterance. The addition does not allow Luther to define a new, immutable context as if he were now in possession of the "true" call. Rather, the call to the ministry of the Word, this call that Luther defines as an *accessio,* this addition, is like the baptismal "pulling out" of the water, the "being clothed" in new garments—that is, being clothed in Jesus Christ. This pulling out and this being clothed are not acts of a human subject: they are the redefinition of the subject. The "addition" witnesses to the fact of survival.

But, as we saw in the previous chapter, *accessio* also implies something like an assault, an onset, a repeated approach, perhaps even an excess that is not controllable. The inaccessibility of event, context, subject opens the door, so to speak, to an "addition," but an addition that is qualified as an onset, as the return of something that cannot be totally grasped but that demands expression or translation. Luther expresses this return in old theological language, though the old now refers to something totally new: he understands the return as a "call"—a call to the ministry of the Word, not a call that is a voice directed specifically at him as subject but a call that arises through the realization of survival, a call that arises out of departure and return, a call that is added to his life as a strange, "passive" form of survival. This addition witnesses to the fact that, in the midst of departure, Luther was pulled out and given life. In this sense, the "addition" always bears a double mark: the mark of a departure and the mark of something life-giving. I will argue that this life-giving mark is continually irrupting as the force of a return, the return of an event, the Christ event. The Christ event is, then, event that remains inaccessible and "known" only through its iterable irruption, intervention, return, addition in life.

This passive survival is characterized by a not-so-passive surprise or awakening—the addition, the return, is unexpected; the survival is unexpected. This unexpectedness is curiously and singularly iterable—iterable because it is a repetition that never dulls the unexpected. The unexpected does not become "expected" or routine through continuous repetition. The unexpected remains iterable. But the iterable nature of this survival does not suggest that there is a core experience that somehow, mysteriously, defines or exerts its influence as a code or pattern. It does not suggest that there is a subject who, through iteration, takes control of the event(s) as in a sort of mastery, as children, in a game, seek to master or control that which surprised them or which they found unpleasant. The unexpected is another term for that which cannot be grasped in the event, that which cannot be contained by "experience" or neatly represented; it is the hole, the abyss, the absence in everything. But how is this unexpected assimilated? Does memory hold a trace of this unexpected excess? Does the unexpected continually return to "haunt" memory, as, for example, the elusive tower experience haunted Luther's autobiographical writing? Is the notion of a tower experience itself simply a type of hallucination that attempts to account for the unexplainable, the unexpected—and, as such a hallucination, is it really a betrayal of remembering? How is the unexpected remembered?

Luther's critique of medieval reading and writing brought biblical exegesis back to "words," back to the canonical events. Luther attacked the allegorizing mode: we are not to look for what is behind or underneath the text, the hidden meaning or the mystery; rather, we are to take the words and the events as the core, as the locus of any meaning. These are to yield "meaning" through their very resistance to meaning.

Luther's *res absens* (that in event, in words, something absent is apprehended only through faith) resists and displaces the meanings we too easily construct—"we," that is, our body, our memory, our intellect, our consciousness. Any signification that the *res* yield through absence confronts the reader and the writer. It cannot be celebrated as eternally valid—the meaning that confronts the reader is already and in some way always disrupting meaning, disrupting the attempts to systematize or theorize. The meaning yielded through resistance will always confront the reader with a continual absence or push toward a departure. Though this absence runs the danger of opening the field to the possibility of a plurality of meanings (and, therefore, no meaning), it accomplishes precisely the opposite. This absence in things does not mean that events cannot refer, nor does is it imply a necessary absolutizing of meaning in order to avoid a possible dissemination. Rather, the absence, the departure, the inaccessibility that the departure enacts opens context to the possibility of something returning, of the force of a return.

This is the entry point of trauma. The Christ event itself is the traumatic event. It is a rupture, a departure, but it is also a return. The addition or the "call" in Luther is the return of that traumatic event. This addition, this "something that returns," breaks open the realm of understanding, of theory. This addition, as "something that returns," blurs the distinction between theology and life. Luther found the place of this blurring, the iterated intervention, in the liturgy.

The addition does not push the subject back into a world of idealized or romanticized experience (including the reinforcement of a romanticized "self"); rather, it calls the subject into an iterated disruption of event, context, subject. This dissemination of event, context, subject, is again not a negation but a calling to life in the world posited in terms other than those of consciousness. I will argue, with the help of one thinker in particular, that this dissemination is a giving of self toward the other—that this displacement is a thrust toward responsibility.

Trauma Theory: Survival and Return

Several terms have been introduced or reintroduced: *reference, survival, return, remembering, responsibility*. These terms have already been applied to Luther's struggle with event, survival, and the translation of that displacement. In this application, the work of Cathy Caruth has already been present. It will now be further outlined by calling on a particular approach to experience (history) developed through trauma theory in her book *Unclaimed Experience: Trauma, Narrative, and History*.[1] Central to Caruth's thinking are the notions of survival and the force of a return that cannot be grasped or controlled. This notion of return I believe to be already operative in Luther's own attempt at translating the "addition" that arose out of a departure. In Luther's thought, this return is life giving. It is not the negation of reference or action in the world but actually pushes to an ever deeper dissemination of subject as response to the call of the other, the "neighbor" in scriptural language. This force of a return and the possibility of its life-giving character can be better understood when we read Caruth and her development of the notion of return.

The implications Caruth draws for trauma theory, literature, history, and the possibility of reference highlight a displacement continually operative in trauma, in theory, in history. Though largely unnamed, I believe that this displacement is inscribed in Caruth's text as a force that breaks open all forms of exclusive theoretization. This force is not transcendental in its power; it is not a philosophical principle or an eternal theological truth (such as grace). On the contrary, it is best summarized by a question that Caruth uses to disrupt the discussion of trauma theory: What does it mean to survive? This question continually disrupts the scene of thought and living. It interprets a certain understanding of "force of a return" that is already operative in Freud's *Beyond the Pleasure Principle*, which Caruth is reading. *Beyond the Pleasure Principle* is already asking the question whether history could be understood as the history of a trauma.[2] As such, added to the notion of trauma as a directly experienced horrific event is the notion that history itself bears the mark of a traumatic event, an event that Freud traces in *Moses and Monotheism* to the invented murder of Moses. Caruth expands on this historicized notion of trauma to ask what it implies for individuals and communities.[3] It is in this application that she proposes that history is the question of survival.

> What Freud encounters in traumatic neurosis is not the reaction to any horrible event but, rather, the peculiar and perplexing experience of survival. If the dreams and flashbacks of the traumatized thus engage Freud's interest, it is because they bear witness to a survival that exceeds the very claims and consciousness of the one who endures it. At the heart of Freud's rethinking of history

in *Beyond the Pleasure Principle,* I would thus propose, is the urgent and unsettling question: *What does it mean to survive?*[4]

Of course, embedded within the question of survival is always the traumatic event that occasions the surprise or shock of survival. However, that traumatic event is not accessible. The question of survival, then, is not only the astonishment that "I survived" a particular event (though of course, in certain circumstances, this can be the case, such as for Holocaust survivors, rape victims, and so forth) but also the translation of an indirect awareness of the traumatic event. What is surprising, Caruth points out, is the indirectness involved. She writes: "If a life threat to the body and the survival of this threat are experienced as the direct infliction and the healing of a wound, trauma is suffered in the psyche precisely, it would seem, because it is *not* directly available to experience."[5] The return of the traumatizing event, the force of a return, is not available to consciousness as sensation or knowledge but is repeated precisely because it is not available, because it is experienced only indirectly. The force of a return questions consciousness and the place of consciousness in time and space, in context.[6] It implies both a return (of the traumatic experience, if only indirectly) and a departure, the displacement of consciousness.

The indirectness of the return of the traumatic experience is precisely its inaccessibility. Because we cannot know the event in its entirety, because the event takes us "by surprise," in an unexpected manner, we continually repeat that surprise as a question of survival. Caruth writes: "The breach in the mind—the conscious awareness of the threat to life—is not caused by a pure quantity of stimulus, Freud suggests, but by 'fright,' the lack of preparedness to take in a stimulus that comes too quickly. It is not simply, that is, the literal threatening of bodily life, but the fact that the threat is recognized as such by the mind *one moment too late*."[7]

The traumatic event was not recognized in its happening. In other words, the traumatic event disrupts the subject and its context by breaking the spatial, temporal, sensory conception. Caruth writes: "The shock of the mind's relation to the threat of death is thus not the direct experience of the threat, but precisely the *missing* of this experience, the fact that, not being experienced in time, it has not yet been fully known."[8] The event is experienced as "traumatic" only later when the subject realizes that it has survived. Because the threat to life (the traumatic event) is missed—that is, cannot be captured—it is experienced as something that continually returns, something that is iterated. Freud suggests that this iteration of the enigma of survival is actually the death drive. Caruth puts it this way:

> As a paradigm for the human experience that governs history, then, traumatic disorder is indeed the apparent struggle to die. The postulation of a drive to death, which Freud ultimately introduces in *Beyond the Pleasure Principle,* would seem only to recognize the reality of the destructive force that the violence of history imposes on the human psyche, the formation of history as the endless repetition of previous violence.[9]

The approximation of death and life within trauma theory blurs the distinction commonly drawn between these two realities. The traumatic event itself—or, more specifically, the missing of that event—the traumatic event that could have meant death, returns as the enigma of survival. Life is, then, the enigma of having survived death. Although Caruth follows Freud in understanding the return as the return of previous violence, her own writing of that return as the enigma of survival points toward a displacement of the repeated violence. The term *displacement* indicates or suggests that the repeated violence itself does not have the last word. I want to argue that the repeated violence itself does not define history or humankind or the human community. Caruth's writing, in the very notion of survival, points toward the irruption of death within every context but then also toward the call to a responsibility: death continually irrupts not as a negative force but as something that demands a relation; the interruption demands a response that becomes then the responsibility of every human being and of every community. The force of return or the survival is experienced in the locus of the community. The introduction of the idea of displacement here underlines the realization that together the missed traumatic event and its return as a question (as the enigma of survival) form a movement out of a given context. The context is not impermeable; the subject is called out by the irruption of the other. Displacement is inscribed with the notion of the other, with the fact of alterity, an alterity that does not permit a systematization or a theorizing of life/death but that continually iterates the unexpected, the ungraspable, the unmanageable.

At the beginning of the chapter on Freud's *Beyond the Pleasure Principle,* Caruth asserts (and then insists throughout the remainder of the book) that the notion of trauma does not eliminate history. It is a rethinking of reference and history.[10] The reconnection between literary theory and "history" (understood as event) diffuses the critique of post-structuralist theory that it relativizes meaning (and, therefore, of course, ethics and the possibility of action in the world). This reconnection plays an important role, as we will see, in Caruth's writing: bringing "event" back into theory. But this "return" of event into theory is not the return of a perceptually confirmed and cognitively verified fact. History—or event—arises in our understanding where "*immediate understanding may not.*"[11] Immediate understanding (knowing defined as immediate perception of the "here and now") is displaced. There is "something" in experience, in event, that cannot be grasped by understanding but which arises and asserts itself. We could perhaps say that history is "known" by something within it that *makes itself known*—something over which we have no control. This "something" is like a force that continually returns to haunt the field of simplistic historical vision, breaking in to disrupt meaning though not negating the possibility of meaning/reference.

This "something" is, of course, elusive. We saw Luther struggling to understand what was hidden in the *res* of history (particularly canonical history) and suggesting that only faith apprehends those absent things—in other words, not immediate understanding. But how is this "something" that is absent translated? How is that which is inaccessible experienced? Caruth, reading Freud, suggests that there is something in experience that cannot be fully known but this "not-knowing" is not an eternally shut door; rather, it points to something latent in history, in event. That which is "not fully known" is latent in history and continually returns and manifests itself not as concept or theory but as question: Why did I survive? Commenting on the shift from the individual to the communal with reference to Jewish history, Caruth writes: "I would propose that what returns in monotheism—the monotheistic idea that comes back after the latency of the Jewish people—is not simply the missed event of the violent separation but the incomprehensible sense, precisely, of having violently separated from Moses *and survived.*"[12] Latent in the Jewish experience was the traumatic event (murder of Moses) and the fact of surviving that separation. The question—why did I survive?—required translation. In the case of the Jews, this survival is experienced as chosenness, the "incomprehensible fact of *being chosen for* a future that remains, in its promise, yet to be understood."[13] This chosenness is compared to being "shot into a future that is not entirely one's own."

But here another displacement occurs. The latency within history does not function on only the individual level. The Jewish example, Caruth argues, points to a characteristic of history as the "passing on of a survival that can only be possessed within a history larger than any single individual or any single generation."[14] This enigma of survival can take on different forms—that is, different historical manifestations—but as a "passing on" it will always implicate a community of persons: "We could say that the traumatic nature of history means that events are only historical to the extent that they implicate others."[15] This notion of history exceeds individual bounds.[16]

The enigma of survival in Caruth is the paradoxical realization that survival requires a continual displacement—that is, the continual irruption of death within contexts that humanly construed mythologies would rather keep hermetically sealed. Survival demands the continual iteration of death or the possibility of death in order to be survival. The question, however, remains: How is this displacement inscribed in Caruth's writing? How does Caruth's own writing enact trauma theory? In order to pursue this question of displacement, two interrelated notions—inaccessibility and the force of *Annahme*—will be the focus of study.

In the case of Jewish history, chosenness as expression for the enigma of survival, as a manifestation of the "fact of latency," again displaces the person or community of persons. As such, "chosenness" is not just a call of privilege that establishes the people in a special relationship or communication with God; it also exposes the people to eradication, to death. As such, this "chosenness," continually oscillating between life and death, is witness to something not fully understood in Jewish history. Chosenness displaces a perceived situatedness (a knowing defined as perception of the here and now); it imposes on every context, in every situation, something that cannot be controlled. Death confronts every context and therefore displaces every context. The displacement of context is nothing else than the realization that the world we construct around us is not eternally valid or perfectly construed—or the realization that something remains inaccessible.

This irruption of death in every context—which some theologians and even philosophical pragmatists have criticized as a postmodern obsession—is, I believe, that which is absent in every event, that which confronts subject and context through event. This irruption of death is translated, in the Jewish example Caruth cites, as chosenness. This sense of chosenness is then something *added* in that it expresses a fundamental dependence on something else. It is *added*—not chosen, but being chosen. The sense of chosenness is not something the individual or community invents; rather, it is something received through event, through that irruption of death, through that disruption of every context. It is the translation of the confrontation by self and context. It is also an awakening to a reality that it does not control, that it receives as "call"—as call to responsibility.

When Caruth, however, understands the sense of chosenness as expressing that which cannot be grasped, that traumatic event that cannot be known, the inaccessible, the enigma of survival, she does so by shifting the metaphor of transition or transmission from "passage beyond" to a repetition or a "passing on." Initially, in rendering Freud's insight, she writes: "The survival of trauma is not the fortunate passage beyond a violent event, a passage that is accidentally interrupted by reminders of it, but rather the endless *inherent necessity* of repetition, which ultimately may lead to destruction."[17] Surviving the traumatic event is not passing beyond a violent event (as if, at some later stage, that event could be represented, if even only metaphorically). Survival is the very "passing on"—the repetition—of that violence (individually, communally, historically). The individual does pass beyond the violent event but, in some way, is condemned to repeat it, almost ritually repeat as if still a victim, still a sacrifice to that violence. But this ritual repetition is, then, also displaced. If there is a drive toward death—a death drive as defined by Freud—it is continually repeated, and for Caruth, it is "passed on" as the question of survival. Referring to the history of the Jews, Caruth writes that they cannot fully claim their own experience and that, because of this inability, there is a "passing on of the monotheistic religion": "This passing on of monotheism is the experience of a determining force in their history that makes it not fully a history they have chosen, but precisely the sense of being chosen by God."[18] The formation of history then becomes "the endless repetition of previous violence."[19]

This "passing on" is the response to an imperative, in this case the imperative to remember the monotheistic religion of Moses (whom they murdered). This "passing on" is operative as an imperative. It is further developed by Caruth reading Lacan's reading of Freud's dream interpretation. Freud tells the story of the dream of a father:

A father had been watching beside his child's sick-bed for days and nights on end. After the child had died, he went into the next room to lie down, but left the door open so that he could see from his bedroom into the room in which his child's body was laid out, with tall candles standing round it. An old man had been engaged to keep watch over it, and sat beside the body murmuring prayers. After a few hours sleep, the father had a dream that his child was standing beside his bed, caught him by the arm and whispered to him reproachfully: "Father, don't you see I'm burning?" He woke up, noticed a bright glare of light from the next room, hurried into it and found that the old watchman had dropped off to sleep and that the wrappings and one of the arms of his beloved child's dead body had been burned by a lighted candle that had fallen on them.[20]

The question uttered by the child is an imperative to the father to wake up and take action: "Father, don't you see I'm burning?" But what is strange is that the imperative comes from a dead child, from a place of death. Neither the child nor the father can ever truly "possess" these words, that is, perfectly understand or respond to them. Language itself is not possessed by the individual conscious subject—the subject itself is always already possessed by language, by language that is gift, something that is given for which the individual did not even ask. As Caruth writes: "Neither the possession of the father nor the possession of the child, the words are *passed on* as an act that does not precisely awaken the self but, rather, *passes the awakening on to others*."[21] What gets "passed on" is not the actual meaning of the words but the imperative to respond, to awaken. This imperative establishes an ethical relation to the world rather than a representational one. And then Caruth's astounding conclusion: "The passing on of the child's words transmits not simply a reality that can be grasped in these words' representation, but the ethical imperative of an awakening that has yet to occur."[22]

The inaccessible cannot be represented, and therefore the only response (relation) to it is an ethical response. I want to propose that this "ethical" response first appeared in Caruth's text as the sense of chosenness of the Jewish people. The possibility of an ethical response resides in the very fact that something in history cannot be grasped or that history can *only* be grasped "in the very inaccessibility of its occurrence."[23] Since the inaccessible cannot be grasped, it is repeated, but this repetition is not just blind, compulsive repetition. The inaccessible is "grasped," but only indirectly, through what I have been calling a translation. The inaccessible—that enigma of survival—calls for translation. Translation here is understood as an attempt to live the inaccessible in experience or event. The inaccessible asserts itself not through what it renders visible or represents but in a continual return (repetition). Translation of the enigma of survival into the cultural reality of individuals, then, takes on the form of a confrontation with the not fully perceived that pushes the individual or the community to a response, an ethical response. The inaccessible in every occurrence necessitates or calls on translation as a displacement in which something is added, something that embodies the call to responsibility, something that strangely represents the other.

To these numerous displacements inscribed within Caruth's text, I will propose yet another, even broader displacement. The displacement of the metaphor of passage (moving beyond death to life, beyond the traumatic to healing) is also a *displacement of the repeated violence* that apparently constitutes history. For what is repeated is not the previous violence but the inaccessibility of every event. Caruth develops this last form of displacement, as we have seen, more fully in the concluding chapters, particularly in her reading of Lacan's reading of Freud. Caruth's work to reconnect poststructuralist literary theory and history or cultural reality, the attempt to introduce the complexity of event into theory, is best described as a "gathering in"—that which is inaccessible in event is brought into theory not through a newly discovered representation of the inaccessible but through a continual repetitive action that displaces the subject always outward. What is repeated is precisely an awakening from violence; it is "the experience of waking into consciousness."[24] It is a waking to the enigma of survival, to the discovery of the inaccessible or absent in every situation (and every theory), and to the possibility of translation and iteration. But this waking up is intimately related to displacement for it is only the survivor who, aware of an absence, is able to witness to the inaccessibility of event. What is repeated—that which is gathered in—is actually the possibility, even the call, to disseminate or scatter hegemonic theory, myth, system. Witnessing to this displacement calls, then, upon the profoundest responsibility.

It is this call to responsibility that, I believe, is latent throughout Caruth's text. All of the displacements operative within her text point toward a displacement of the self or context by the other. This "other" is often unwritten or appearing in disguise. For example, in the concluding chapter, in the father's dream of his dead child calling him to wake up ("Father, don't you see I'm burning?"[25]), the other takes the form of a child. But what is to distinguish this child in a dream from the beggar who knocks at the door asking for bread? We translate the beggar into a world of dreams where we have no responsibility; Caruth brings the dream back to irrupt within reality. The other displaces us—our selves, our world, our theories—and calls us to love.

But the "other" is already deeply embedded in Caruth's first question: What does it mean to survive? The surprise of survival is not simply escaping the threat to life, to one's personal life. The surprise is a continual surprise, an iterated surprise—as if surprise could be repeated! A child, when she discovers that she can actually surprise her parents with a sudden appearance, will repeat the "arrival" unceasingly and expect her parents to respond with the same surprise each time. The adult has lost, on a conscious level, this ability to be surprised repeatedly except here, when expressed as the question, Why did I not die? Not only is this the question of victims, for example, of the Holocaust, but it is the question of their children and grandchildren: Why am I here? It is the question of a parent confronted by a severely handicapped child, by a child in whom death is continually present: What does it mean to live? It is a question every community and nation should ask itself when confronted by death—that is, by starvation, illness, injustice, torture, war, poverty in the world: What does it mean to live in luxury? It is the biblical question posed within a place of death: the dead rich man calling on Lazarus to bring him comfort (Luke 16).

This witnessing to displacement, this call to responsibility, occurs not only in the displacement of passage by repetition but also by the strangely present first-person singular pronoun in both Caruth's and Freud's text, as if Caruth and Freud themselves become the "other" calling us. Caruth herself will always delicately but insistently point toward these displacements—"I will argue . . ."; "I will suggest . . ."; "I would propose . . ."—as she pushes Freud's *Beyond the Pleasure Principle* toward *Der Mann Moses und die momtheistische Religion*, as she suggests that the compulsion to repeat is not a form of mastery of previous violence (the traumatic event, for example) but the submission to something inaccessible and a call to responsibility.

In this way, Caruth is repeating the same displacements already written in Freud's text. Freud's own displacements are often introduced as well with the first-person singular pronoun: *"mein Ich"* or *"Ich glaube."* In the second chapter of *Beyond the Pleasure Principle*, Freud introduces the crucial reflection on an infant's game with the simple "At this point I propose . . ." Freud moves from "the dark and dismal subject of the traumatic neurosis" to "children's play" in two short lines.[26] The child's game displaces the discussion of the traumatic dreams of World War I survivors. The displacement surprises the reader for it is eventually a displacement, a departure, that does not know or necessitate a return. This displacement is not a passage ending in victory (as the passage from death to life or even, dare I say, from cross to resurrection). It does not engender a teleological ethics in which we aim toward a supreme reward; it is a displacement of this very passage, pass-over and its teleology. It is the repeated shock of survival witnessed by and continually displacing time, space, and the "I".

Freud and the Turn to Ritual

What we have engaged here, through the writing of Cathy Caruth in particular, is a displacement of the meaning of repetition. This displacement, of course, already began in the preceding chapter when repetition was distinguished from iterability. Repetition is understood as that which closes the event in on itself and creates the illusion that we have captured the event. Iterability, however, "repeats" the rupture, the absence, in any event. The utterance or possibility of intervention constitutes the event as iterable—that is, it opens the door to an iterability that does not dilute or compromise the singularity of event.

Freud approaches the question of iterability through a child's game—the game of *fort und da*. What is particularly intriguing in Freud's turn to a child's game is that this game is a repeated game, a game that is actually an enacted ritual. Freud had observed, in the house where he was staying, a little boy throw out his toy in order to retrieve it. When he threw the toy away from him, he exclaimed, "O-o-o-o," and when he pulled it back, "A-a-a-a!" As it turns out, this little boy was his grandson, and both Freud and his daughter (the boy's mother) interpreted the exclamations as signifying the words *fort* and *da*. What Freud later understands is that the child is enacting the departure of his mother, who would be gone for long hours of the day, but also, in a strange way, the child was also repeating the final departure of his mother (who died).

The game intrigues Freud because it apparently contradicts the pleasure principle. Freud asks: "How then does his repetition of this distressing experience as a game fit in with the pleasure principle?"[27] Though Freud proceeds to explain the repetitive nature of the child's game as in some way working out the pleasure principle (by making an unpleasant association—a departure—pleasant), he remains perplexed and goes back and forth himself on whether this example implies something beyond the pleasure principle. The perplexing character of the child's ritual, and that which finally brings Freud to positing the death drive as something "beyond" the pleasure principle, is the repeated nature of the *fort* on its own. The child repeats the departure without the pleasurable return. It is a repetition of a departure, the repetition of death or the attempt to enact a death, to bring a death, a departure, a displacement into the realm of life.

This gathering in or breaking in of death through the repetition of the *fort* and its curious relation to the *da* play out in several ways throughout Freud's text. Already in the first chapter of *Beyond the Pleasure Principle*, Freud raises questions as to both the smooth functioning of the pleasure principle and the too easy explanations that can be given. He begins the first paragraph with a description of what happens in psychological theory and presents a *"Darstellung"* (representation). Freud throws out for discussion a metapsychological picture or representation. In the next paragraph, he immediately retracts this by stating that with the presentation (*Aufstellung*) of the pleasure principle, he has no interest in seeing how close he can come to a philosophical system. He writes: "Priority and originality are not among the aims that psychoanalytic work sets itself."[28] Any theoretical speculation is always grounded in the facts of daily observation. He warns that we are dealing with "the most obscure and inaccessible region of the mind" and that, if we cannot help contact with it, we need the most flexible, *lockerste Annahme* (the least rigid hypothesis).[29]

Two observations need to be made. First, as already stated, Freud is beginning to play the game of *fort und da* through his own hesitancy in writing: proposing theory, retracting his ambitions, restating the need for theory but now as an extremely flexible approach—an *Annahme*. This is further underlined in chapter 2 after the introduction of the child's game. An "obvious" interpretation is given to the game.[30] But this interpretation is also questioned because "the first act, that of departure, was staged as a game in itself and far more frequently than the episode in its entirety, with its pleasurable ending."[31] The game does not apparently fit the theory.

Freud then states that "no certain decision can be reached from the analysis of a single case like this."[32] He then proceeds to explain and deconstruct different ways in which this playful repetition could be interpreted. The child's game, the *"fort und da,"*[33] can be interpreted as reproducing the mother's departure in order to reproduce the pleasurable return; by repeating the experience, the child was able to turn something passive into something active—but this would be simply a means of control, a means of exercising an instinct for mastery, indirectly venting anger at the mother by throwing objects or simply trying to transpose oneself into the adult world (which only suggests that repetition is a derivative form of imitation). Despite this long list of possible (and seductive) interpretations, despite giving the reader satisfactory answers to the questions surrounding this curious child's game, despite bringing everything back, pulling the toy back and explaining with joy, *"Da!"*, Freud throws us back out again with a strong exclamatory, *"Fort!"* Freud remains unsatisfied because the theories we use to approach such cases all presume the dominance of the pleasure principle. These theories do not "witness" (*zeugen*) to the effect (or operation) that other tendencies might have, tendencies that are beyond the pleasure principle, tendencies that are more originary and independent. All possible explanations, "are of no use for *our* purposes since they presuppose the existence and dominance of the pleasure principle; they give no evidence of the operation of tendencies *beyond* the pleasure principle, that is, of tendencies more primitive than it and independent of it."[34]

Departure and return are not only the "subject" matter of this text entitled *Beyond the Pleasure Principle;* departure and return are written, inscribed, in Freud's text itself. Freud's writing is event. And, in this writing, we are left with the impression that there is "greater pleasure" in departure.

The second observation is related to this departure and return. We see another example of *fort und da* surfacing in the word *Annahme.* This word is preemptively translated by "hypothesis" in English. (A strange parallel is to be read here between Freud and Luther. The disruptive characteristic of their writing is tamed through translation into English, tamed by science in the one case and tamed by the "church" in the other.) The Standard Edition of Freud's work translates: "This is the most obscure and inaccessible region of the mind, and, since we cannot avoid contact with it, the least rigid hypothesis, it seems to me, will be the best."[35] We are led to believe that, if we are to have contact with this "obscure" (or unclear, unintelligible) region, it must be through the least rigid hypothesis, a flexible theory. But Freud's text suggests something very different. Read it again: "Es ist das dunkelste und unzugänglichste Gebiet des Seelenlebens, und wenn wir unmöglich vermeiden können, es zu berühren, so wird die lockerste Annahme darüber, meine ich, die beste sein."[36] The region is described first of all in terms of light, specifically, a lack of light. It is a dark region, in fact the darkest and most inaccessible region. Freud avoids a pairing of obscurity and understanding as if understanding were able to pierce into that dark region and formalize it, as if darkness could put order into the chaos. The approach to this region, any contact with this dark and inaccessible region, happens—in the writing at least—through the word *Annahme*, that is, through adoption (literally, of a child), taking in, gathering and accepting.

The obscure region is not clarified through theory; rather, theory itself adopts the obscurity. In order to reach beyond the pleasure principle to those *"ursprünglicher"* and *"unabhängig"* tendencies, theory itself needs to gather in the obscure, to adopt the inaccessible. Obscurity, in other words, is brought here (*da*), although there is no indication that this darkness will be understood or mastered. In fact, we can argue the contrary: this adopted obscurity, this *Annahme* of the most inaccessible region, displaces theory. As such, theory does not even accomplish the act of adoption; rather, the darkest, inaccessible regions assert themselves on theory and displace it. They continually break open theory. Put in terms of the perplexing child's game: the *"da"* moment in the game is in some ways already a *"fort."* And isn't *Beyond the Pleasure Principle* itself the writing of a disruption, a continual game of displacement, of the pleasure principle?

Caruth also forcefully argues for the "return" of the repressed as the return of an unconscious force: "As a consequence of the repression of the murder of Moses and of the return of the repressed that occurs after the murder, the sense of chosenness returns not as an object of knowledge but as an unconscious force, a force that manifest itself in what Freud calls 'tradition.'"[37] And I am proposing that this return of the repressed, this unconscious force stated in terms of Freud's reflection on theory, is the *Annahme* of the darkest regions. The theory, any theorizing, will be inscribed with what is obscure, inaccessible, with what is absent—beyond understanding.

As Freud suggests, this *Annahme* does not have the luxury of being a definitive theory explaining the dark and inaccessible region. If the *Annahme* were an explanation of the dark and inaccessible, it would again be a game of mastery. The adoption of the darkest and most inaccessible regions, those regions that are never fully captured or conceptualized, is an iteration of this obscurity, this enigma of survival, this absence. In the word *Annahme,* Freud holds both the departure and the return in a curious juxtaposition. The *Annahme* embodies ritual, and ritual is marked by the iteration of an obscurity, an absence, the enigma of survival.

Going out and coming back, giving and taking, *fort und da,* departure and return . . . and the curious realization dawns upon the reader (or the same interrogation arises for us as it did for Freud),[38] namely, that there is more "pleasure" in the departure. The *fort* is repeated much more often alone, without the *da.* Or the *da* becomes itself a form of *fort.* I would argue that the *fort und da* in Freud's text is not an enacted repetition seeking a pleasure-giving return—that is, it is not an active repetition—but, rather, it is continually struggling with the force of a return, the return of that dark and inaccessible region. The child's game as it becomes enacted in Freud's writing is, curiously, a passive repetition. It is the stabbing in the dark, enchanted forest. It is the throwing away of the toy without retrieving it. If the action of throwing away—the *fort*—stands so often on its own, it is not as a prerequisite for the *da* but as a response to the *da.* The *fort* does not require a *da* but the opposite: the *da* requires the *fort.* The so-called explanation is greeted by its displacement. Is this not highlighted by the following footnote?

> A further observation subsequently confirmed this interpretation fully. One day the child's mother had been away for several hours and on her return was met with the words "Baby o-o-o-o!" which was at first incomprehensible. It soon turned out, however, that during this long period of solitude the child had found a method of making himself disappear. He had discovered his reflection in a full-length mirror which did not quite reach to the

ground, so that by crouching down he could make his mirror-image "gone" [fort].[39]

When the *da* (the mother's return) manifests itself, the child still repeats the *fort* (the disappearance)—however, not of the mother but of himself. The baby disappears; the baby is *fort*. The *fort* asserts itself as a *da*. The return of the mother is greeted by the disappearance of the baby. The *da* is greeted by a *fort*. There appears to be greater pleasure in the disappearing, in the *fortgehen*. Does the child attempt to turn the *da* into a *fort* and thereby continually repeat the *fort*? Freud discounted this possibility.[40] Or is the *da* itself always pushing toward a departure, toward a displacement? The whole *fort und da* game would then be considered as the iteration of a continual departure.[41] This iteration, however, is like an adoption (*Annahme*). The adoption of the darkest and most inaccessible regions, those regions that are never fully captured or conceptualized, iterates this obscurity, this enigma of survival, this absence. In the word *Annahme*, Freud holds both the departure and the return in a curious juxtaposition.

Beyond the Pleasure Principle begins with the troubling experience of World War I survivors and the recurrence of traumatic dreams, dreams that do not "fit" the theory of wish fulfillment. The traumatic dreams of these survivors are far more complex. Freud realizes that the trauma is perhaps more in waking from the dream—the fright of waking, or what Caruth calls the shock of survival—than in the dream itself. Caruth writes: "It is *the experience of waking into consciousness* that, peculiarly, is identified with the reliving of the trauma."[42] As we have seen, Freud attempts to refer this traumatic awakening through the example (analogy?) of the child's game, the *fort und da*. What happens, however, is more than an analytical explanation of trauma. Theory itself becomes "traumatized" and reoriented in that awakening. Freud reorients the movement—if it can still be called movement—that attempts to reconcile or simply relate practice and theory, daily observation and system, reference and abstraction, empirical reality and transcendental philosophy. The movement is not from lower to higher nor from higher to lower. Psychoanalytical theory is not trying to "explain" (which implies a movement from an obscure to a clear point of view, from a lower, chaotic, murky state to a higher, more lucid one) but is simply an attempt to repeat a movement. This iteration is not one of mastery or control (which suggests progress in dealing with crises) but one of confrontation.

The road "back," the road of return, has been obstructed. As Freud writes: "The backward path that leads to complete satisfaction is as a rule obstructed by the resistances which maintain the repressions."[43]

Psychoanalytical theory is then presented as an adoption (*Annahme*), that is, as a taking in, or taking upon itself, an *adopting* of the dark and inaccessible reality of the mind. If theory "refers" to history or context, it is to what is not known in event, to what is obscure, dark, even absent in event. But *Annahme* is not a solitary movement: that which is adopted never truly "belongs" to us. As utterance, it is also disruption. The child's game of *fort und da* is simultaneously return and departure, taking in and going out. The *Annahme* as a gathering in of the inaccessible, can we say, as the adoption of a child, maybe even a dead child, is like a continual return of that unexpected call of that child but that return sends it always *fort* once again; it passes on the call. As such, the "passing on" is an iteration of something that cannot be captured, the impossibility of a pure repetition or a mastery of event. Written within Freud's text, in the actual *fort und da* of the text, is a resistance to theory, to that which can be simply repeated or proven "in experience." And this resistance comes to expression in the very word for theory itself, *Annahme,* or "hypothesis."

If simple repetition of the event (whatever the event) is resisted, then how do we remember? Freud draws a surprising distinction between repetition and remembering. The patient "is obliged to *repeat* the repressed material as a contemporary experience instead of, as the physician would prefer to see, *remembering* it as something belonging to the past."[44] Repetition, or what we have called iteration, is not the memory of something past but a displaced reliving of what was latent, inaccessible, absent in the event; that which cannot be known in the event displaces facile remembering; that which confronts us in the event, in experience, is not an object that can be remembered or mastered (or theorized). The event is accessible only through an *Annahme* as a continual question of survival. The question calls on iteration: iteration of that which cannot be remembered. Context itself, then, as always historical, is broken open, or, as Derrida suggests, is "never absolutely determinable." [45] It is not self-contained but knows the irruption, the return, of a force.

Adoption/*Annahme*—the writing of theory—in Freud is at the same time the continual disruption of theory rather than conclusive systematization. It is the disruption caused by the child's ritual of sending forth, of playing the departure, of adopting the dark and inaccessible region. The *Annahme*, this adoption of (by) a child, as both theory and disruption of theory opens the field to that question Cathy Caruth posed: What does it mean to survive? The question of survival, or, in the Jewish case, the sense of chosenness, is like an addition, something that continually returns and calls to be enacted. The *Annahme* in Freud is both the writing and unwriting of theory that occurs through the ritual of a child's game. The resistance to theory, to systematization, in the field of psychoanalysis that Caruth enacts in her own writing through the question of survival and the continual displacement of the subject by the imperative of the other, that resistance is also a ritual move in that it "passes on" a responsibility, a call from and toward the other. This "passing on," this call, this addition, is, I believe, also operative in communal ritual and particularly in the Christian liturgy. Could we say that the dark and inaccessible region—the execution of God on the cross—returns and haunts Christian liturgy as the question, How could someone die for me? How could God die? And, in even greater surprise, how could God die for me? Once again, the enigma of survival is posited: Why did I survive? This surprise itself displaces the easy notion of death, of God's death, as a sacrificial act. The surprise displaces the theory of sacrifice by the enigma of death and the question of survival.

In both Freud and Caruth, theory itself is disrupted (and displaced) by the call of the other. The call of the other—the fact of alterity—finds expression in their writing through a reference to ritual—to the iterability of something not totally grasped or known. In Freud, the reference is explicitly to a child's ritual; in Caruth, the reference is to the iterability of a theological notion (the sense of chosenness of the Jewish people) and perhaps also to that subconscious human ritual of dreaming. To our surprise, we will now discover that this same move to ritual—to a liturgical form or language—is found in Luther, a move that profoundly rewrites our understanding of liturgy and, in particular, begins the rewriting of an eucharistic hermeneutic.

Writing the Return as Liturgical Event

Freud questioned the impermeability of his own theory—*beyond* the pleasure principle. And, as Caruth has eloquently suggested through her addition of the enigma of survival to Freud's questioning, the permeability of theory disables a totalization. The permeability of theory exposes a break, a rupture, through which "something" of past events resurfaces and reasserts itself as a force that returns, a force that cannot be controlled or captured (whether cognitively in theory or actually in analysis). Caruth has understood this return as the enigma of survival and the awakening to responsibility that such an enigma implies. In order to approach this force of a return, Freud turns to the ritual of a child's game that does not repeat a pleasure but apparently repeats a death, a departure. Caruth, as well, ritualizes the enigma of survival. The enigma of survival is in its core a repetition of that something that returns. This repetition is not just individual, it is communal: a people are defined by this ritual repetition, as in the case of the Jews and the sense of chosenness.

In both cases, the fact of a repetition, of a ritualization, points toward the idea that something has not been comprehended in history; something has not received *representation* and therefore returns as a force, as something uncontrollable. The turn to ritual repetition is necessitated by the fact that that in history which returns cannot be represented, cannot be "logo-fied" in theory. The notion of force displaces the more habitual sense that we can represent or imitate the past (especially significant, "meaning"-making events) as if the past were accessible. The turn to ritual in order to express this force of a return also reconfigures our relation to "meaning"—meaning is not something we can know but is something absent that continually imposes itself or asserts itself as a force, as an addition, as something we cannot capture.

I want to argue that we have already witnessed this displacement of meaning by force in our reading of Luther. Luther, before Freud and Caruth—and perhaps, strangely, as unrecognized father of Freud and Caruth[46]—witnesses to that which is absent or inaccessible in every event, in everything, and which disrupts every context and subject—and resists theoretization. Unlike Freud, though, Luther does not "return" to the imagined murder of Moses as past event that haunts the Jewish people in the form of monotheism and chosenness. Luther returns to the murder of Jesus as a theology of the cross. He returns to that execution as something that cannot be known through the metaphysical speculations on being and supreme being or through a metaphysical cosmology of two spheres or through the mystical climbing of a ladder to ever deeper heights. Luther returns to the Christ event as something that is known only through the force of its return, as something that continually irrupts in the present moment.

Luther struggles with *res*—with what is absent in event, context, "thing." He cannot pinpoint the "event," the Reformation breakthrough. His own tower (context) is destroyed, disseminated into multiple languages—that is, translation is required. Luther is confronted with a force of dissemination. However, this dissemination is experienced not as negative destruction but precisely as a force through which something else returns. The dissemination is experienced, as we saw in his struggle with words, as a confrontation. Meaning is not hidden behind or under the words or things and discovered through allegory and mysticism. The Christ event returns as a force that confronts every subject in every context through a disruption of subject and context. The confrontation is not itself a new presence forcing its entry on the scene but a continual disruption of the scenes we create. The Christ event is confrontational by its very absence—that is, by its absence apprehended by faith alone.

But Luther, too, is constrained to find a language for this force of a return. He, too, is obliged to find words that will displace representational knowledge in favor of a theology of the cross. He is forced to find words for this God event. And Luther turns in his struggle to the place where the struggle was most intensely experienced: in the singing of the liturgy. Luther can only find liturgical language to translate this force of a return. Luther turns to liturgical, and specifically baptismal, language to render a sense of displacement. In the *Præfatio* to the Latin writing, we discovered inscribed in Luther's writing a passive sense of survival, a sense of being "pulled out" of the waters of death, a sense of being called. The baptismal language stresses the passive nature of call: it is not Luther as subject who accomplishes the "pulling out"; it is not Luther as subject who organizes the chaos of events and defines himself as new creature. Luther as subject does not "choose" baptism, whether baptism is understood as enacted sacrament or language or simply as affirmation of a new self and context. Rather, the sense of call, the sense of being "pulled out," translates "something" that returns but cannot be grasped.

But long before he wrote the *Præfatio* to the Latin works, Luther was aware of a shifting context (the monastic vows). The monastic context could not justify eternally valid vows. The medieval monastic vows had been understood as a second, justifying baptism, as if the vows themselves, as if the active recitation of these vows, procured new life or ensured access to eternal life (heaven). Now, Luther, through the event of writing, understands baptism as a passive reception, as "God," not human being, acting, as "God" strangely acting through events that cannot be ordered, systematized. Now Luther understands "God" acting through words that cannot be "understood" (represented), through words that confront reader and believer. Now, Luther understands the displacement of event and context as the impossibility of accessing the "hidden meaning" of event and the absolutely determinable context, in fact, the disruption of any hidden meaning in itself. For Luther, every context, every subject, is exposed to a force that returns, the return of the cross, the death of God.

Even this understanding, however, is not a victory of human consciousness, as if reinforcing the supremacy of the subject. The execution of Jesus (the cross) cannot be known or imitated: it calls for conformity, that is, for a passive surrender, for the surrender to a gift, a call, the surrender to faith alone. "Knowing" is then submission to a call, to an onset, a return. Is this not what Luther also suggests in the conclusion of his letter to his father? He writes: "I could not have refused to obey you without endangering my conscience unless [Christ] had added the ministry of the Word to my monastic profession."[47] The word was *added*, not "actively chosen," not "granted" because of or by human works, but simply *added*. Something intervenes as utterance. And this addition works a passive conformity to the ministry of the Word that transforms both subject and context.

In the midst of the dissemination of meaning, an addition is made (the addition of the ministry of the Word). This "addition" or "call" is not the direct appellation of an individual to serve God as if the individual "heard" the voice of God calling. Rather, this "call" is the call to an impossible responsibility—to a ministry that is continually disrupting, moving out, departing toward the other because of the other, a ministry that is conformity to the cross, to the death of God. This call to an impossible responsibility is perhaps best described by the ancient Greek word *leitourgia*—the work or ministry of the people for people, the response to a communal urgency or need, a work that is both totally gratuitous and also implies a quantitative loss of resources.[48] Given this implication of liturgy as disruption by the other, it is not surprising that when Luther "writes" the return, when he appropriates theologically the force of return, he does so through liturgical action and in liturgical language.

But the dissemination of meaning (or of context and subject) is not simply the negative return of a force disrupting, destroying, demolishing. It is not simply the repetition of past acts of violence. The return of the cross as addition, as call, points to a blurred distinction already operative in the cross: the blurred distinction of death and life. Baptismal language, for example, encompasses both loss and addition. There is the loss of life (the drowning in the water) and there is the addition (clothed in new life, clothed in Christ). Luther is continually thrown back on, confronted with, events, words, that elude systematization, and in that confrontation something returns. This "something" is first "experienced" as loss—as the displacement of event, context, and subject, the reality of an absence in everything. But it is also the discovery of an addition, the discovery that meaning is not to be found hidden behind things but that a new language for meaning is required. This language of loss and addition becomes the language of a force, the force of a return.

The "discovery" as such is not really a discovery. When Luther understands the force of return as a call (the addition of the ministry of the Word), this sense of being "called" is in itself a type of translation. The addition, the call, translates the sense that Luther is part of a history that he has not chosen but which passively submerges him. This "call" as translation is then the sense that nothing in event, context, or in himself as subject (as person) can justify or define either event or context or subject, and perhaps even more surprisingly, that nothing can justify or put event, context, or subject in an immutable relation to God. Nothing.

Nothing human beings can accomplish will justify them in their existence and in their relation to "God." The late medieval concern about one's place in the afterlife is now itself disrupted. The medieval concern absolutized the way toward "God"; it created the perfect context (life, way) by which the individual can attain eternal life. Luther attacks the attempts of medieval church to secure a place for the human being in heaven as simply means of controlling both individuals and God. The realization that nothing can justify is the awakening to the displacement of event, context, and subject. This disruption is brought about first of all by a dissemination of event, context, and subject. It is a baptismal awakening.

The confrontation with events and with words is the disruptive act permeating Luther's writing. This confrontation is perhaps best illustrated where Luther finds it himself—in the words read and sung (!), that is, in the words of a book understood liturgically. If words and event can confront the reader/participant, it is because they are not signs or symbols of some deeper meaning. They confront the reader with a certain inaccessibility of meaning; they confront through a certain absence of meaning. Luther's own struggle with words brings him to writing the inverse of the so-called irreversible sequence. It was not, first, in a divine insight that he achieved a proper theological and grammatical understanding of the justice of God; it was in struggle with the words themselves and with what could not be grasped in those words.

The enigma of survival is an iteration of that which is inaccessible (even perhaps absent) in event and which returns. This iteration is experienced not just by the individual (in the form of a specific traumatic experience) but communally: a people are defined by this force of return, as in the case of the Jews and the sense of chosenness.[49] In both cases (individual and communal—or, could we say, the clinical and the interpretative?), the fact of iteration breaks ritualization open because it points toward that which has not been comprehended in history. Ritual—and, for our example, the sacrament of the Lord's Supper—is not a form of *representation or mastery* but is the continual opening up to the inaccessible that returns as a force, as something uncontrollable. The turn to ritual is necessitated, according to Freud's and Caruth's reading of trauma theory, precisely because the "event" (in this case, the Christ event) cannot be represented, cannot be "logo-fied" in theory. The turn to ritual in order to express this force of a return also reconfigures our relation to "meaning"—meaning is not something we can know but a body that confronts, that continually imposes itself or asserts itself as a force and that disseminates both subject and context.

Luther is constrained to find a language for this force of a return. He, too, is obliged to find words that will displace representational knowledge in favor of a theology of the cross. He is forced to find words for the Christ event. And Luther turns in his struggle to the place where the struggle was most intensely experienced: in the liturgy. Luther can find only liturgical language to translate this force of a return. The Christ event returns as a force that confronts every subject in every context through a disruption of subject and context. The confrontation is not itself a new presence forcing its entry upon the scene but a continual disruption of the scenes we create.

Luther turns to the liturgy because it is through ritual that he understands the demise of all systems. The liturgy can embody the Christ event as traumatic event from which we awaken always one moment too late: Why did I survive? What does it mean that God died and I didn't? Luther reacted against the relegation of the radical singularity of the event (the meal-sharing tradition) by sixteenth-century Catholic sacramental practice. This practice, still current today in different form in all denominations, places an event at center stage—the Last Supper (for example, Luke 22)—and establishes this event as knowable, or commemorating, origin. By placing a theological emphasis on knowable origin, the eucharistic celebration becomes "law" (ritual as rote repetition) rather than that which displaces law/ritual. In the worst-case scenario, the eucharist becomes a law dictating our ritual remembering and repetition as if through ritual remembering we had ever-renewed access to the mystical or divine foundation (the Last Supper) and to some special communication of grace. In this scenario, only the (usually male) presider regulates access to the event, and the meaning of the event is controlled through faithful observance and imitation of the law (of the knowable event). This is not what Luther proposed.

Luther's proposal is most clearly witnessed in his vehemently polemical writing against Zwingli: *That These Words of Christ, "This Is my Body," etc., Still Stand Firm against the Fanatics.*[50] As the Reformation was taking root in the lives of people, in certain practices of prayers and religious culture, one of the strongest objections to Luther's liturgical theology came not from the Roman church but from more radical reformers. Zwingli condemned what he called Luther's slavery to the older Roman sacramental system: Christ was not really present in the bread and the wine of the eucharist, but the bread and the wine were merely symbols or representations of Christ. Luther saw a great danger in this position (which he labeled "fanatic"): when the body of Christ is merely representation or memorial, it becomes a disembodied body, a dis-membered body.

Luther's insistence on the literality of the words "This is my body" is the insistence on a reality that cannot be captured or contained by the senses or reason. These words do not have a hidden (metaphysical) meaning, nor do they simply "signify," that is, stand as a memorial sign of what it is to be a Christian (against Zwingli). These words, "This is my body," confront the believer, and for the one who tries to cover them up or conceal them by explaining them away, they stick like an "everlasting splinter" to the flesh.[51]

The argument Luther pursues in this fiery treatise is twofold. First, there is the simple meaning of the words. The reader, interpreter, translator is not to seek different meanings to words that are clearly stated: "For anyone who ventures to interpret words in the Scriptures any other way than what they say, is under obligation to prove this contention out of the text of the very same passage or by an article of faith."[52] In other words, we are obliged, so Luther argues, to take the words "This is my body" literally when referring to the bread. We are not to interpret "is" as "represents" and "body" as "sign of the body."[53] The reader (the interpreter and finally the participant) is confronted by the literality of the words.

> Now, here stands the text, stating clearly and lucidly that Christ gives his body to eat when he distributes the bread. On this we take our stand, and we also believe and teach that in the Supper we eat and take to ourselves Christ's body truly and physically. But how this takes place or how he is in the bread, we do not know and are not meant to know. God's Word we should believe without setting bounds or measure to it. The bread we see with our eyes, but we hear with our ears that Christ's body is present.[54]

Our senses are disrupted by this bread and wine, which is Christ's body. The senses of seeing and hearing are in an irreconcilable tension. Our body is confronted physically by this Other body.

The "fanatics" (as Luther called Zwingli and those who insisted on a symbolic interpretation of the words) wanted "to eliminate the words 'This is my body' and say: 'Christ took bread, gave thanks, and broke it, and gave it to his disciples saying, "Take, eat, do this in remembrance of me."'"[55] The fanatics wanted to eliminate the confrontation, the tension, that the words "This is my body" introduced into the human quest for knowledge and faith in God.

The fanatics attempt to keep God "locked up in a closet."[56] They do not believe that God is present in the outward Word—that is, they do not believe that God could in some sense *return* in the outward celebration of the Word. The sense of "presence" here needs to be read in light of this confrontation the words create. God is not present in a fully accessible conscious form but in the bread that has these words ("This is my body") *added* to them. This addition, of course, is not the accident of Aristotelian metaphysics—as something that is simply added to the essence, the accident of a substance. The traditional Catholic approach to the eucharistic celebration (integrating the ritual into an ecclesial hierarchy that controls the dispensation of the sacrament and theologizes this sacrament as "sacrifice") falls into the same trap as that of the radical reform approach: both incorporate the sacrament into structures of representation. The use of representation or symbolism perpetuates the illusion of a control that blocks out (or at least attempts to block out) the possibility of a singular utterance or return, whereas Luther is attempting to lift up that which is inaccessible in the event—that which confronts the participant. Through the bread with the Word added to it, the Holy Spirit is given with all its gifts.[57]

The literality of the word—"This is my body"—confronts us again with the nonsaturable context, with the break, the rupture in context exposing the subject to the force of a return, an addition. Something in event and context remains inaccessible, and this something inaccessible "confronts"—that is, it precludes systematization or theorizing and sends the "subject," so to speak, out the door. The inaccessible in event, this rupture in context and irruption of a force, this possibility of an addition, is, for Luther, best witnessed in an iterated event of the eucharist. Here, in this liturgical celebration, Word and body cannot be understood separately. The body is comprehended in the Word and is in fact necessary "in order that our faith may be correct and consistent with the Word, because the two, Word and body, are not to be separated."[58]

Here, in the eucharistic celebration, iteration as continually failed remembering allows the body to return. Liturgical iteration does not establish a new line of communication with the divine or ensure a participation in the heritage of the new covenant. Liturgical celebration, and particularly the eucharistic celebration, confronts us with this failure of meaning—with the failure of the self, of the individual, to define meaning. Rather, a body returns or confronts the self in this eucharistic celebration—a body that cannot be controlled or captured. The ritual gathers in the darkest regions, the violence of an execution, and in this *Annahme* that ritual embodies ritual; ritual itself is marked by the iteration of an obscurity, an absence, the enigma of survival. In this *Annahme*, ritual confronts the participant with the dissemination of event, context, and subject in the world and points toward an impossible responsibility. Both ritual and participant are rewritten.

Luther writes: "The one faith says: This is Christ's body. The other: This body is mine. Do not come forward without this faith."[59] "This body is mine"—the believer is conformed to Christ's broken, disseminated body. The believer is conformed to the suffering, needy, indigent body of the neighbor.

The sacraments, and particularly the eucharist, make us aware of the other in his or her need. They point us to the other who, by his or her appearance in our midst, somehow points out the failure of our often insular and hermetically sealed rituals. The eucharist makes us not only attentive but responsible for the cry of the other. It is the voice of a dead yet living body, calling out: do this in remembrance of me. A dead voice calls in iteration, as resurrected voice—a voice over which we have no control, a language we cannot possess or capture but that always awakens us and displaces us.

> Nevertheless, God says: "I do not choose to come to you in My majesty and in the company of angels but in the guise of a poor beggar asking for bread." You may ask: "How do you know this?" Christ replies: "I have revealed to you in My Word what form I would assume and to whom you should give. You do not ascend into heaven, where I am seated at the right hand of My heavenly Father, to give Me something; no, I come down to you in humility. I place flesh and blood before your door with the plea: Give Me a drink! Instead, you want to erect a convent for Me.[60]

God is not "experienced" in the heights, in the invented narratives of our interpretative whims, in the systems we establish to order meaning. Rather, God intervenes as an utterance, like the wounded voice of the other calling us to what seems an impossible responsibility. It is the voice of Jesus. And outside of this voice, "outside of Christ, there is no God."[61] And this voice is heard in the immense suffering in the world: God experienced in a confrontation with the Word inseparable from the body.

Something "returns" in the sacramental celebration, an utterance, an absent voice that does not place us, once again, in the security of our contexts but intervenes as cry, as call, as addition. The cross "returns" liturgically and pushes the hearer/participant out the door to be confronted by the body in the world, to find the broken body of Christ in the world, in the cry of the "other."

Chapter 5

Writing Disruption

Eucharist and Law

Luther's turn to liturgical celebration and language underscores liturgy as a place of return, as a place where the iterated return of the Christ event continually disrupts subject and context through a continual conformity/unconformity to that traumatic event. Trauma theory now calls us to question more closely the notions of both iteration and remembering and how these are developed in Luther's writing. The radical difference between imitation and conformity (*imitatio* and *conformitas*) in Luther's thought accentuates the question of remembering. *Conformitas* for Luther is the passive tense: being conformed to the Christ event not through human effort but by what returns, what remains inaccessible, singular in that event, experienced as an addition. *Imitatio* is simply the repetition of the event by memory as if memory knew what happened, as if consciousness had captured the event either through re-actualization (anamnesis) or through an unbroken communication (testament). But how does Luther write the passive tense of conformitas? How does Luther break the powerful influence of imitatio, of repetition and remembering?

We began this study with a discussion of event and the difficulty involved in defining or pinpointing event (other than through mythology or hagiography). Luther himself was not able to pinpoint the happening of the assumed "historical" event, the tower experience. In the *Præfatio* to his Latin writings, the inaccessibility of event finds expression through liturgical and, more precisely, baptismal language. Luther frames this autobiographical text not in terms of a unique insight through divine revelation but as a story of continual baptism. Baptism works as an open-ended metaphor through which Luther expresses something about his involvement in the happenings of the Reformation. The baptismal

125

metaphor, of course, underlines the passive character of Luther's involvement in things he did not always understand or control. The baptismal narration of Luther's life does not transform events into a new order; it does not create a heroic hagiographic narration in which events point to hidden meanings perceived only by the hero or saint. Baptismal language allows Luther to simply acknowledge (confess) that he could not bring order to the chaos of events but that, strangely, the events conformed him, Luther, to the Christ event. He can therefore continually refer back to that chaos, to the events that make up the chaos, without needing to justify them. The baptismal narrative does not supersede and relegate events to an indistinguishable background but permits the events to stand in all their uncertainty and chaos. The events themselves resurface throughout the writing in all their inaccessibility.

These events (if we are speaking historically), these "things" (if we are speaking philosophically), these "words" (if we are speaking linguistically, exegetically), these *res* contain something that is not known. They do not simply hide "meaning" as if meaning were a deeper layer to reality; rather, they confront us with something we cannot capture or understand—with a new grammar. And in that confrontation, the singular event, the absent thing in history becomes strangely accessible, not through cognitive knowledge or faithful representation of the event but through a traumatic return—as "something" that returns, something of that past event, the Christ event that returns as a strange absence, a call, as addition, as an utterance, perhaps, of the Holy Spirit.

This baptismal language was also present already in Luther's letter to his father that prefaced *De votis monasticis*. For Luther, the realization that the monastic context was not eternally valid, that in a strange way no context is eternally valid or could demand absolute obedience (he acknowledges the authority of his father as disrupting the authority of the monastic vow only to take away the authority of his father later in the letter), came with or through the realization that he had already been "claimed" by Christ—this is the core baptismal proclamation. "As many of you as were baptized into Christ have clothed yourselves with Christ" (Gal. 3:27); and, in the Large Catechism, Luther writes: "Therefore let all Christians regard their baptism as the daily garment that they are to wear all the time."[1] Luther understood that any context that human beings create for themselves can never negate or surpass that first baptismal claim. There, God's call to ministry is understood not as a conscious, personal, self-establishing act but simply as an addition, an *accessio*—something that continually comes back, like an onset, as a force that returns and continually disrupts. In order to write this "something" that returns, this addition, Luther turns to the liturgy and liturgical language. He finds embodied in the liturgy this disruption of subject and context.

The writing of the liturgical treatise "That These Words of Christ, 'This Is My Body,' etc., Still Stand Firm against the Fanatics" exemplifies perhaps even more directly than these two other works Luther's reliance on liturgical language. For Luther, the language and enactment of the liturgy express that which always remains indirect, not graspable, in history (and, in Luther's case, a history that he always understood as salvation history). Heiko Oberman perceptively noted that traditional Luther scholarship separates into two different chapters the narration of the "insight" of justification through faith alone and Luther's eucharistic theology. And yet it is in the language and celebration of the eucharist[2] that Luther hears the continual return of the promise of justification—a promise that cannot be "adjusted to fit the categories of human ratiocination."[3] (We shall return later to the problem of the rationalization of the promise of God.) Cutting off the liturgy (and particularly the eucharistic celebration) from the doctrine of justification by faith alone does not witness simply to a certain prioritization by scholars, as if the "doctrine" of justification were higher up than a theology of the liturgy on an imaginary intellectual ladder; it also witnesses to a misunderstanding of Luther's turn toward the liturgy as the place of a return that confronts the participant, reader, believer. Even Oberman expresses this misunderstanding with that curious exclamation mark inserted into Luther's text on the singing of the Liturgy of the Hours—as if practice and study belonged to different realms.[4]

The confrontational function of the liturgy, and particularly of the eucharistic liturgy, not only disrupts our senses but shifts or displaces context and subject. In this disruption, the promise is "heard" in life—not as something we can grasp or systematize but as something that continually and unexpectedly returns as gift. As such, Luther's turn to the liturgy is not only the use of a new metaphor to disrupt what is understood by the word *meaning* but also the turn toward enacted language—like a child's ritual game—a ritual/language that resists theory and pushes theory beyond itself.

Luther's own resistance to theory, his radicalization of the crack within the metaphysical tower, occurs through the words and performance of the liturgy and, in particular, through these words: "This is my body." It comes then as no surprise that it is these words that have occasioned the most intense debate among theologians resulting in the deepest divides within the Christian community, sadly even wars. How is the "body" remembered? What is the proper form for the repetition of this meal act? What does it mean to "do this in remembrance of me"? What does this meal mean or signify or represent?

For traditional eucharistic theology, of course, the basic components of this liturgical practice are not hotly contested. An event happened—traditionally called the "Last Supper." So-called high liturgical traditions (those emphasizing shape, pattern, and strictly ordered ritual) have approached this event through a sacramental understanding: "anamnesis" is an enacted remembering of the event. Contemporary scholarship has focused more on the event of the cross and resurrection than on the Last Supper, but the Last Supper remains a model that speaks "in time" of an unrepeatable event.

Alexander Schmemann suggested that the eucharist curiously repeats an unrepeatable event: "The worship of the Church has its real center the constant renewal and repetition in time of the one unchanging Sacrament; unchanging, that is, in its meaning, content and purpose. But the whole significance of this repetition is in the fact that something unrepeatable is being recalled and actualized. The Eucharist is the actualization of one, single, unrepeatable event."[5] Anamnesis is here described as the re-actualization of an unrepeatable event. Though the event is described in terms similar to ones developed here—the event as both singular and unrepeatable—it remains knowable or accessible.

Other liturgical traditions will push more toward a memorial of the event and consider their "remembering" as simply an act of public allegiance, as a token of their faith that distinguishes the community as belonging to that past event (Zwingli's voice, of course, is the primary representation of this option). Other traditions will consider the event "present" through the Word, as though the Word collapses the need for any ritual (religious) action or repetition (remembering becomes devotion, prayer, and preaching). In all of these cases, however, a previous occurrence (or event) in salvation history (the Last Supper, the proclamation of the good news, the Word, the death of Jesus and his resurrection, the gift of the Spirit) is remembered or appropriated by a current/present act. The repetitive ritual act is, in itself, a "communication" of the event.[6] No matter which classical liturgical approach to the "Christ event," they all engage ritual (even when they deny the use of ritual or consider ritual suspect) as if the event to be "remembered" and "enacted or "communicated" were already known.

Luther, of course, opposed both such appropriations of the eucharistic event by his insistence on the liturgical character of the event. He opposed the control of the promise through Aristotelian metaphysics that made the focus of the celebration the manner through which the bread and the wine actually became the body and the blood. Luther recognized that the Aristotelian/Thomistic explanation and the strict rules governing its performance took precedence over the actual words "This is my body" and the promise embedded in these words. But Luther also vigorously opposed the theology of Zwingli as if the eucharistic celebration were merely a memorial, a simple remembering of something Jesus did and that we should do in order to be members of the "club."[7] In both cases, Luther confronts different forms of remembering the event and opposes the possibility of its repetition. I want to suggest that Luther decidedly moves toward that deeper separation of remembering and repetition that Freud pointed toward three and half centuries later.

But how does the liturgy, and particularly the eucharistic celebration, confront and confound our forms of remembering and repetition? How are remembering and repetition separated in the eucharistic celebration? Where is the resistance in the eucharistic celebration to theory or systematization (even theological systematization)?[8] We have already witnessed the danger of approaching any issue through the dangerously enticing "what" question.[8] If we ask the "what" question—What is the eucharist?—we will always be tempted to return to a presupposed origin. We will want to know what really happened and, if possible, we will want to "see," to reenact and relive, the scene as in a movie. But through which lens are we going to view the scene? Through the passion? Through the resurrection? Through a notion of sacramentality? Through Aristotelian or Thomistic metaphysics? Through the notion of sacrifice or perhaps through testament? Through a question of "direction"? Through memorial or anamnesis? Perhaps through the Word alone? No matter how forcefully each argument is stated, these approaches all have one thing in common: they all apply a hermeneutic to the eucharist.[9]

But is Luther not making a radically different proposal?

Christ, in order to prepare for himself an acceptable and beloved people, which should be bound together in unity through love, abolished the whole law of Moses. And that he might not give further occasion for divisions and sects, he appointed in return but one law or order for his entire people, and that was the holy mass. . . . Henceforth, therefore, there is to be no other external order for the service of God except the mass. And where the mass is used, there is true worship.[10]

These words come from another treatise, an earlier, less polemical treatise, on the eucharist, the "Treatise on the New Testament" (1520). I believe that Luther, in these words, rather than applying yet another theory to the eucharist, is proposing that a hermeneutic—the very possibility of a theology—arises out of the event called the eucharist. And further, I will suggest that Luther understands the force of a return, the continual return of the Christ event through the eucharist as an unexpected promise or call that alone opens up the possibility for the believer to relate promise to life—their life, the life of the neighbor, the life of the world in its vastness.

The Singularity of Event

The strange and unexpected irruption of the phrase "one law" (or order) in the passage cited above requires some analysis. Why would Luther employ a word or play with a word that he normally sets in juxtaposition to gospel? As a hermeneutic for the exegesis of the Scripture and preaching, the "law and gospel" dynamic is considered by many scholars a "trademark" of Luther and Lutheran scholarship. The distinction, however, between law and gospel in Luther's writing remains surprisingly elusive, even in the thought of one of the finest readers of Luther in the twentieth century, Gerhard Ebeling. Ebeling, however, makes several proposals that are worth developing in ways that he may not have expected.

In his exposition of the law and gospel dynamic in Luther, Ebeling points out that Luther was pushed to develop an exegesis that rendered Scripture "actual" for the reader, an exegesis that would enable Scripture to encounter (almost confront) the reader: "so that it speaks directly to the reader, affects the reader and comes to life in the reader's heart?"[11] The reader of Scripture assumes a passive role. From the outset, Ebeling posits Luther's development of "law and gospel" as an attempt to write the impact of an encounter and, I would argue, the force of a confrontation or return.

In its simplest form, the distinction between law and gospel can be described in this way: law is something that requires strict adherence and obedience, something that places a demand (that it cannot fulfill), whereas gospel is always promise and gift. However, despite this succinct definition, Ebeling confesses that a law and gospel hermeneutic is neither a single "idea" nor a twofold thought; it strangely avoids being at any center, whether it be the center of a circle or the double center of an ellipse.[12] The difference cannot be encircled. Law and gospel hermeneutic is not a new organizing principle around which Luther builds a new theory or metaphysics. Again, the distinction, for Ebeling, is much more the impact of an encounter that is experienced and that cannot be easily systematized or even verbally repeated.

Remaining a moment with Ebeling's writing, we discover that the difficulty in writing the law/gospel dynamic finally pushes Ebeling to question the meaning of "difference" ("What does 'distinction' [or difference] really mean here?").[13] Ebeling's questioning of difference cannot be pursued in the present study other than to state that, in Luther's distinction of law and gospel, Ebeling understands something that strangely resists theoretization.

> A distinction here does not mean a difference which simply exists, and has only to be established, understood and recognized. The issue is a serious one for the very reason that the difference does not exist in practice, but is rather experienced only in a mixed and confused form, and that even where it is clearly recognized, it must be repeatedly clarified, and can only be maintained against a constant and pressing threat of confusion.[14]

The distinction between law and gospel is actually a difference that "factually" (*faktisch*) does not exist (*nicht besteht*) but is known (or comes) only through unexpected experience. Is Ebeling suggesting that the difference is something that cannot be represented or "known" perceptively? Is Ebeling already suggesting that this difference embodies something not known, something that cannot be grasped? He then goes on to state that where the difference is "clear" (*klargestellt*), it pushes toward a repetition so that it can be made ever clear again (*immer neu klargestellt werden muss*). Difference is neither a separation nor a paradoxical binding but a challenge[15] and something like a trauma that requires repetition in the hope of understanding what it means.

Despite the spiral of ever-increasing difference within Ebeling's own writing of the distinction between law and gospel, he still clings to that basic, commonly accepted theological distinction of law as demand and gospel as promise. However, inscribed in his writing, we read a growing ambiguity on the actual nature of the distinction. This ambiguity reflects further "differences" written into the nature of law. Ebeling writes: "The distinction between the law and the gospel results in a distinction with regard to the law itself."[16] One difference engenders other differences. This growing chain of differences is already present in Luther's writing. For Luther himself to write the difference, he develops two uses of law: first, God uses the law to restrain evil and to maintain order in creation (the civil or political use of the law); second, God uses the law to reveal sin, to terrify conscience, and to put to death the old creature by driving it to Christ (the theological use of the law).[17]

The first use of the law is the most usual and perhaps the most universal. The notion of law is associated with the ordering of society and the maintenance of balance between the rights of individuals and the collective interest. "Law," in this sense, takes on even a symbolic force as a system that represents, protects, and, when invoked, reenacts the rights of a people. The second use of the law is more properly theological in that it brings the human being to a realization of depravity and through that recognition to God. The "law," then, as both regulatory of human affairs and as instrument of God, assumes certain mystic proportions. Though Ebeling does not explicitly refer to this power of a mystic characteristic of the law, he does state that we must not "play" with the law. It carries with it a danger.

Even before Ebeling can write about this power or danger inherent in the law, he is pushed to reassert, within in his own text (perhaps out of fear of that very power or force), the singular power of the gospel. This reassertion, however, turns the power of the gospel into a hegemonic authority. The following lengthy citation (though, in German, all one sentence!) is necessary in order to grasp the strength of Ebeling's assertion, his need to reinforce the power of the gospel against the law, and perhaps his fear of the inability to properly define the notion of difference.

> For if "good news" [gospel], that is, preaching which brings joy and liberty, which increases courage, reveals hope and creates faith, is not to be a mere interlude which provides a passing relief, a diversion, a slight illusion, a momentary forgetfulness, and a kind of opium, but instead is to dominate the future, be adequate to all temptations, resolve all confusion and shine brighter than all darkness, then it must be a word which is unequivocally clear, true and certain and cannot be shaken or explained away. It must be a word which is true unconditionally and without qualification, which is reliable and therefore evokes trust, and which illuminates the man [sic] who permits it to be spoken to him, liberates him from the curse of the lie and brings him the truth, sets him free from doubt and gives him certainty, saves him from death and hell, and gives him life and blessedness.[18]

Here, Ebeling reasserts the power of the gospel over and against the power of the law. Here, Ebeling displaces the power of law by positioning the gospel in an even more compelling and comprehensive role. The gospel, for Ebeling, is this unique, single-minded force that is not just an intermezzo or interlude, not just an illusion or opium-induced state, but something that levels out all difference, even time (*Zukunft* and *Anfechtung*). These assertions (and this fear that demanded the assertions), however, belong to Ebeling, not Luther. Faced with the ambiguity and power of the law, Luther does not turn to the gospel as an overriding, centralizing, hegemonic principle; Luther turns to the gospel as utterance that comes to expression in the eucharist, in a liturgical action.

But then the phrase "[Christ] appointed in return but one law or order for his entire people, and that was the holy mass" becomes even more puzzling. Why would Luther equate what he considers the heart of the gospel with "law" that orders society and symbolizes the power of systematization? Even if we were to read "law" in the passage from "Treatise on the New Testament" according to Luther's second use of the law, we would still need to ask why Luther would equate the words of promise of the eucharist with a law that terrifies and kills. How is the grammatical peculiarity of this phrase to be understood? Could our previous statement that Luther turns to the eucharist as an expression of the gospel's disruption of the law be incorrect? Could the young Luther actually be leaning toward an understanding of the eucharist not as gospel but as a single and new absolute law, "one" liturgical law that would replace the official metaphysical cosmology?

In light of Luther's reticence toward a legalism of form (and particularly within the liturgy), in light of Luther's resistance to the construction of an impermeable context, we need to answer with a resounding "No"! It would be better to reformulate the question: Is not Luther breaking open, disrupting, the notion of "law" by setting it side by side with the eucharist? The intrusiveness of the word *law* in this passage yields, I believe, an initial hermeneutical insight: law and its power (authority), whether understood as regulatory and hegemonic or as terrifying consciences, is profoundly destabilized or displaced by a liturgical act, by a liturgical iteration of an event—by the gospel. Law itself is displaced within a Christian context by the iteration of the Christ event. The dangerous power of the law is not restrained or reinserted into a system through a gospel hegemony or gospel (logo-)centrism. The ambiguity of the law and the shifting notion of difference between law and gospel is not abrogated by an even more powerful theology of the Word.

The gospel does not become a new law that itself controls the interpretation of the Christ event as if "gospel" were a new theological systematization of event or as a means of accessing the meaning of event. This gospel (logos) imposition would simply relegate the event to a particular place within a grammatical construction (even if that place is originary and privileged) and deny it the possibility of returning, of encountering, of confronting the reader/participant. The eucharistic event is not distilled or rendered accessible by law; rather, event—in this case, the eucharistic event—interprets and even disrupts the law.

Luther, through liturgical reflection, disrupts the two narratives as he reverses the relation between law and event, and particularly between law and gospel event. The first disruption concerns us more immediately: the disruption of the narrative of the discovery of justification through faith alone. The second disruption can be only suggested and left for later development: the disruption of the ancient coupling of law and liturgical practice and, in particular, the use of the law in order to explain and justify liturgical theology and practice—*lex orandi, lex credendi*.

The narrative of Luther's discovery of the theological insight "justification through faith alone" has already been unveiled as invented narrative, especially when it is considered from the perspective of a supremely conscious subject assenting to divine revelation. The breakthrough in Luther's life and thought could not be pinpointed to any place or time, but, as Luther himself narrates, this change or turn was itself the sense of "being pulled out." Luther did not have a revelatory insight but, rather, was imbued with a sense that life was a continual baptism. The understanding that neither law nor work could justify the human being standing before God, the understanding that justification "happens" through faith alone, presented Luther with an inextricable situation: How could this justification, how could this "faith alone," be written without turning it into new law or work?

Here, again, the answer for Luther lies in the turn toward the liturgy and liturgical language. The celebration of the eucharist—the holy mass—stands as the moment of iterated disruption of law and works. Luther does not turn to the speculative theology of the late middle ages; he does not turn (forgive the anachronism) to the speculations of nineteenth- and twentieth-century "systematic" theology. Luther does not turn toward the systematic development of a theological premise (faith alone or Word alone). By "not turning" to a theological premise, Luther disrupts the narrative of a passive justification that establishes the idea of faith alone or Word alone or any other theological use of the word *alone*. Luther turns not to a theological premise or system but to the disruptive celebration of baptism and eucharist; in that turn, I believe, Luther redefines the promise that is uttered as justification and the status of every human being standing before God *(coram Deo)*.

The second narrative, though not directly related to Luther or addressed by Luther (yet hinted at above), must be briefly considered for we will discover, already here in liturgical iteration, an unsettling of the notion of law. The narrative in question is the ancient coupling of "law" and liturgical practice and the uncritically held notion of law operative within theological reflection. This uncritically held notion revolves around the invention of the aphorism *lex orandi, lex credendi*. The original form of the aphorism appears in a text of Prosper of Aquitaine: *"ut legem credendi lex statuat supplicandi."*[19] The development or the application of the aphorism *lex orandi, lex credendi* does not, of course, correspond to what Prosper originally wrote. Though we rightly credit Prosper with the citation, its subsequent narration remains surprisingly mysterious—despite a presumed (that is, unquestioned) historical certainty. Despite the consistent and regular use of the phrase *lex orandi, lex credendi* by liturgical theologians, the genealogy of the aphorism remains unknown. The mysterious origin of this curious reduction is perhaps best described in the words Jacques Derrida employed to speak of the so-called origin of authority and the force of law—its "mystical foundation."[20] The deferral of the origins of law to a mystical foundation, of course, suggests that law does not have an origin, that the source of law cannot be pinpointed. "Since the origin of authority, the foundation or ground, the position of the law can't by definition rest on anything but themselves, they are themselves a violence without ground."[21] It is this non-origin of authority and law that renders law so powerful as a regulating and defining force.

The liturgical aphorism, in its appeal to a law of believing and a law of praying, in its invention of law dissociated from human need or lack (*supplicandi*), defers believing and praying to a force of law that controls (logo-fies) believing and praying. The shift from *ut legem credendi lex statuat supplicandi* to the shorter phrase *lex orandi, lex credendi* was perhaps necessary to avoid the reference to a particular historical context (Prosper's text and the debates of the fifth and sixth centuries around Augustine's theology). But this shift was also necessary to establish a mystical foundation of law and to universalize the hegemony of the term *law* over believing and praying.

As already noted, the "originary" phrase was *"ut legem credendi lex statuat supplicandi."* In the form in which it first appeared, a relationship is established between a rule of believing and a rule of supplication. It could be argued that this rule of supplication is not even necessarily liturgical in that it could also be translated as the rule or the condition of begging. Prosper appeals not to a universally imposed practice or law but to a law of begging,[22] a law of supplication, an appeal to unceasing prayer. The need of all humanity before God is itself a continual prayer and, for Prosper, this prayer—this need both silent and spoken—is expressed through liturgical practice.[23] The appeal to law in Prosper is not the appeal to the universality of law or rule; rather, Prosper directs the reader to the universal condition of humanity as needy humanity; it is an appeal to unceasing prayer rather than to a uniform liturgical law or practice of prayer.

Prosper's appeal to unceasing prayer, to the condition of needy humanity as the "law" of liturgical practice implicitly acknowledges a foundation that does not rest in any institutional church, in any magisterium, even in any liturgical tradition. It stands in opposition to the imposition of law as hierarchical control or as hermeneutical principle. The foundation of the "law" is not the solid, unambiguous (and untraceable) certainty of a mystical origin that proclaims eternal truths, that insists on absolute values, that appeals to universal principles, that unfailingly distinguishes between "right and wrong," but, in the words of Psalm 42, the foundation is "deep calling to deep"— strangely, oddly, deeply abyss, need, hole. The law's foundation is in humanity's need.

The aphorism *lex orandi, lex credendi* witnesses to a dynamic within liturgical scholarship that created a slippage toward the notion of law. This slippage toward a law of believing and praying disguises the fact that law itself is an invented term[24]—as much as the liturgical aphorism itself is an invented term. The invention of the aphorism *lex orandi, lex credendi* is a deferral to law; it is the imposition of a universal to maintain order, an imposition that is justified by an appeal to a foundation—a mythic, idolized, even mystic foundation. In other words, the law's foundation becomes nonnegotiable, beyond criticism and questioning.[25] But the invention of *lex orandi, lex credendi* also reflects an explicit attempt to ground both theology (belief) and liturgical practice (prayer) in "law." The word *lex* overshadows discussions of belief and prayer, of theology and liturgy, in liturgical scholarship. The insistence of scholars on the term *lex* displaces both *supplicandi (orandi)* and *credendi*. The equation of supplication and prayer with law brought with it a suspicion of the liturgy within scholarship originating in the Reformation—a suspicion that persists even today. Strangely, the same suspicion was not applied to the notion of belief, of theological explanation and systematization. The unmasking of the imposition of law over practice, however, exposes an implicit desire to control practice, to prevent the irruption of practice or event into the established and controlled systematization of God's revelation. Or, as in Ebeling's writing, the need to appeal to the gospel is an all-powerful force that levels all differences—as a form of new law— rather than turning to the sacraments as Luther does.

Though the concern about the overwhelming role that *lex orandi, lex credendi* plays in liturgical scholarship is a contemporary concern, Luther implicitly undermines the hegemonic control of the notion of law (and, therefore, also the idea of a mystical foundation) by interpreting the law through the eucharistic event. Through his use of liturgical language, Luther disrupts uncritically held notions of law. When the foundation of the law is not a mystic origin or a transcendental source but humanity's need of grace expressed through liturgical practice, then both law and its foundation are shaken. By displacing the law and its foundation through liturgical practice—specifically, the liturgical act known as the eucharist—the law itself is awakened to its characteristic not as absolute but as invention. Through its displacement by the eucharistic event, the "one law" questions its own "origin"—it is called to recognize the deep, the abyss, the hole; it is called to respond to that need; it is called to responsibility.

Luther's intention is now perhaps clearer: by placing "law" and "eucharist" together in one phrase, he places intense pressure on the term *law*. Luther contrasts the "one law" that is the eucharist with the old law of Moses. In other words, the "one law" is contrasted with that older law that has constituted for itself a mystical foundation. The "one law" that is the eucharist displaces the "law," which posits its origins in an absolute authority, in a mystical (or divine) source. The eucharist is the "one law," the law alone—it is not "a" law but, rather, the one law that effectively ends the mystical character of all law. Luther is questioning, displacing, the violent imposition of a "law" in order to reach the profound "unity through love" for the entire people. (Though to effect this displacement, he still employs the old word *law*.) The "one law" that is the "holy mass" challenges uncritically held conceptions of law by interrupting, irrupting, awakening the reader/participant—by awakening "us"—from the realm of mystical foundations, absolute origins, eternal testaments, perfect memorial.[26]

In stating that the holy mass or eucharist is the "one law" for the entire people, Luther disrupts the notion of law by displacing its "origin." A liturgical act—the eucharistic event—breaks open the mystical origins of the law. Or, put another way, when we say that Jesus Christ is gospel—new law—the "mystical foundation" of all law and religion is challenged. This challenge addresses itself to the Thomistic understanding that "the 'eternal law' from which natural law is participated is nothing other than God as providential maker and governor, as artisan."[27] Luther disrupts the *primum analogatum* that is eternal law—that is, the eucharist celebration proclaims the death of God, the death of eternal law as the foundation for mystical authority (whether written or unwritten authority).

Of course, for Luther, Jesus is "God" but not the God of mystical origins and absolute heights, not the God of eternal law and first analogies. Jesus is God in the manger and on the cross.[28] In other words, when we "run" to God, we do not run to the "law" (or ascend to its mystical origins) but we run to the manger and the cross.[29] We run—dare I interpret it in this way—to the singularity of an event.

Disruption of Remembering

The singularity of an event, however, presents the liturgical theologian with a considerable problem. The disruption of the law—or theory, for behind the notion of law has been the lurking danger of the gospel becoming theory or new metaphysics—through the eucharist and, more broadly, through liturgical action raises the question of the relation between liturgical action and gospel, or between eucharist and the Christ event. This question could also be posed in terms of Luther's writing: Why does Luther turn to liturgical language in order to write the events of his life? Throughout this study, the focus has been on what is inaccessible in event, on something that cannot be grasped, on the *res absentes* that Luther suggests are apprehended only by faith. "The words of the spirit announce an absent thing, not-to-be-seen, but apprehended by faith."[30] But if the singularity of event is known only through the return of something inaccessible in event, if history arises in our understanding only where "immediate understanding may not,"[31] then how is the singularity of event—how is that which resists systematization or capture—accessed, remembered, repeated? This is profoundly a liturgical question: How is the Christ event remembered?

This question in itself presupposes a historical perspective, for, in order to ask the question, something necessarily occurred. Remembering the event, remembering that which occurred, implies, for a traditional understanding of "remembering," that the reader/participant look back as if the event—call it the Last Supper, for example—could be localized. However, this commonsense notion of "looking back" in order to grasp a historical moment defines the event as an ending, as something contained within itself that can be known, as something resolved, as something that can be kept as a memorial. The consequence of our reading of Luther, Caruth, Freud, and Derrida has demonstrated though that event is not an ending or a saturated context; rather, it is like a beginning that continually irrupts, something unknown that continually returns and strangely calls.

The force of a return—of something that cannot be grasped in the singular event—the continual irruption of that event in life, both individual and communal, is here opposed to simple imitation, repetition, and memorial. Something in the event—its singularity—cannot be captured by our memories, by any act of mimesis, imitation, or remembrance. This singularity continually disrupts the ordered patterns of lives and through the force of that return disseminates principles, rules, laws, foundations (even mystical foundations), and, of course, reference points of faith.

But in what way is this different from the classic meaning of anamnesis in liturgical studies? Alexander Schmemann holds that liturgical remembering in the eucharistic celebration is the actualization of that past, single, unrepeated event.[32] For Schmemann, there is no difference between remembering and repeating. Repetition serves memory. Liturgical repetition is the actualization in the present (through remembering) of an event that is known. The Christ event—defined as cross and resurrection and embodied in the Last Supper—is embedded in the ritual action of the eucharistic celebration: the liturgy (supposedly) invites people into a participation in this divine reality. Anamnesis is, then, primarily a form of communication for divine revelation, a re-actualization of the promise of God: the revelation of salvation, forgiveness, and life eternal.[33]

What we have discovered in Luther, however, is the impossibility of such a communication or a resituating of the terms. Not only does the meaning of the unexpected, singular event remain inaccessible—or absent—but this absence puts into question the very possibility of meaning and its communication. The absence questions the meaning-making context. The context of our performative acts (our lives) is not defined by the meanings we create, meanings that, in the end, are nothing but conventions, even if sometimes validated by divine or eternal language. The monastic context for Luther was not eternally valid, and the recognition of that invalidity—that no human context can be a second baptism—brought with it the realization that no human context can assure us a relation, a communication, with God. For Luther, all life is a baptism, that is, a continually dying and rising again. The historical, meaning-making context is displaced by a liturgical act that attempts not to imitate (or repeat) an event or communicate with and through divine revelation but to confront the reader/participant in an iteration of a return. This iteration continually disrupts any form of "actualization"; it continually disrupts the illusion of communication and the boundaries of what has been labeled the "present" context. This iteration quietly but insistently suggests that the term *meaning* itself is in need of a new approach.

The dynamics of liturgical iteration, then, focuses on the singularity of the Christ event that cannot be captured or remembered. Liturgical iteration itself is a strange iteration of an absence, of something that cannot be grasped in the event and that precisely returns, as a force, in the celebration to disrupt context anew. In the liturgical celebration the completeness or fullness of the event is not reenacted or re-lived or experienced as if it were divinely communicated. "Fullness" is experienced only as it continually disseminates, as if "fullness" could only be experienced as a continual scattering. The question we initially posed now becomes this: How is this continual dissemination "remembered"?[34]

This second question flirts on the edges of another: What constitutes, in the event, the singularity that resists capture or remembering? Michel de Certeau writes: "An event is not what can be seen or known about its happening, but what it becomes (and, above all, for us)."[35] He is writing about an event (the "revolution" of May 1968 in France) that had been witnessed and that had, as its own testimony, the chronicles of innumerable newspapers. Yet, a sensory and intellectual/emotive conceptualization does not constitute the event. The event is in its becoming, in its coming to be, and, parenthetically, in a continual and nonexhaustive "coming to be" through the limitless "us."

However, this "coming to be" is not the actualization of the classically understood anamnesis of liturgical theology (Schmemann). In terms of Christian theology, the singularity of the event opposes the actualization of divine revelation or of meaning in predetermined contexts. It opposes the facile historical perspective as it opposes the facile theological positing of an origin or mystical foundation as if these could be "explanatory." The singularity of the event is known only in what cannot be known of it—that is, it returns as a force that disrupts knowing. In other words, "remembering" as active participation in the divinity is an active participation that is only human work. Luther, on the other hand, pushes toward a passive reception where "remembering" becomes "return," a return that cannot be grasped but is only experienced as onset, call, addition. In other words, idealistically construed liturgies or correctly defined sacraments or memorial acts or even broad ecumenical consensus are merely attempts to capture the Christ event through "remembering" rather than submissions to the addition, to the return, of that event.

The singularity of event opposes the facile positing of an origin as if the event could be understood in its absolute impact. The singularity of the Christ event, for Christian theology, then confronts the mystical foundation (or mystical origin) that is traditionally claimed as source for remembering and liturgical repetition, for the actualization of the event. Luther's turn toward the liturgy as the "place" where such confrontation is maintained suggests that the singularity of event is not only a "resistance to remembering" on the cognitive level (a resistance to knowledge) but a resistance that engages the body as well. The resistance to facile remembering is a dissemination of context and subject; we might say that it is a "dis-membering" of personal identity, of life and knowledge, of body and blood. The event returns and irrupts in the present moment, in the present context through continual dissemination.

The radical singularity of the event and its uncontrollable return has been relegated to a corner by traditional eucharistic theology and practice, perhaps, precisely because of its unexpectedness. For traditional eucharistic theology, an "event" is placed at center stage—the Last Supper (for example, Luke 22), or the Last Supper as prefiguring the cross and resurrection. This event, as has been noted, is established as "origin" that can be remembered or actualized or ritualized. But by placing a theological emphasis on "origin," on a known central event, the eucharistic celebration receives a new mystical foundation. The eucharistic celebration itself becomes "law" or authority regulating life rather than that which interprets and displaces law, authority, theological principle. In the worst-case scenario, the eucharist becomes a "law" dictating our ritual remembering and repetition as if through ritual remembering we had ever-renewed access to the mystical or divine foundation—to some special communication of grace. The eucharist as "law" becomes a new technology that can be mechanically repeated (for example, in assuring that the "direction" of the liturgical action is correct—from God to us) and therefore its effect continually assured. In this scenario, only the (usually male and/or heterosexual) presider regulates access to the event, and the meaning of the event is controlled through faithful observance and imitation of the law. This is not what Luther proposed when he wrote that the "one law" inspires unity through love.

A Liturgical Intervention: The *Didache*

The unexpected return of something past—the adoption/*Annahme* of a force—can be frightening. We prefer a scenario in which we remember by repeating. We memorialize or commemorate. We repeat in order to remember, for example, a particular event, a person, a context. We repeat and remember in order to be connected—connected to that past event, continuing its significance in the present day. But the *Annahme* of a force displaces our remembering and our repeating, for it is the repetition or, more precisely, the iteration of that which is unavailable to consciousness but continually intruding on sight.[36] The force that unexpectedly returns is perhaps a connectedness with an event but a connectedness we cannot control. It is the iteration of something that paradoxically cannot be remembered. Iterability is separated from remembering, and because it is separated from the simple memory of an event it opens up "a larger relation to the event that extends beyond what can simply be seen or what can be known."[37] In other words, the nonsaturated context, the possibility of event "becoming" today, is invoked.

Inscribed in both Freud's and Caruth's writing is the force of a return—a return, however, that cannot be captured. It may be described as a traumatic return—that is, the return of the repressed, the return of a violent event—or it may be described in terms of the enigma of survival, in which case it is a question of the community of the living, all of the living. Perhaps the "survival" in question is second degree: perhaps I am not a Holocaust survivor, but I may be the child of a Holocaust survivor. I may be the child of a victim of Nazi oppression, I may be the second or third or fourth generation, but my survival will always in some way depend on the survival of the preceding generation. History itself is then marked by the enigma of survival.

I have suggested that this force of a return is also inscribed in Luther's language and particularly in his turn to liturgical language in order to describe the disseminated, the disrupted, context and subject.

The inaccessible that returns as a force in Luther's writing is that which cannot be known about the Christ event—the dissemination of God and, therefore, the dissemination of all meaning. This return strangely iterates the initial trauma, whether that trauma is expressed as a question of survival (how do I survive the death of God?) or, as Luther does when confronted with the disseminated context (and vow), in terms of an addition or a call.

Luther's turn to the liturgy and liturgical language in order to write the force of this return, in order to continually write the disruption of law and the dissemination of both origin and context and subject, Luther's rewriting of remembering not as active participation but passive reception, dare I repeat, Luther's rewriting of remembering as return is encountered through a specific liturgical rite: the holy mass or eucharist. This turn to the celebration of the eucharist, to a specific liturgical rite and text, as embodying a disruption, I want to suggest, is not specific or unique to Luther. Another liturgical text, a liturgical example that predates Luther (and one that Luther did not know) will help clarify, through its own enigmatic "remembering" (!) of the Christ event, this resistance to remembering that is inherent in liturgical iteration, a resistance that Luther indisputably put in the foreground of his writing.

The first-century church document in question—the *Didache*[38]— pushes the reader/participant to reformulate the notion of liturgical or ritual repetition as the force of a return. The *Didache* is particularly noteworthy for our study because, first, it disrupts the narrative of the eucharistic event. The "remembering" of the *Didache* does not call back upon an originary event or moment. It does not ritualize a source to the exclusion of all other events and narrations. But second, the *Didache* also disrupts the narrative of liturgical history and theology. It disrupts liturgical writing, a disruption that prompted liturgical theologians to relegate it onto the shelves of non-eucharistic texts. The *Didache* occasioned a violent selectivity as to "what" constitutes the eucharist.

Though the text of the *Didache* (Teaching of the Twelve Apostles) was only discovered in 1873 by Archbishop Philotheos Bryennios,[39] it is one of the earliest witnesses to the liturgical life of the nascent church. The *Didache* is also the first witness of a genre that became known as "church orders"—writings that defined the practice of the liturgy and the exercise of ethical life. The *Didache* is an assembled text with chapters dating from the first to second centuries. The oldest known manuscript presents the work of an eleventh-century scribe. We do not know at what earlier date the assembly or editing occurred, but our discussion here will focus on chapters 9 and 10—two chapters that have attracted the most attention because, I believe, they are the most threatening for current understanding of liturgical practice and tradition. Numerous commentaries attempt to explain their place or nonplace in the history of eucharistic celebration and theology.[40]

Chapters 9 and 10, which present a form of eucharistic instruction, were classified as a non-eucharistic meal because of the absence of certain traits that theologians believe belong to a eucharistic celebration—for example, the Words of Institution ("On the night in which he was betrayed, our Lord Jesus took bread, and gave thanks; broke it, and gave it to his disciples, saying: Take and eat; this is my body, given for you. Do this for the remembrance of me. Again, after supper, he took the cup, gave thanks, and gave it for all to drink, saying: This cup is the new covenant/testament in my blood, shed for you and all people for the forgiveness of sin. Do this for the remembrance of me."). The dismissal of these chapters was (is) necessary if the eucharistic celebration as a remembering and actualization (anamnesis) of a fixed past event was to be maintained. The dismissal of these chapters from the history of the eucharist was necessary in order to maintain the illusion of an access to the "Last Supper" as an event with historical continuity, with event as a historical category, as institutionally justified tradition, as ritual power.

Recently, however, the *Didache* has sparked renewed interest particularly in light of research that has uncovered other eucharistic texts without the customary Words of Institution.[41] This scholarship has shown that the contested chapters 9 and 10 should be dated as early as the middle of the first century (around 50 CE),[42] which would mean that they predate the written Gospel accounts, are probably coterminous with the oral tradition of Matthew's Gospel and Paul's preaching, and were perhaps even transcribed within a few years of the death of Jesus.[43] There is also a growing scholarly agreement that these chapters depict a eucharistic celebration and not just simply a ritual or agape meal.[44] The *Didache,* which soon after its discovery was confined to a dislocation, of disjuncture, within the narrative of the historical development of the eucharistic tradition, now returns to question the very reasons for forgetting and remembering.

The *Didache,* I believe, offers an example of displacement, of a profound resistance to the efforts of memory to capture the event and define speech. It questions our memory, our historical, institutional, ritual remembering of an event, by questioning our understanding of the Christ event. The question, then, before us is not what the text (the *Didache*) actually remembers (what "event" is at the source or origin of the text and liturgical celebration), but how this text disseminates memory, how it dis-members a historical and ritualized remembering of the event. I believe that chapters 9 and 10 do not look back to a particular, fixed, central event but embody within their liturgical and ethical instruction the force of a return, a return experienced as an imperative to become, and, above all, to become for others.

Chapter 9 of the Didache outlines the "eucharistic" celebration for the community. It contains the blessing over the cup and over the bread and concludes with a prayer for fulfillment and a warning about participation. It begins with instruction, clearly stating its purpose in the opening line: "Peri de tés eucharistias" (for thanksgiving). But two things are strangely absent from this account of the celebration of thanksgiving: the Words of Institution and any explicit reference to the cross—to the death and resurrection of Jesus Christ. These two missing references unsettle common theological assumptions: Is the "what" of memorial, the "what" of ritual action, the "what" of "event," no longer clearly definable? Here is an early Christian community, in fact probably one of the earliest of which we have a record, celebrating the central liturgical rite of thanksgiving yet not remembering Jesus' actualized presence in the community by means of either the Last Supper or the cross. Communication with those "central" events is textually absent. How does this community then "remember" the Christ event?

The question that arises for us is a question of reading: the reception of the text has been determined by the expectation of the reader. We have already mentioned the selectivity that dismissed the *Didache* as a eucharistic text by some scholars because the Words of Institution are absent. Since the liturgical (eucharistic) celebration is a remembering of the event of the Last Supper (prefiguring the cross and resurrection) and since the performative words that ensure a continuum (or unbroken context) are absent, they argued, these chapters of the *Didache* cannot be a eucharistic celebration. But others who have argued strongly and convincingly for the reception of the *Didache* as a witness of an early eucharistic celebration also argue on the assumption of a continuum between the event of the Last Supper and liturgical actualization in the mass or eucharist today even if actual reference to the Last Supper is absent in the text. This is the case of the admirable work of Enrico Mazza, who, through historical analysis and biblical exegesis, reframes for us the questions that have been posed.

For Mazza, the criterion that decided whether an anaphora (the text of the thanksgiving/prayer that actualizes the consecration of the bread and the wine) is eucharistic is not the presence or absence of the Words of Institution. Rather, the criterion depends on two related movements: (1) that the celebration "corresponds to what has been established and instituted by the Lord. With the anamnesis, the Church establishes a line of continuity between our celebration and what happened in the Upper Room (cenaculum) at the Last Supper";[45] and (2) "the entire celebration is a true memorial of the Lord only if it is, in fact, in conformity with what he [Jesus Christ] did, and therefore what he instituted; the Church makes this conformity its theme, by telling of what he has instituted and by explicitly pronouncing its own obedience to his command."[46] In other words, a celebration of the meal is eucharistic when it is in a line of continuity with the Last Supper (and the cross and resurrection of Jesus), a continuity established by obedience to what Jesus commanded in that meal and what he fulfilled on the cross. This connection between the present-day celebration and the command of Jesus in fact assures the validity of the consecration whether the Words of Institution are present or not.[47]

What, then, is the command of Jesus that demands such faithful repetition? The command is summarized in the text "Do this in memory of me" (Luke 22:14-23). But the "do this" is not simply the repetition of a meal celebration. In terms of a classical theological explication, Jesus was preparing his disciples, through this meal, for his death on the cross and his resurrection. Or, as Mazza writes: "For this reason the supper, loaded with these structures, was proclamation of the death of the Lord. This content was objectively inside the supper, even if the events had not yet happened historically."[48]

Mazza proceeds to demonstrate how one verse of the *Didache* (10:3) is in conformity with the command of Jesus: "You, almighty Lord, created all things for the sake of your name, and you gave food and drink to human beings for their enjoyment, so that they would thank you. But you graced us with spiritual food and drink and eternal life through <Jesus> your servant."[49] This verse is evocatory of the command given by God in Deut. 8:10 ("You shall eat your fill and bless the Lord your God for the good land that he has given you"). *Didache* 10:3 is "a kind of 'reference to the institution' of the Jewish religious meal."[50] And in the Jewish context of this very early Christian community's practice, this text of institution (*Didache* 10:3) would have been understood as referring to the command of Jesus "Do this." Of course, *Didache* 10:3 lacks any reference to the "promised land," but this also underlines Mazza's point. The eucharist of the Didache "is the bearer of a new revelatory content and gift (ἐχαρίσω) from Jesus the παῖς of God."[51] It is embedded in the tradition of Jewish meal ritual but it is also transforming that tradition. Jesus himself becomes the origin of an entire meal-sharing tradition, and the gift now revealed is grace.

Rather than questioning the strange absence of the Words of Institution, Mazza reinserts, albeit indirectly, the Words into the *Didache*. The Words of Institution are not absent but are disguised, at least for modern readers, behind other words. The early Christian community, he argues, had no need of an explicit reference to the meal because they implicitly understood the meal as a command of God; they implicitly received the meal as connected to the Last Supper. In other words, the Words of Institution are not absent in the *Didache*. This connection became more tenuous as the growing church community developed geographically and lost its rootedness in Jewish meal ritual. It was at this later stage that the Words of Institution were inserted into the text to reestablish the connection to the meal Jesus celebrated before his death.

The necessary insertion of the Words of Institution as cultural and religious memory failed or was absent in the growing Christian communities is suggestive of the power of these words to invoke the event. The words *Jesus used* are necessarily cited in every eucharistic celebration; these words have become like a watchword for the eucharist. Repeating the Words of Institution creates the illusion that the worshipping assembly is repeating something that Jesus did, something Jesus instituted, something Jesus founded. The cross event itself cannot be repeated every Sunday, but this meal can be repeated and the community can thereby "remember" the passion. Mazza's exegesis of the *Didache* reflects this assimilation of repetition, memory, and continuity and covers up the force of an absence within the text.

The possibility that the words are simply absent and, as such, that nothing in the text refers to the command of Jesus is not entertained.

I would like to argue that this liturgical text, however, remains a eucharistic celebration despite such a radical absence. The *Didache* disrupts our remembering, and it does so at that critical moment in the liturgy when the celebrants (ordained and lay) think they are at the most crucial and intimate moment of "remembering." The *Didache* pulls the rug out from under the assumptions of liturgical theology. It questions the historical, institutional, and ritual remembering of an event by questioning our understanding of that event. The very absence of the Words of Institution confronts the reader/participant with the question, How is the Christ event "remembered" in the eucharist? This question can be posed historically: Is the eucharistic celebration, a centralizing remembering of only one meal, only the Last Supper? I believe that, by its silence on the Last Supper and, in particular, on cross and resurrection symbolism, the *Didache* disseminates both the "event" and liturgical "remembering" of that event.

These chapters of the *Didache* point not toward one story or act of the meal (the Last Supper) but to the entire meal-sharing tradition that Jesus practiced.[52] Jesus proclaimed the kingdom of God through his table fellowship, through the ancient ritual action of a meal. This act of "open commensality"[53] radically disoriented and reoriented the participants in relation to their accepted cosmology.[54] When the meal "event" in the gospels is examined, something peculiar surfaces: Jesus was breaking every ritual norm when he celebrated a meal. He would eat with those deemed unworthy (or ritually "unclean"). When he ate with "religious folk," he always introduced an element to unsettle the ritual purity of the event (Matt. 9:9-13; Luke 7:36-50; Luke 19:1-10). Whatever Jesus' intent in the unexpected pattern of these meal events, one thing is clear: the meal sharing became, already in the gospels, a ritual act that pointed away from itself as ritual or liturgical act and toward a disruption, not a random disruption but a disruption by an other, by one unexpected who calls the reader/participant to a responsibility. The so-called Jesus movement that gathered around the celebration of the meal gathered not around a death—for the death was, in some way, too horrible to remember—but around this disruption of the closed circle, the displacing of the purity law toward the other, the absent one, toward the breaking open of exclusionist theory. The meal event as celebrated by Jesus was so radically new and different (displacing), so radically life giving in its displacement, that the sharing of bread and wine—and not the symbolism of cross and resurrection—became the central act by which the early Christian community repeated that disruption, repeated that reversal, repeated that which could not be captured other than by living out a responsibility.

Liturgical iteration, then, already in this text that is "closest" to the event, is not the "remembering" of one event but the continual return of that which cannot be captured in the event. Rather, it is the continual disruption of all forms of remembering; it is the return of a disorientation and reorientation of this radical commensality. The *Didache* and, of course, the gospels stand as witnesses. Disorientation and reorientation are consequences of the force of a return, the return of the singularity of the Christ event into daily life. In the text of the *Didache*, we are surprised to discover this force of a return in yet another way: the text presents us with a church, a Christian community, in the process of itself encountering the resurrection as something that continually irrupts. The resurrection itself did not "happen," like a source or an origin or a new mystical foundation. The resurrection is encountered at the table.[55] Now, "remembering" is not "looking back" or "calling to mind," but the return and the dissemination (or scattering) of our lives so that the event can "become for us" (de Certeau). The iteration of the meal is not control but dispersal in life and ethics and hope.[56]

We do not know how the eucharist "became" for the community of the *Didache*. We do have, however, a witness in the structure of this text: the "meal-sharing practice" finds expression in a particular relation to the world, to the community, to strangers, and to the poor. The concluding chapters of the *Didache* reorient the notion of hierarchy in the community and propose a radical generosity, a strong welcome, and an equally strong discernment. This reorientation can perhaps be understood as the firstfruits of the beginnings of a knowledge of Jesus Christ: the beginnings of the resurrection as continual disruption.

The literary form of the *Didache* further underlines this displacement and resistance to memory. For example, Jesus is not the grammatical center of this liturgical text. In fact, the name of Jesus itself is disseminated in the text. The cup and the bread (the promise) do not refer directly to Jesus but come to the participants through (*dia*) Jesus. The emphasis is on the promise of God—the promise of life, knowledge, Spirit, reconciliation—that comes through Jesus. The emphasis is not as much on the person of Jesus (subject) and what

Jesus did (context) as it is on what comes through; perhaps we could write, the emphasis is on what returns. This is in sharp contrast to later canonical literature (particularly in the Words of Institution) in which Jesus is the primary referent. In the Gospel of John, Jesus becomes the vine and the community becomes the branches. The name of Jesus is imposed through direct reference and speech: "I am the vine, you are the branches" (John 15:5). The need for a direct, clear reference, the need to capture the event in the "I am" or the "This is my body," overpowers the call to disorientation, displacement, and reorientation.[57] The eucharistic witness of the *Didache*, however, orients the reader (the participant) not to a single referent, not to a single name, not to an imposition, not to a "law" (and its mystical foundation), but to a radical interrelationality (the call to live as community in and through the sharing of all things, material and spiritual, in the concluding chapters of the *Didache*). The dissemination of the referent and the subsequent displacement of the participant are perhaps the return of the singularity of the Christ event (the return of a series of related events—the meal gatherings by Jesus).

The eucharistic meal in the *Didache* suggests that performative ritual embodies the force of a return—or the awakening to the impossibility of capturing the event per se. The *Didache* witnesses to the impossibility of "remembering," even to the impossibility of remembering or capturing the meaning of the horrific execution of Jesus by crucifixion. For the community of the *Didache*, Jesus could not be remembered by this cruel mode of execution. We might even argue that the silence of this text about the cross witnesses to the trauma of such an execution—a trauma that cannot be named but that is continually iterated.

Instead, for the community of the *Didache*, the "presence" of Jesus as the one who overcame this death was enacted through a meal in which he continually disseminates traditional knowledge, faith, and life. The meal was the iteration of something that the disciples, the first community, could not grasp—the iteration of something inaccessible in the event. Curiously, even Enrico Mazza points to this tension in the meal— a characteristic of resistance that disrupts the boundaries of the event— when he suggests that the logic of the parable requires or demands "the possibility of containing in itself something which is superior to itself and irreducible in itself: something which has its actualization elsewhere."[58] There is something "irreducible" in the meal, something, I argue, that cannot be remembered or repeated. The meal itself was as a force that returns, confronts, disseminates, awakens,[59] and has its "actualization elsewhere."

The witness of the *Didache* to the meal event that Jesus practiced is a liturgical witness to a dissemination that cannot be remembered but only iterated as the force of a return. The return through liturgical iteration first expresses the dissemination of event: not only is the bread broken, disseminated, but the "utterer" (the presider) is also disseminated, scattered in plural, grammatical forms. Any connection between remembering and repetition is broken in this dissemination. This return and dissemination do not reduce the eucharistic event to a historical fact or moment, they do not send the reader/participant off into the unfathomable grounds of a mystical foundation, nor do they focus primarily on death—the death of God—as if the resurrection were denied. Both movements—both death and promise—are inscribed in this return and dissemination.

Liturgical iteration does not connect the worshipping assembly with a source or origin or foundation, not even with the event. The eucharistic celebration is not the imitation or mere repetition or simple memorial or even anamnesis of the final meal of Jesus but a witness to the continual dissemination initiated by Jesus. Liturgical iteration is the opposite of imitation, for imitation would repeat a closed, self-containing event, a direct referent. Liturgical iteration confronts the participant with a continual dissemination that breaks open every context and disseminates every subject. In this sense, liturgical iteration is always already an anti-liturgy.[60] The eucharistic celebration witnesses to a death (God was broken, fragmented, displaced, disseminated) that cannot be remembered (the promise). Liturgical and especially sacramental practice is called toward dissemination. But this is not simply death. Liturgical iteration points toward dissemination as both death and promise—even as a profound disruption of the law/gospel dichotomy.[61] The something that returns in the eucharistic celebration points the reader/participant away from any easy "meaning" that might be attributed to the event or the liturgical enactment. The promise is, in fact, meaning itself disseminated, sent out through the door as many broken pieces of bread.

The iteration of the meal in the eucharistic celebration has brought back dissemination, not as a negative incapacity but as promise.

"Remembering" has been displaced by the force of a return—the return of something absent, a hole, an abyss, something that cannot be grasped but that is still becoming "for us." This dissemination of meaning permits the promise of God to be promise, that is, not human work but something that can only be received, added on, calling out—something over which we have no control.

Chapter 6

Rewriting Promise

Broadening Law and Gospel

THE INTERVENTION OF AN EXAMPLE—the specifically liturgical example of the *Didache*—has disrupted what is understood by "remembering." The intervention of this text, as utterance, points not only to what cannot be known, what remains absent in event (to cognitive recognition), but to this absence as a force of a return. Remembering, if you will, is taken out of the realm of human cognitive work. It is no longer "our work," but the strange work of history—read traumatically—within us.

This notion of return is experienced in and through liturgical enactment and liturgical language. A liturgical utterance (the *Didache*) has disrupted traditional liturgical (and theological) remembering (or anamnesis); it has fundamentally disrupted the law of praying and, I also would argue, the law of believing; it has disrupted the presupposed divide between theology and practice. This raises, then, the question about the character of liturgical action. Why does Luther turn to the liturgy in order to disrupt theology? Is liturgical practice simply human action, or is there something more? Is it from God, or is it from people? Is liturgical action merely about our prayers, our thanksgiving to God, or is it also hearing God's word to us? If only the former, liturgy may too quickly fall into the realm of sacrifice (law); if only the latter, liturgy risks becoming simply magical (requiring no response on our part). The issue at stake is about "direction."

This metaphor of direction, however, has its own complexity, as we have already seen. When "remembering" is no longer our cognitive ability to repeat, embody, enact one of the central events of faith (the giving of God's word to us in the celebration of the meal) but the "return" of something that has never been fully assimilated or known (God's death for us, God's murder at our hands), then our celebration as traumatic remembering is a passive act in which we receive something through an iterated structure. gospel, in this scenario, and law are not as easily distinguishable as some would like to make them to be. They cannot be reduced simply to a question of "direction," whether from us or from God. I may add, at this point, that my insistence on the use of the word *eucharist* for the Lord's Supper is intended to highlight the complexity of direction in this sacramental event.

We need then, first of all, to return again to the discussion of law and gospel in Luther and to ask whether this force of return, this something that returns and disrupts both remembering and law, finds a witness in Luther's enigmatic coupling of law and mass: "[Christ] appointed in return but one law or order for his entire people, and that was the holy mass"? How does the sacrament "communicate" the promise of God without becoming itself something like a new revelation, like new tablets of the law, without it becoming a work of sacrifice or privileged access to a heavenly realm? The desire, arising out of human nature, is of course to have a pure sacrament—one that either channels faithfully God's grace to us (for example, in a theology grounded in the metaphor of "means"—"means of grace") or that bequeaths unfailingly, as through a testament, the forgiveness of sins upon us. Both metaphors, however, do fail. As noted above, "direction" cannot be purely defined.

The ambiguity in the very notion of direction highlights the conundrum that Gerhard Ebeling already found himself in when trying to distinguish law from gospel. Ebeling, it will be recalled, needed to explore the meaning of the word *difference* in order to distinguish law and gospel and even then concluded that gospel (promise) is strangely dependent on law:

> Thus the gospel is not present in a pure and undefiled form when its stands on its own, untroubled and undisturbed, with its relation to the law never considered. For the gospel only comes into action when it does so in distinction from and in opposition to the law—and when as a result the law is really the law.[1]

The gospel is defined in its relation to law. It is "known" in the midst of struggle or temptation *(Anfechtung);* it is "known" in the struggle with unexpected experience, perhaps, precisely as that absent something in event. The gospel is known only in its opposition to or in its distinction from the law. The gospel, as an experience, is known as distinction. Or, dare I put it this way, the gospel is not known metaphysically (as if we had access to a divine illumination).

Ebeling appears to suggest that the gospel is known as difference. Where does the distinction, the difference between law and gospel get played out? He admits that the distinction cannot "be carried out by means of a theological definition."[2] The only place of meaning—the only place where theology works itself out for Ebeling—is in a liturgical task: in preaching. Preaching here, Ebeling writes, "must be taken in a very broad sense, or more accurately, in the very exact, real and consequently very comprehensive sense of the word which is spoken and must be spoken, in concrete circumstances, for Jesus Christ's sake."[3] This is an important point. In the world of experience, we suffer the impact of the confrontation but we need a word to help us recognize or live or step into that distinction. The concern of preaching, for Ebeling, is to put into practice the distinction between law and gospel, and in that distinction, practiced in preaching, salvation takes place.[4]

Ebeling descends into the depths of the distinction. Relying on the preaching task, he states that failure to make the distinction in preaching results in a confusion that is evil. Failure to preach the distinction results in the abandonment of the gospel, and we are left with only the law. But an overemphasis on the gospel results in a loss of the law that in turn is a loss of the gospel. He struggles now to understand gospel and finally concludes that the distinction itself is gospel.[5] After making this amazing assertion, Ebeling comes back to his question: "But to what in fact do these two terms, the law and the gospel, which become more enigmatic the more we use them, actually refer?"[6] I want to argue that his insight that gospel is in the distinction suggests a deconstructive function for gospel (much like Derrida's understanding of justice as deconstruction).[7] The gospel, as such, is not a "thing" we can possess. It is not a direction that we can construct. Rather, it is the continual deconstruction of all of our attempts to ensure its presence. We might say that it defies the "what" question!

Gospel is that word that deconstructs law, that deconstructs the prison in which human words bind us. But the gospel is also that word of God that imparts faith. Can we say that the distinction between law and gospel, that distinction that encounters us, that affects us in the present moment through experience and in proclamation (in the liturgy), is the impact, the addition, the gift of faith?

Is not Ebeling's struggle to write the difference between law and gospel and the force of its impact on us inscribed by the same difficulty found in Luther's writing? Law and gospel do not stand before us with a duality, with two separate realities. In a sense, we never stand before the law or before the gospel. Rather, our lives, the events of our lives, are immersed in this law/gospel difference. In a sermon on St. Thomas' Day (December 21, 1516), Luther writes:

> God's alien work, however, is to make human beings sinners, unrighteous, liars, miserable, foolish, lost. Not that God actually makes them such, but that the pride of men *[sic]*, although they are such, will not let them become or be such, so much so that God makes use of a greater disturbance, indeed God uses this work solely to show them that they are such.[8]

God's alien work is the revelation of human failing—the failing of all our attempts to construct a world in which everything is explained, including sin and grace. Human beings do not want to give up the meaning they create. This is what Luther means when he says that human beings don't want their Adam killed. And because of this, they do not come to God's proper work that is the justification or resurrection of Jesus Christ.

Here both law and gospel are God's work. One is not opposed to the other. In fact, as Luther states in this sermon, that "conformity with the image of the Son of God [cf. Rom. 8:29] includes both of these works." The work of the gospel is the work of both law and gospel. The alien work of God is still a gospel work, though Luther will call it a "strange work of the gospel."[9]

The metaphor Luther employs in this sermon is a surprising one. "Therefore the gospel magnifies sin in that it so broadens the law that no man can be found just, that there is none who does not transgress the law."[10] The gospel magnifies sin and *broadens* the law. The gospel opens the law wide open so that all are pulled in and absolutely every aspect of life is pulled in. Nothing now escapes the trauma of the law—we might even say the law continually recalls trauma—and yet this is still the gospel's doing; this is the strange work of the gospel.

Jacques Derrida hints at a similar metaphor: "I want to insist at once to reserve the possibility of a justice, indeed of a law *[loi]* that not only exceeds or contradicts law but also, perhaps, has no relation to law, or maintains such a strange relation to it that it may just as well demand law as exclude it."[11] Derrida is asking about the possibility of a justice in this world (note this well—not a justice in heaven or at the end of time), but about the possibility of a justice in this world that exceeds, contradicts, and even broadens the law to such an extent that we do not recognize the law. Derrida is asking about a justice that is not a force of violence, an imposition, a new law. And he calls the relation between this justice and law a strange relation.

We want to ask about a gospel that is not itself a demand, a law, a question of channeling or direction, a violent imposition but, rather, a continual difference, a distinction that cannot be limited, confined, or hemmed in. Whenever we attempt a systematization of the gospel, whether as means of grace or as testament, the distinction becomes manageable. This difference between law and gospel, however, is primarily witnessed as a continual broadening of both law and gospel, a certain heightening of the "strange relation." For Luther, this distinction is described in a place that itself knows of no explanation, that is traumatic. The broadening that encompasses both law and gospel and defines their strange relation is, for Luther, found in the suffering of Christ: "God's alien work, therefore, is the suffering of Christ and sufferings in Christ, the crucifixion of the old man and the mortification of Adam. God's proper work, however, is the resurrection of Christ, justification in the Spirit, and the vivification of the new man."[12] Luther describes this strange work of the gospel, this alien work of God—law—as Christ's suffering and all sufferings in Christ. The broadening of the law is found in suffering, in a suffering that we cannot explain, a suffering we can never imitate. The broadening is the broadening of trauma. It is the continual resurfacing of what is latent, the suffering (implicit and explicit) that is passed on. The broadening is the force of a return, the continual return of suffering that breaks all of our contexts.

And resurrection? Resurrection or, to use a perhaps more accessible word, vivification comes not in an explanation of that suffering, not in a capturing of the moment (whether the moment of suffering, for example, the cross, or the moment of resurrection, for example, the forgiveness of sins) ritually or systematically. Resurrection does not come in a solution to suffering, not in a movement that gets the "direction" of grace right, not even (necessarily) in a healing, but through an intervention, through an utterance, a word to the dead.

This question of difference and broadening has taken us to the problem of suffering as a place where the juxtaposition of law and gospel and its tension is heightened. But does Luther not contradict or negate this tension himself? Does he not fall back into a legalistic approach in which law and gospel are clearly delineated when he writes that the holy mass (the gospel) is the one law for the entire people and through his own, very practical insistence on the use of the Words of Institution at every celebration of the sacrament.

Luther strongly argued that the only proper celebration of the eucharist was with the use of the Words of Institution (that is, without additional prayers of thanksgiving, invocations, smells, and bells as distinguished from those words).[13] If we are to understand this sacrament, Luther writes, then we must "first grasp and thoroughly ponder the words of Christ, by which he performed and instituted the mass and commanded us to perform it. For therein lies the whole mass, its nature, work, profit, and benefit. Without the words nothing is derived from the mass."[14] Does not this insistence contradict the conclusions drawn from the absence of the Words of Institution in the *Didache*, namely, how this absence displaces remembering (the memory of the event) by the force of return? Is not Luther attempting to capture remembrance in speech, in a ritual act? We are forced to ask: Is not Luther's insistence on the Words of Institution a new law?

This insistence on the Words of Institution can be read in several ways. In Lutheran scholarship and ecclesial debate, this insistence has resurfaced among contemporary theologians adhering to a non-geographic ecclesial association within the larger Lutheran community: the Word Alone Network. The insistence, among these theologians, echoes Luther's insistence: that the celebration of the Lord's Supper be clear in its direction from God toward the believer. The only necessary component, then, of a proper celebration is the Words of Institution and that these be "heard" clearly as proclamation (as coming from God to us). Any action on our part toward God (even thanksgiving) is considered sacrifice. "Christ's gift is what matters, not our thanksgiving, celebration, or sacrifice."[15]

The key word in the Words of Institution that expresses metaphorically the proper direction is *testament*. Believers are heirs of a testament—the forgiveness of sins. Christ bequeaths a promise and seals the testament with his blood. Believers are the heirs of this testament.

But what is happening with this insistence on the Words of Institution and, in particular, on the word *testament?* The Words of Institution now ensure for the believer a proper remembering of an event—the bequeathing of a testament by Christ at the Last Supper. The Word Alone Network will also insist that the proper nomenclature of this remembering is the "Lord's Supper" (and not "eucharist," for example, a word that evokes human action through thanksgiving). And yet, this nomenclature itself places great value on a particular event as if that event can be repeated, as if we have, through this repetition, an infallible access to God's promise. The notion of testament itself curiously places this theological perspective in a direct communication with a past event, with one event, as if we were still in control of both remembering and event.

The Word Alone statement on worship points out that eucharistic prayers, or any prayers for that matter that accompany the Words of Institution, do not make Christ present: "Our act of remembering Christ does not cause him to be present in the Supper nor to do his work of forgiving sins."[16] The suggestion, of course, is that the Words of Institution as remembrance do make Christ present. We are once again caught in a facile remembering that seeks to capture the promise ritually (speaking the Words of Institution over the bread and the wine is itself a deeply ritual gesture even when actions and adornments are kept to a minimum).

However, as we have seen, liturgical remembering is not constituted by our conscious, cognitive act spoken ritually. Rather, in the celebration of the eucharist, something returns; something over which we have no control both confronts and vivifies. "Remembering" is not simply repeating or rehearsing a past event today; it is a dis-membering and a re-membering. Liturgical remembering is an awaking to something that is inaccessible in event and that intervenes as utterance for us "today."

The believer does not "participate in Christ's deed" as if the believer were in some form of continuum, communication with the event of deeding. Testament language, just as sacrificial language, risks giving the participant direction communication (as direct "heirs") with what Christ instituted. Testament itself becomes a law that rests on a notion of unbroken communication with the event.

As already stated, Luther's insistence on the Words of Institution can tempt the reader in the direction testament understood as law. Could Luther still be clinging to a representational form of remembering? Could this insistence be another expression of his inability to undress and abandon the monk's cowl and tonsure? Could Luther be resisting the very disruption he reads in the words "This is my body"? Luther's coupling of law and holy mass, I believe, resists this facile interpretation. By turning to the eucharist's central act—the Words of Institution—as embodiment of the gospel promise, Luther accomplishes what the *Didache* enacts *without* those same words. Luther not only preserves the gospel from law but disrupts the notion of law and all human attempts at remembering. By insisting on the Words of Institution, Luther insists on an intervention, on an utterance that disrupts the context that humans wish to create theologically and ritually. The Words of Institution themselves become, as the silence in the *Didache*, a witness to a traumatic event that cannot be represented.

The Little Word "Alone"

Let us recall what has already been written. Luther turns to liturgical language, specifically baptismal language, to write the reversible sequence, to write the nonsaturable context, to write *illuminatio* as *tentatio*, to write that which is inaccessible in event, to write the force of a return that cannot be theorized. Luther turns to liturgical language, in one sense, to circumvent the ever-present danger of the belief that we could access event, that we could put order into the chaos of events, that we could write the meaning of event (history). This turn to liturgical language is a form of resistance to memory. Luther resists a form of remembering that captures the event. This resistance to the assertion of a new meaning is the resistance to a new meaning that would once again establish a new, eternally valid context. Luther does not turn to liturgical language—to the sacraments—to construct what he has deconstructed. Luther turns to liturgical language to write a continual dissemination, a continual disruption of context and subject, but a dissemination that is not only deconstruction, a death that also implies a promise.

In the midst of the deconstructive moment—as Luther experiences the demolition of his monastic context—something is added: a call to ministry. In the moment of deconstruction, the ministry of the Word is added. The demolition of the tower—the tower of Babel, the *Turmerlebnis*, the tower of the Roman church—is understood by Luther as God's work, not human work. Luther participates in that demolition, and there *(da)* experiences the addition, the call to ministry. The call is not received as a possession that simply reasserts Luther's conscious subject. The call is something added, something that continually surfaces as onset, as repeated approach, as return. The addition, the call, is itself like a promise of life that returns in the moment of dissemination. The addition—the ministry of the Word—is itself an enactment of disruption. The moment of dissemination does not negate the promise but, strangely, is the promise.

The "content" of the promise of God in classical Christian theology, stated summarily, is forgiveness of sins through Christ and the gift of life eternal. The Reformers understood this gift to be a totally free gift.[17] This understanding of the promise, however, reinserts the promise— reinserts the gospel—into the categories of context and subject. The promise has a content that defines a new context of forgiveness and justifies the subject. However, in the preface/letter to his father, Luther recognizes the promise of God as addition precisely in the disruption of context and subject, his own context and subject. Luther recognizes the promise of God in the impossibility of accessing the event, of capturing the event (and the source of event, God) through remembering.

The narrative of life, the narrative of the subject—of the self in relation to God—is rewritten through the promise. The promise does not comfort the believer in a self or culturally created identity but pushes the subject constantly toward a baptismal understanding of life. If the Words of Institution contain the promise in its most succinct form, it is not in order to reinsert the subject in an indelible, pure communication with the event of God. The celebration of the eucharist and the use of the Words of Institution confront context and subject and *scatter* them. Constructed identities, mythologized contexts, theological affirmations, systematic formulations are forgiven (that is, scattered)—nothing can appropriate, approach, capture the Christ event. "The words of the spirit announce an absent thing, not-to-be-seen, but apprehended by faith."[18] And this absent thing, this Christ event, that cannot be captured is apprehended by faith—by faith alone, by faith standing alone.

In other words, the gospel promise, embodied in the eucharist, is a dissemination that gifts faith standing alone. What does this mean? Let us focus, first of all, on the word *alone*. The little word, of course, captivates, even hypnotizes, scholars of Luther. It surfaces as the metanarrative of "justification through faith alone"; it asserts itself as a fundamentalism (*sola Scriptura, sola Dei*); it even imposes itself as opposition in the title of a polemical movement already cited (Word Alone Network). Curiously, in the metanarrative of Lutheran scholarship and polemic, the use of the *alone* actually supplants Word, Scripture, God, faith. The word *alone* becomes its own metanarrative; it replaces God and event. The word *alone* becomes law. It manifests itself in a violent imposition.

Luther's use of the word is surprisingly different. As Luther himself describes it, the word came through a grammatical necessity of translation. To translate into German the central passage in Paul's letter to the Romans—"For we hold that a person is justified by faith apart from works prescribed by the law"(Rom. 3:28)—the word *allein* (alone) is necessary. "In German when you affirm one thing and deny another you use the word *solum (allein)* with the word *'nicht'* or *'kein.'*"[19] Luther needs to add the word. The Reformation "insight" so elusive to theologians—pinpointing the breakthrough, the origin, the center of the Reformation tower—turns out to be not a divine revelation or intuition but something linked to a question of language and translation. Yes, for Luther the word *allein* is a key theological reality—in Rom. 3:28 Paul expresses the central piece of Christian doctrine.[20] But this key theological reality comes to expression oddly and unexpectedly as a moment of translation.[21]

This discovery of translation, though, is not really that important. First, what is significant is Luther's critique of those who have misunderstood his translation. The papist scholars make the mistake of translating his *allein* with *sola* when it should be *solum*.[22] *Allein* should be read as an adverb rather than an adjective. Luther's critique—not theological at first but grammatical—stands firm against Lutheran scholars today as well who continue to only read *allein* as *sola,* "alone" as "only." In other words, *allein* does not just describe a substantive state (whether it be faith or Scripture or Word) as if that state could, in some form or other, be communicated to the believer and become a possession. *Allein* performs a displacement of event, context, and subject so that gospel faith, in this life, is faith standing alone—there is nothing else.

Rather sarcastically, Luther writes that the papist scholars stand as a cow before a new gate when they see the four letters *s-o-l-a*.[23] And he points out that, here too, he was pushed to this addition of the word *allein*.

> Now I was not relying on and following the nature of the languages alone, however, when, in Romans 3[:28] I inserted the

word *solum* (alone). Actually the text itself and the meaning of St. Paul urgently require and demand it. For in that very passage he is dealing with the main point of Christian doctrine, namely, that we are justified by faith in Christ without works of the law. And Paul cuts away all works so completely, as even to say that the works of the law—though it is God's law and word—do not help us for justification.[24]

The "meaning" of Paul in this passage demanded and forced Luther to add the word. This addition is curiously paralleled by something being cut off. Works are cut off, just as Abraham's foreskin was cut off. The addition is also a cutting off. Can we not then argue that it is the addition of a call (the promise) that also cuts off, disrupts, identity and context? The believer is not saved by works—Abraham was not saved by circumcision—but all works are completely cut away (*"schneit alle werck so rein ab"*).[25] The cutting off (circumcision) did not save Abraham; now works are cut away—but even that does not save or justify the believer. For this cutting away can easily become work in itself; circumcision can become a ritual that justifies, and a liturgical enactment can become law again. But a word is added—a word is added that disrupts context and subject. A word is added that cuts away all invented structures of meaning.

This added word, the heart of the gospel, the promise of God—apprehended through faith alone—is spoken through the eucharistic celebration, in the Words of Institution. It is an addition that is out of human control but that comes to the reader/participant/believer as an intervention, as onset, as repeated approach, as something that continually returns. For Luther, this addition was sung. The enactment of the Words of Institution consisted in singing them to the gospel tone[26] at the very place of what had been the "sacrifice" of the *Stillmesse* (the silent mass). The promise of God—apprehended through faith alone—is apprehended itself in a moment of displacement. The singing of the Words in the gospel tone was a displacement of both sacrifice and law.[27]

Faith alone is nothing less than the addition of the promise, a spoken promise. "Is Christ's death and resurrection our work, that we do, or is it not?"[28] By what work, Luther asks, can we possess and hold the death and resurrection of Christ? The believer cannot control or hem in the event. The gift is not intended to create a new context or establish a single practice. The believer can only receive the *selbige, allein,* faith[29]—receive it, that is, as addition, receive it as an encounter of the resurrection.

Faith alone as gift, as addition, as iterated promise, is nothing less than the dissemination of God, the death of God, the inaccessible in event, the absent thing that cannot be captured but that continually returns *as resurrection*. Faith alone, then, is truly faith standing alone, for it disrupts, cuts off, all works, all constructed contexts and self-invented subject. As such, Luther's insistence on this addition runs counter to the attempts of every culture to define faith itself as human work. And yet, the departure or dissemination (death) of God holds, strangely, paradoxically, the promise of life.

We then need to ask: does this promise call for ritualization? And if so, what form of ritual or liturgical iteration? Luther's insistence on the ritual use of the Words of Institution pushes the reader/participant to a radical departure from which there is no coming back. When Luther writes that Christ "appointed in return but one law or order for his entire people, and that was the holy mass," he turns to the liturgy in order to disrupt the law—in order to disrupt any construal that might be called law (whether it be Aristotelian/Thomistic metaphysics or Lutheran reductionism or human mythologies). Luther turns to the eucharistic celebration that disrupts all forms of liturgical repetition *(imitatio)*. Rather, for Luther, the believer, the participant, is brought into conformity *(conformitas)* with the Christ event through a liturgical iteration, the iteration of a promise that resists the transformation of gospel into law, that resists the reduction of the difference between law and gospel. The iteration of this ritual meal has inscribed within it the radically rewritten gospel promise as baptismal dissemination.

A Dead Voice Calling

How is the promise ritually heard? The *accessio,* or addition, in Luther, is deeply the dissemination or demolition of the tower. It is also closely linked to a spoken word. To write the impact of this dissemination and avoid its reinsertion into theory, Luther turns to liturgical language. Language, of course, refers here not only to the spoken word—to the words pronounced during a liturgical celebration, and particularly the eucharistic celebration—but to the entire action of the liturgy as a language or, perhaps more precisely, a grammar. "This is my body" are spoken words, but as words added to the bread and wine, they become enacted words. Liturgical language—and, more specifically perhaps, sacramental language—disrupts even the categories of language.[30]

Luther turns to liturgical language as a type of grammar in order to approach something about event. We have already, in the first chapter, called this grammar a grammar of event. The grammar of event, as grammar of the disrupting return, heightens an awareness of the *res absens,* of that which is absent in every event. The designation "grammar" is significant because grammar itself does not contain or embody meaning or sense. Grammar is not understanding as information but as demand, imperative. It calls upon enactment, upon a response. In Luther's turn to liturgical language as grammar, he rewrites the presumed access to meaning not as something that can be described, represented, or understood but as something that is like an addition, something that comes to him, something that he may resist but that continues to demand and continues to return as a force.

Event "becomes for us" in that imperative, in that demand for a response, in that call to responsibility. This imperative, however, does not reinstitute the ancient formula *do ut des*.[31] The response does not consist in giving something back—as if the participant *could* return something to "God." Responsibility defined as "giving back" would be only "works" once again.[32] The imperative, the demand for a response, is the imperative of an impossible responsibility. This impossible responsibility, however, does not immobilize; rather, it renders the individual and the community attentive to life—life in its suffering and need and in its joy.

The imperative without work, the impossible responsibility—how is the disruptive return to be written? How, Luther might have asked, is meaning itself to be rewritten in light of the chaos of events, in light of events that do not offer any discernible order? Luther was able to answer this (imagined) question only by accomplishing a shift away from the notion of event as simple historical occurrence in a space-time continuum—from a questioning of event as happenings—to the enactment of event (the enactment of the return) through ritual, and, particularly, through the eucharistic event. In the liturgical act, the imperative is heard again and again as an addition, as utterance. The promise as addition is always a word, a liturgical voice—a public voice. The promise continually confronts the reader/participant through liturgical iteration as addition, as both dissemination and call.

The turn to liturgical language (grammar) has, of course, implications for the understanding of liturgy itself. Liturgy is cut off from the realm of remembrance and repetition. Liturgy is dissociated from the notion of a ritual mastery—whether of chaos or sin or other ailment. And, of course, it is dissociated from the realm of entertainment, where the participant is a mere spectator. If the event "itself" cannot be repeated, if the event is "known" only through what is not known about the event, if the event is known only as a continual disruption or return, then we should not be surprised if there is resistance to this dangerous iteration and to this rewriting of liturgical hermeneutics. The return can be frightful.

> And suddenly there was a great earthquake; for an angel of the Lord, descending from heaven, came and rolled back the stone and sat on it. His appearance was like lightning and his clothing white as snow. For fear of him the guards shook and became like dead men, But the angel said to the women, "Do not be afraid: I know that you are looking for Jesus who was crucified. He is not here; for he has been raised, as he said" (Matthew 28:2-6).[33]

Not the narration of a death, not the memory of an event, and not the re-actualization of a moment become sources of repetition. Repetition itself is displaced by an awakening, a sudden (even frightful) awakening, a disruptive return. And this return is always a return to beginnings that have never been fully understood.[34] At the heart of the liturgy is a dead voice calling, a resurrected voice iterated that continually interrupts, unexpectedly. Liturgy is this return, this awakening, that is a continual yet impossible repetition.

The liturgy, then, is not the facile remembering or simple repetition of an event, an anamnesis, but a surrendering, a submission, through an iterable structure, through and in the realization that someone died for me. It is the iteration of a question that has haunted Christian theology throughout two millennia: Why did God become human (*Cur Deus Homo*)?[35] Or, in other terms: How could the child die before the Father? How could God die? How could someone die for me? Why did I not die? Liturgy is the iteration of this dissemination but it is also the surprise of awakening to life—to the continual return of the resurrection. If, for Freud, the death drive is "precisely the experience of having passed beyond death without knowing it,"[36] then, I would argue, the particular ritual iteration of the Christian liturgy is the continual return, addition, onset, of both the survival of God's death and the impossible imperative, as response to that death, as a response to that gift. This impossible imperative that seems to demand response, to demand work, is nothing less than an immersion in God's own death and life. It can be called discipleship.

A liturgical intervention has raised this further characteristic of the return as imperative: the return is experienced not only as the repetition of past violence or disruption but also as the imperative to live out an impossible responsibility. This imperative is already developed in the text of the *Didache*. The chapters following the description of the eucharistic celebration of chapters 9 and 10 (the concluding chapters of the *Didache*) outline the ways—teaching—in which the community shall live among themselves and vis-à-vis the world. Caruth also describes this imperative: "It is precisely the dead child, the child in its irreducible inaccessibility and otherness, who says to the father: *wake up, leave me, survive; survive to tell the story of my burning.*"[37] Caruth points out that the force of a return is also a voice calling the living to a responsibility.

Who or what is this *voice calling?* In the voice calling, we discover not only that the return is an iteration of something inaccessible or absent (the death of God on a cross) but that the return is audible as a voice of promise.

The voice that calls, for Caruth, is the voice of the dead child calling the father to recognition in the dream described by Freud and commented on by Lacan.[38] Caruth points out that the survival of the father is not merely "an accidental living beyond the child, but rather as a mode of existence determined by the impossible structure of the response."[39] Survival is considered a different mode of existence, a mode of existence that cannot respond—in this case, to the voice of a dead child. No response can make the child live again. No response can assure the father of a victory over death, the death of his child and also his own death. The father cannot by his own work, by his own response, save either his child or himself.

The impossibility of responding to a dead voice highlights, I believe, several notions that will require development. Of course, first, the impossibility of responding underlines once again the inaccessible, the absence—that which cannot be known in event and returns to awaken us. But this voice, this dead voice, this voice that cannot be possessed, also pushes toward life, but life not as "possession." This could be stated, in theological language, as the impossibility to justify or save oneself—that is, the impossibility of works (response) to ensure life (eternal) or a right relation to God. In other words, the response itself is not a "work" or something that the subject possesses. The response contradicts the move to spirituality or asceticism when these are conceived as *imitatio Christi*, when these understand the "goal" of spiritual life to be centered or focused on the life of Christ. The response calls the believer into a life beyond death, an almost impossible life, into Christ's life that is already a life disseminated, noncentered, nonoriginary.

The response is a consequence of the voice calling, of the addition, and, as such, as response, does not claim life but attempts to disseminate, to scatter, to share life. One cannot respond to this dead (and yet not dead) voice, to this voice of the resurrection, other than by also witnessing to the impossibility. The only witness is gift. The only witness is faith alone that demolishes all other possible responses.

But there is a second aspect to this dead voice calling: it reveals something of the iterable structure of event. The voice that returns and calls is a voice that disseminates context and subject and, as just noted, a voice that reveals human impossibility. No humanly constructed context or identity is righteous or righteous making. This impossibility—the impossibility of works—is, however, also a mode of existence. It is not merely negation. It is the ungraspable, the trauma, in history itself that humanity carries. Luther recognized this impossibility as mode of existence as he wrote the demolition of the monastic context. Luther surrendered himself to the force of a return that he hears (and bears) as an addition, an addition that implies a response. Caruth writes, "To awaken is thus to bear the imperative to survive: to survive no longer simply as the father of the child, but as the one who must tell *what it means not to see*."[40] Luther is pushed to write the dissemination of context and subject. Luther is forced to preach the dissemination of the Word, of what it means not to see, to possess, or to capture, but to stand passively as recipient. In the letter to his father, he wrote the voice that returns and calls, the voice that disseminates, as an addition, *accessio*. He wrote that which calls him as a responsibility (the ministry of the Word). Luther enacted the promise as that life-giving dissemination, as discipleship.

For Luther, the voice returns or is also iterated as promise in the eucharistic celebration and, specifically, in the Words of Institution.

Here, the words confront the participant as an intervention. The Words of Institution do not validate the context. They do not validate the performance of the eucharistic consecration. The Words of Institution are like an intervention, an utterance that cannot be controlled, an utterance that disrupts all theory, all hermeneutics, an utterance that is apprehended by faith alone. The Words of Institution are themselves like an *epiclesis*[41]—an invocation and acknowledgment of the Holy Spirit, who continually disseminates reference.[42] The work of the Holy Spirit itself is here rewritten. The work of the Spirit is the work of inscription: it is the work of something inscribed (as return) within the structure of event, as absence within *res*, as the ungraspable within history itself that is continually recalled.

Curiously, the Words of Institution and this disruptive Spirit—these words as testament, if we wish to bow momentarily to that language—are words spoken by a "dead" voice, by a voice that we cannot possess, that comes to us from elsewhere—dare we say, from a resurrection voice? This "dead" voice coming from an indeterminate location intervenes as utterance, as Spirit, in the midst of life.[43] This dead (yet strangely alive) voice intervenes and we cannot respond to the voice. We can only submit to the iteration of this voice as it calls us from outside the sphere, outside the ritual circle.

An Unexpected Return and an Impossible Responsibility

Earlier, the assertion was made that Luther, rather than applying yet another hermeneutic to the eucharist, is proposing that a hermeneutic— the very possibility perhaps of theology—arises *out* of the event called the eucharist. This assertion now appears problematic. This study has not set out or systematized what Luther clearly understood but has, in its own meanderings, continued an implicit (and sometimes explicit) critique of hermeneutics, of systematic theology. Can we turn to theory where Luther turns to the liturgy? The assertion is problematic not only for the writing of theology, as we will see, but also for the practice of the liturgy. Perhaps, rather than proposing a new hypothesis or theory, we are entering the realm of *Annahme* that is much more the realization of being adopted, of being pulled out. Perhaps we are entering a baptismal realm?

By enigmatically equating the "one law" and eucharist, Luther displaced the origin and foundation of the "law." The "law"—no law—gives us access to the singularity of an event. Rather, "law" itself is disrupted, displaced, and reinterpreted through a liturgical iteration. Denying the reader/participant access to immutable, transcendental, mystical truth and origin, Luther directs his reader to the singularity of an event, to an ongoing event—the Christ event. As ongoing event, it disrupts the reader/participant with the impossibility of remembering and ritual repetitions, thereby suggesting a new mode of existence as continual dissemination. We also saw how the liturgical practice of the *Didache* embodies this confrontation by focusing on the radical disorientation and reorientation of the meal-keeping practice of Jesus. Liturgical repetition is not repetition of a memorial as such but the iteration of a continual dissemination.

The impossibility of capturing, imitating, remembering, or repeating the singularity of an event plus the recognition that any form, whether new or old, inadequately expresses the singularity, creates a temptation and a dilemma. The temptation, of course, is the persistent human tendency to create foundations, to rebuild the walls of the demolished stronghold. Luther may have saved the word of God from "tradition," but Lutheran orthodoxy and current forms of Gnesio-Lutherans have reified the Word again into the "letter." Who will now save us from the Word, we might ask with Lessing?[44] Who will now save us from the Word as law?

The dilemma follows and reacts to the temptation. Is it possible, when the eucharist is considered as an event always breaking our rituals open, always pointing toward an abyss or absence, always disseminating, is it possible to discern a hermeneutics? How is the dissemination of event, context, subject—of presider, people, things, and world in liturgical celebration—to be written without laying new foundations? How is trauma recalled that does not succumb to trauma, that does not simply repeat past violence, but recalls trauma as responsibility? The dissemination of both context and subject through the singular event witnesses to a profound need of rewriting of history and reference. This writing of dissemination, however, curiously resists writing. Once again, we find this resistance inscribed in Luther's writing, but now we find it inscribed in liturgical language, in words about the liturgy, words that resist not dissemination but theory.

Luther understands the significance of the sacrament—the holy mass or eucharist—as a fellowship of saints.[45] And this fellowship "consists in this, that all the spiritual possessions of Christ and his saints are shared with and become the common property of him who receives this sacrament. Again all sufferings and sins also become common property; and thus love engenders love in return and [mutual love] unites."[46] The word *love* now makes a more prominent appearance. It was already present in the central passage of chapter 4: "Christ, in order to prepare for himself an acceptable and beloved people, which should be bound together in unity through love, abolished the whole law of Moses."[47] The passage, of course, concludes with the juxtaposition of eucharist and law. In other words, this strange juxtaposition of eucharist and law, this juxtaposition that has led to the disruption of law, simultaneously binds together in unity through love. The question that we now ask is perhaps self-evident: What is love? How is love a unity that binds without being a law? How is love to be understood in this dissemination of event, context, and subject?

But allow me to step to the side for a moment. Intra-Lutheran debate has placed much more emphasis on Luther's later writing on the holy mass or the sacrament of holy communion, especially in the polemical writings against Zwingli in the late 1520s. The one concession, perhaps, is the "Treatise on the New Testament" (1520), from which some derive the testament language and Luther's insistence on the Words of Institution. Luther's insistence on the sacrament as fellowship (from a 1519 sermon) receives far less attention. However, the mention of love is central to both the treatise and the sermon. In the treatise and in our central citation from that treatise, the eucharist disseminates the law in order to prepare and bind a people together through love.

Luther's insistence, in the same treatise, on the Words of Institution as an everlasting testament and on the sacrament as binding in unity through love are not in contradiction. In fact, the voice that utters the Words (of Institution), the dead voice that pronounces the testament, is an iterated voice. As iterated voice, it is not alone but implies the other, implies the irruption of the other. The Word—and this cannot be stressed enough—is not simply originary on its own as if rhetorical bravura alone constitutes justification. The Word is never heard or understood or received outside of the community, outside of its liturgical enactment (it is constitutive of and dependent upon the community).

In the sacrament, according to Luther, the participant receives the "immeasurable grace and mercy of God."[48] This gift is not to be possessed but occasions an undressing, a giving away, a dispersal of misery and tribulation (*Anfechtung*). Misery and tribulations are laid upon Christ and upon the community of saints.[49] Something in the sacrament comes to the participant, something strangely returns, continually returns as addition, as gift, as call, as the other.

> So it is clear from all this that this holy sacrament is nothing else than a divine sign, in which are pledged, granted, and imparted Christ and all saints together with all their works, sufferings, merits, mercies, and possessions, for the comfort and strengthening of all who are in anxiety and sorrow, persecuted by the devil, sins, the world, the flesh, and every evil. And to receive the sacrament is nothing else than to desire all this and firmly to believe that it is done.[50]

The sacrament of the eucharist imparts Christ *and all saints together*. Luther will almost never mentions "Christ" without adding "and all the saints." Christ becomes Christ in the saints, and the believer is once again directed to that other mode of existence, that dissemination of life, the dissemination of Christ now in the other. Incarnation and community are inseparable. The neighbor and the believer are both caught up in the gift of God's continual dissemination through liturgical iteration, through the celebration of Word and sacraments. Through the participation in the eucharist, we are made one with Christ and all the saints in their works, sufferings, and merit.[51] Union with Christ is not the inception of an individualistic piety (Jesus and me) or a new religion. "Christ with all his saints, takes upon himself our form, fights with us against sin, death and all evil. This enkindles such love that we take on his form, rely upon his righteousness, life and blessedness."[52]

When believers are "conformed" to this disseminated Christ, they are conformed to the other, to the neighbor in suffering and need. "Again, through the same love, we are to be changed and to make the infirmities of all other Christians our own; we are to take upon ourselves their form and their necessity (*gestalt und notdurfft*)."[53] The key phrase here is not "take upon ourselves" (as if we were putting on a new cowl) but "through the same love." Through this love that first took upon itself all our need, through this love that revealed itself through death, through dissemination, are we also then to "take upon ourselves" the sufferings of others. What the believer receives in the celebration of the eucharist is Christ with all his saints, that is, what returns, what continually returns in the movement of this liturgical iteration, is the other, the other in need and in blessing.

The liturgical iteration does not establish a new line of communication or ensure a participation in the heritage of the testament. The believer is not simply transformed into a new substance. The believer is reoriented in relation to event, context, and self. The sacrament confronts the participant with a new (and perhaps impossible) language about history and self: "meaning"—all the meanings humans construe—are inventions. The liturgical celebration, and particularly the eucharist, confront us with this failure of meaning. The eucharist confronts us with the dissemination of event, context, and subject, leaving faith alone. "The one faith says: This is Christ's body. The other: This body is mine. Do not come forward without this faith."[54] "This body is mine"—the believer is conformed to Christ's broken, disseminated body. The believer is conformed to the suffering, needy, indigent body of the neighbor. Life, knowledge, truth, and yes, even communion are promised in dissemination.[55]

Liturgical theologians have a strange name for this dissemination—one that they will probably not recognize as such: the "means of grace." The "means of grace" clearly focuses on the sacramental gifts of bread and wine and water but also, even more importantly, on the promise these hold. However, this focus is not on the "means" as a form or method of communication or assurance but, rather, as a means of dissemination in love. Through the "means of grace," people are invited, gathered in, to participate in a dissemination of all referents, all foundations, all laws.

The "one law," the juxtaposition embedded in the eucharistic event itself, does not defer to a mystical foundation but takes the believer to the crux of a sacramental act—and, subsequently, to a rewriting of liturgical theology. The sacramental act is not the bridging of the gap between the sacred and the secular; it is not our "peephole" into God's reality or our high-speed Internet connection to God or any form of privileged communication. The sacramental act is the enactment of a return, an encounter with something inaccessible that continually returns, that confronts the believer, perhaps frightens and awakens the believer to both a death and a resurrection. In that encounter, all human need becomes a call, a voice, a responsibility. And is this not what has been called grace?

Grace is the displacement of all mystical foundation; it is the displacement of God in vulnerability, need, suffering.[56] This grace is the absent thing in every event, the permeability of every context, the dissemination of subject in order to find life through faith alone. The liturgy itself disseminates and juxtaposes rather than systematizing and concluding. It points to the hole, the abyss, in which the "promise" can be truly promise, truly testament.

The "means of grace" is nothing less than this dissemination—this way to the cross—and this return, this encounter with the resurrection. The believer is brought back from the temptation of inventing new mystical foundations, from the presumptive notions of piety, from the desire to possess the "means." The believer is brought back to the death and resurrection of Jesus Christ, to a communion in the paschal mystery, to the heart of the eucharistic practice as conformity to Christ and neighbor. The believer is brought back to eucharistic practice as gift, as grace.[57] Through the bread and the wine and the Word, the believer is brought back to the body and blood of Jesus Christ, to his life offered for everyone.[58] But is this not in contradiction to the earlier statement that the "means of grace" confounds our very method of thinking and remembering? What does it mean to go to the cross? Are we again idealistically remembering that past event as if we were all gifted with liturgical hypermnesia?[59] Are we somehow miraculously taken back to the crucifixion as in a film?

When the event, the singular event, finds iteration, when the "means of grace" takes the people to the cross—it takes them to the cross disseminated in the world today. The "means of grace" take us to the cross in human lives, to the cross in the life of family, community, society, nation, world. When the "means of grace" take the assembly to the cross, it takes the assembly to the promise: the promise as event, as profound dissemination of context and subject. In that promise, justification, reconciliation, forgiveness, and life are disseminated and then known as an addition, as a call, as an impossible responsibility. In and through liturgical iteration (the "means of grace"), the participant hears God's promise becoming today. Liturgical iteration directs the assembly to the cross, to the hole, the abyss, to that which cannot be remembered or captured or explained or repeated. Liturgical iteration takes the participant to that which continually returns as call, to a new mode of existence. It takes the participant to the place of God's suffering in the world.

> Then the king will say to those at his right hand, "Come, you
> that are blessed by my Father, inherit the kingdom prepared for

you from the foundation of the world; for I was hungry and you gave me food, I was thirsty and you gave me something to drink, I was a stranger and you welcomed me, I was naked and you gave me clothing, I was sick and you took care of me, I was in prison and you visited me." Then the righteous will answer him, "Lord, when was it that we saw you hungry and gave you food, or thirsty and gave you something to drink? And when was it that we saw you a stranger and welcomed you, or naked and gave you clothing? And when was it that we saw you sick or in prison and visited you?" And the king will answer them, "Truly I tell you, just as you did it to one of the least of these who are members of my family, you did it to me" (Matt. 25:35-41).

Writing a New Mode of Existence

A new narrative is proposed. Luther's writing his own narrative pushes us toward an un-writing and a rewriting of the core theological notions of promise and grace.

Turning the cross—or the Christ event—into a sacrifice or a testament that we ritualize in the celebration of the eucharist is just a human attempt to control that which is traumatic, that which is inaccessible in the event. Trauma theory here opens a door to the possibility of a move beyond a repeated ritualization of violence or sacrifice. It allows us to approach the Christ event (and the way in which we ritualize that event) as something that Jesus suffered—not something he controlled. It was, precisely, traumatic. And this event, this death, continually returns, in ritual iteration, but an iteration that shifts the focus of ritual away from violence toward a question of life, of awakening. The "force of return" is encapsulated not in repeated violence but, rather, in the question of survival.

The new narrative displaces the narratives of both sacrifice and testament, of works and of memorial. It is writing the end of violence, the end of a superimposed hermeneutics that always becomes law. The narrative is, strangely, writing the death of the God of mystical foundations. The dead voice, the resurrected, iterated voice calling, dispels the power of violence and the perpetuation of violence by ritually returning not a graspable, spiritually accessible presence but an absence that precisely cannot be held.

This narrative speaks to human suffering by placing that suffering in the perspective of a traumatic return, of something that remains inaccessible and yet, as utterance, as voice calling, continually awakens us to an impossible responsibility, to discipleship that is no longer violent, no longer self-imposed work or sacrifice or new asceticism or demand, but gift precisely in the midst of human need. It is a dead voice, a suffering voice, that calls as resurrection, as life. "Don't you see I'm burning?"

Liturgical iteration and, in particular, the celebration of the eucharist invite "life" into the continual dynamic of dying and rising in Christ, a spiritual baptism, which has no end until bodily death and resurrection. This confrontation with dying and rising is not merely an emotional or psychological drama—such a drama would situate the participant once again in the realm of the representational. The equation of "awesome" religious emotion with a sense that something has been given up "for God" is imaginary. The dying of which Luther speaks is a concrete participation—*conformitas*—in the death of God and in the suffering of others. This death is not a spiritual discipline. It is not an emptying of oneself or a centering or a sacrificial religiosity. This dying, first realized in baptism, is a submersion in event and a being pulled out. It is a dissemination of context that permits something to be added, a return, a call to live. The "service of God" as eucharist or, as Luther puts it, "the real fellowship" and "the true significance of this sacrament,"[60] calls the participant through an iterable, that is, liturgical, structure to live out a responsibility. The "one law" awakens us to this almost impossible responsibility—continually sent out of the closed circle, out of the community, out of the old law, out of a hermeneutics, disseminated but also reoriented, to find God already displaced, disseminated, outside waiting.

Life itself is disseminated and reoriented: here is promise, here is faith alone, here, offered in liturgical disruption. Here Christ prepares an acceptable and beloved people; here Christ appoints in return "one law" for his entire people, and that is the holy mass.

Abbreviations

LW   Martin Luther, *Luther's Works: American Edition.* 55 vols. Philadelphia: Fortress (Muhlenberg) Press, 1958–1986.

WA   Martin Luther, *Luthers Werke. Kritische Gesamtausgabe. Schriften.* 65 vols. Weimar: H. Böhlau, 1883–1993.

WABr   Martin Luther, *Luthers Werke. Kritische Gesamtausgabe. Briefwechsel.* 18 vols. Weimar: H. Böhlau, 1930–1985.

WADB   Martin Luther, *Luthers Werke. Kritische Gesamtausgabe. Bibel.* 12 vols. Weimar: H. Böhlau, 1906–1961.

WAT   Martin Luther, *Luthers Werke. Kritische Gesamtausgabe. Tischreden.* 6 vols. Weimar: H. Böhlau, 1912–1921.

Notes

Preface

1. T.S. Eliot, *The Complete Poems and Plays:* 1909–1950 (Boston: Houghton Mifflin, 1952), 68.

Introduction

1. David W. Noble, *Historians against History: The Frontier Thesis and the National Covenant in American Historical Writing since 1830* (Minneapolis: University of Minnesota Press, 1965).

2. "Don't we see in the history of the people of God many institutions, that in order to maintain themselves through time, have lost the provisional nature of their beginnings?" Frère Roger, *Dynamique du provisoire* (Taizé: Les Presses de Taizé, 1965), 128.

3. Dietrich Bonhoeffer, *Letter & Papers from Prison,* ed. Eberhard Bethge (New York: Macmillan, 1972), 300.

4. Parts of the following two sections have appeared in my article "Trauma Theory and Liturgy: A Disruption of Ritual," in *Liturgical Ministry* 17 (Summer 2008): 127–32.

5. Sigmund Freud, *Beyond the Pleasure Principle,* ed. and trans. James Strachey (New York: Norton, 1961), 12ff.

6. This is the name given by the American Psychiatric Association in the *Diagnostic and Statistical Manual of Mental Disorders,* 4th ed. (Arlington, Va.: The American Psychiatric Publishing Inc., 2000).

7. Cathy Caruth, *Unclaimed Experience: Trauma, Narrative, and History* (Baltimore, Md.: Johns Hopkins University Press, 1996).

8. Caruth, *Unclaimed Experience,* 62.

9. Caruth, *Unclaimed Experience,* 17.

10. Sigmund Freud, *The Standard Edition of the Complete Psychological Works of Sigmund Freud, vol. 23,* ed. and trans. by James Strachey (London: Hogarth Press, 1958), 158.

11. Caruth, *Unclaimed Experience*, 69.

12. Exod. 34:6-7 NRSV.

13. Cathy Caruth, *Trauma: Explorations in Memory* (Baltimore, Md.: Johns Hopkins University Press, 1995), 151.

14. For an English translation, see Kurt Niederwimmer, *The Didache: A Commentary*, trans. Linda M. Maloney, Hermeneia (Minneapolis: Fortress Press, 1998).

15. Jacques Derrida, "Force of Law," in *Acts of Religion* (New York: Routledge, 2002), 233.

16. Derrida, "Force of Law," 234.

17. *Auslegung D. Mar: Luthers, uber etliche Capitel des andern Buchs Mosi, Geprediget zu Wittemberg, Anno 1524. 1525. und 1526*, WA 16:71, 15–17.

18. On the freeing of speech and its multiple manifestations socially and politically, see Michel de Certeau, *The Capture of Speech and Other Political Writings*, trans. Tom Conley (Minneapolis: University of Minnesota Press, 1997).

19. Michel de Certeau, *Capture of Speech*, 26.

Chapter 1. Writing an Event and the Event of Writing

1. See Bernhard Lohse, ed., *Der Durchbruch der reformatorischen Erkenntnis bei Luther* (Darmstadt: Wissenschaftliche Buchgesellschaft, 1968).

2. See Martin Lohrmann's recent article "Text, for the Record: A Newly Discovered Report of Luther's Reformation Breakthrough from Johannes Bugenhagen's 1550 Jonah Commentary" in *Lutheran Quarterly* 22 (Autumn 2008): 324–30.

3. The concern of a just relation to some absolute power or will or being, of course, is not of such concern today as it was in Luther's time. However, the shift Luther initiates, I would like to believe, exposes the contemporary narrative of its own accomplishments and history for what they are—another form of God—and it thereby exposes the continued belief in a god.

4. Heiko A. Oberman, *Luther: Man between God and the Devil* (New York: Doubleday, 1992). This work has been considered Oberman's systematic theology. See Timothy Wengert's review in the *Journal of Religion* 72 (January 1992): 112–13.

5. Oberman, *Luther*, 165.

6. Oberman, *Luther*, 157–158.

7. Oberman, *Luther*, 164.

8. Heiko A. Oberman, "'Immo.' Luthers reformatorische Entdeckungen im Spiegel der Rhetorik," in *Lutheriana Zum 500. Geburtstag Martin Luthers,* ed. Gerhard Hammer und Karl-Heinz zur Mühlen (Köln: Böhlau Verlag, 1984).

9. Heiko A. Oberman, "Luther and the Via Moderna: The Philosophical Backdrop of the Reformation Breakthrough," *Journal of Ecclesiastical History* 54, no. 4 (October 2003): 641–670.

10. Timothy Wengert, private correspondance with the author.

11. Heiko A. Oberman, "Wenden und Wertung der Reformation. Thesen und Tatsache," in *Reformatio Ecclesia: Beiträge zu Kirchlichen Reformbemühungen von der Alten Kirche bis zur Neuzeit. Festgabe für Erwin Iserloh,* ed. Remigius Bäumer (Paderborn: Ferdinand Schöningh, 1980). English translation of this chapter to be found in Heiko A. Oberman, *The Reformation: Roots and Ramifications,* trans. A. Gow (Grand Rapids, Mich.: Eerdmans, 1994).

12. Oberman, *The Reformation,* 20.

13. As Oberman writes: "*potentia dei absoluta*—The absolute power of God subject only to the law of non-contradiction which leaves the actually chosen order out of consideration. *potentia dei ordinata*—The ordained power of God. This is the order established by God and the way in which God has chosen to act in his opera ad extra, i.e., over against the contingent order outside him. It is the power which is regulated by the revealed and natural laws established by God. Between the absolute and ordained power of God there is no real distinction but merely rational distinction." Heiko A. Oberman, *The Harvest of Medieval Theology: Gabriel Biel and Late Medieval Nominalism* (Grand Rapids, Mich.: Eerdmans, 1963/1967), 473.

14. Oberman, "Luther and the Via Moderna," 656.

15. Heiko A. Oberman, "Via Antiqua and Via Moderna: Late Medieval Prolegomena to Early Reformation Thought," *Journal of the History of Ideas* 48, (1987): 28.

16. Oberman, "Luther and the Via Moderna," 656.

17. Oberman, "Luther and the Via Moderna," 646.

18. Heiko A. Oberman, *The Dawn of the Reformation: Essays in Later Medieval and Early Reformation Thought* (Edinburgh: T & T Clark, 1986), 55.

19. Oberman, *Dawn of the Reformation,* 650.

20. Oberman, *Dawn of the Reformation,* 650.

21. The following discussion of the two spheres or two realms is marked by the medieval distinction between *potentia dei ordinata* and *potentia dei absoluta*. It is not referring to that later distinction Luther makes between the two kingdoms, though there is definitely an overlap.

22. Oberman, *The Reformation,* 16.

23. WA 39 1:175, 11.

24. Oberman, *The Reformation,* 17.

25. *In natura experiential est causa, cur audiamus, et praecedit assensum.*

26. Oberman, *The Reformation*, 19–20.

27. Oberman, *The Reformation*, 20.

28. "Die unumkehrbare Abfolge von Assenz—d.h. lebendigem Glaubens-gehorsam—zur Grammatik—d.h. Schrifttreue—hat Luther zum Reformator gemacht." Oberman, "Wenden," 502–3, and *The Reformation*, 20.

29. Oberman, *The Reformation*, 20.

30. Oberman, "Luther and the Via Moderna," 654–55.

31. "In natura experientia est causa, cur audiamus, et praecedit assensum; in theologia autem experientia sequitur assensum, non praecedit." WAT 1, no. 423; 183, 25–27.

32. Oberman, *The Reformation*, 20.

33. LW 26. Commentary on Galatians 3:3.

34. Oberman, "Wenden," 502.

35. Oberman, *The Reformation*, 19.

36. "Dieser Entdeckungsweg wird ausdrücklich als mühsam und langwierig bezeichnet." Oberman, "Immo," 20.

37. Regin Prenter, *Spiritus Creator* (Philadelphia: Muhlenberg, 1953), 56.

38. Oberman, *The Reformation*, 20.

39. This exclamation mark is added by Oberman to the German text.

40. WAT 5, no. 5247: 26, 18–26.

41. Oberman, *The Reformation*, 18–19.

42. Oberman, *The Reformation*, 20.

43. "Es kann kein Zweifel darüber bestehen, dass 'immo'—wo es mehr bewirken soll als emphatische Zuspitzung—die Aufmerksamkeit des Hörers—bzw Lesers—auf Gottes Wirken *'sub contrario'* lenken will: *'Immo'* ist zur rhetorischen Figur der *'theologia crucus'* geworden." Oberman, "Immo," 32–33.

44. Jacob und Wilhelm Grimm, *Deutsches Wörterbuch*, Zweiter Band (Leipzig: Verlag von S. Hirzel, 1860), 646–58.

45. ". . . das organische da weist auf raum und örtlichkeit und bedeutet demonstrativ ibi, relativ ubi." Grimm, *Deutsches Wörterbuch*, 646.

46. Even in the Table Talks, years after Luther would have sung the psalms in the prayers of the office, these words are still rendered in Latin; unfortunately, the play of two languages is lost in the translation into one language.

47. WA 5, 1519–21.

48. 'Meditari' dicunt id esse, quod disserere, disputare, et omnino verbis exercere, ut ps. xxxvi. *'Os iusti meditabitur sapientiam'*. Hinc B. Augustinus in sua translatione habet, Garrire, pulchra sane metaphora, quod ut garritus avium est exercitium, ita hominis (cuius est proprium officium sermocinari) exercitium sit sermocinatio in lege domini." WA 5:34, 3–7.

49. WAT 5, no. 5247:26, 11.

50. Oberman, *The Reformation*, 19.

51. WA 5:239, 3.

Chapter 2. Writing Life

1. Michel de Certeau, *The Capture of Speech and Other Political Writings*, trans. Tom Conley (Minneapolis: University of Minnesota Press, 1997), 12–13.

2. LW 39.

3. The fourfold interpretation consists of the literal, anagoglical, tropological, and allegorical reading. See Henri de Lubac, *Medieval Exegesis*, trans. Edward M. Macierowski (Grand Rapids, Mich.: Eerdmans, 2000).

4. LW 39:181. "Aber sei ist nott, das nit ein iglicher von ihm selb musteria ertichte, wie ettliche than und noch thun. . ." WA 7:652, 34–35.

5. LW 39:177.

6. LW 39:183–84.

7. LW 39:177.

8. Regin Prenter, *Spiritus Creator* (Philadelphia: Muhlenberg, 1953), 219.

9. "Besset thun die, die ihn nennen *grammaticum, historicum sensum.*" WA 7:652, 24–25, and LW 39:181.

10. LW 39:184–85.

11. "[I]ch bitte, das ir den kern, den rechten Schatz behalten und das furnemester heubtstueck in der heiligen Schrifft, Nemlich, das ir die heilige Schrifft nach der historien weg wol lernet." *Auslegung D. Mar: Luthers, uber etliche Capitel des andern Buchs Mosi, Geprediget zu Wittemberg, Anno 1524. 1525. und 1526,* WA 16:71, 15–17. And further: "Das Heubtstuecke und den grund oder das beste in der Schrifft nenne sie auch die Schalen one die Nuss, als, die historien obenhin lessen und wissen, Du aber lass auch dein bests studieren sein, das wir wissen, wie die historien gehen, wie Abraham im wort Gottesund Glauben gelebet, und wie es im ergangen sei." WA 16:70, 21–27.

12. WA 16:70, 21–27.

13. LW 39:182–83.

14. WA 54:176–87, and LW 34:325–38.

15. WA 54:180, 3–4, and LW 34:328.

16. WA 54:184, 29–30, and LW 34:335.

17. WA 54:183, 27, and LW 34:334.

18. WA 54:183, 21–22, and LW 34:333–34.

19. This phrase comes from the title of Frère Roger's book, *Dynamique du provisoire* (Taizé: Les Presses de Taizé, 1965).

20. WA 54:185, 12.

21. WA 54:185, 12.

22. "Sintemal darrinnen offenbaret wird die Gerechtigkeit die fur Gott gilt welche kompt aus glauben in glauben Wie denn geschrieben stehet Der Gerechte wird seines Glaubens leben. [Aba.2.]" WADB Römer 1, 17.

23. *The Spirit and the Letter*, WA 54:186, and LW 34:337.

24. WA 54:186, 21–24, and LW 34:337.

25. WA 54:186, 27, and LW 34:338.

26. WA 54:186, 30–187, 1, and LW 34:338.

27. WA 54:179, 10–12, and LW 34:327.

28. WA 54:179, 28–33, and LW 34:328.

29. ". . .mei autem libri, ut ferebat, imo cogebat rerum gerendarum nullus ordo, ita etiam ipso sint quoddam rude et indigestum chaos, quod nunc nec mihi ipsi sit facile digerere." WA 54:179, 10–12, and LW 34:327.

30. Literally translated: one (thing) seen or intuited.

31. WA 54:186, 27–29, and LW 34:338.

32. WA 54:86, 25–27, and LW 34:338.

33. "Confirmet autem Deus hoc in nobis, quod operatus est, et perficiat opus suum, quod incepit in nobis, ad gloriam suam, Amen." WA 54:87, 5–7, and LW 34:338.

34. "Solus primo eram, et certe ad tantas res tractandas ineptissimus et indoctissimus, casu enim, non voluntate nec studio in has turbas incidi, Deum ipsum testor." WA 54:180, 2–4.

35. ". . . ita erbium, imo submersum in dogmatibus papae." WA 54:179, 25.

36. *Preface to the Wittenberg Edition of Luther's German Writings*, LW 34:284. Heiko Oberman observes that "Luther prescribes a *lectio* initiated by *oratio* and leading toward a *relectio*. When compared with the preceding tradition, it is striking that Luther no longer regards *lectio* (letter) and *meditatio* (spirit) as two successive stages. In 1539, dealing explicitly with the proper order, it is stated that true *meditatio* is *lectio* and *relectio*. (Italics are Oberman's.) See Heiko A. Oberman, *The Dawn of Reformation: Essays in Later Medieval and Early Reformation Thought* (Edinburgh, Scotland: T & T Clark, 1986), 148.

37. ". . . et tamen salvus fieri ex intimis medullis cupiebam." WA 54:179, 32–33.

38. WA 54:182, 4–8.

39. "Atque hic vide vel in meo casu, quam difficile sit eluctari et emergere ex erroribus, totius orbis exemplo firmatis, et longa consuetudine velut in naturam mutatis." WA 54:183, 21–23.

40. ". . .id quod consequens erat non vidi, scilicet papum necessario esse ex diabolo." WA 54:184, 1–2, and LW 34:334.

41. WA 54:184, 4.

42. WA 54:179, 35–36, and LW 34:328.

43. WA 54:180, 3–4.

44. WA 54:180, 2.

45. WA 54:180, 21.

46. This opens up possibilities of retranslating the "unquenchable fire" in the Gospel of Matthew 3 and Matthew 13.

47. "Interim eo anno iam redieram ad Psalterium denuo interpretandum . . ." WA 54:185, 12, and LW 34:336.

48. "oderam vocabulum, quod est Cap.1: Iustitia Dei revelatur in illo." WA 54:185, 17–18.

49. See Luther's discussion of faith in *De votis monasticis*, especially the categories of faith as developed by late medieval theology and in particular through the work of Gabriel Biel. WA 8:592 and LW 44:275.

50. WA 54:186, 8–13, and LW 34:336–37.

51. WA 54:186, 15–16, and LW 34:337.

52. WA 2:727–37.

53. WA 54:186, 3–4, and LW 34:337.

54. ". . . ibi iustitiam Dei coepi intelligere eam, qua iustus dono Dei vivit, nempe ex fide . . ." WA 54:186, 5–6, and LW 34:337.

Chapter 3. Writing the Other

1. Jean-Paul Sartre, *Qu'est-ce que la littérature?* (Paris: Gaillimard, 1948).

2. Jean-Paul Sartre, *What Is Literature?* trans. Bernard Frechtman (New York: Harper & Row, 1965), 45. "Ainsi la lecture est-elle un exercise de générosité; et ce que l'écrivain réclame du lecteur ce n'est pas l'application d'une liberté abstraite, mais le don de toute sa personne (. . .)." Sartre, *Qu'est-ce que la littérature?*, 57.

3. Sartre, *What Is Literature?*, 64.

4. Jacques Derrida, "*Signature Événement Contexte*," in *Limited Inc* (Paris: Galilee, 1990), 17–51. Hereinafter cited as *SEC*. The English translation is found in Jacques Derrida, *Limited Inc.*, trans. Alan Bass and Samuel Weber (Evanston, Ill.: Northwestern University Press, 1988). Hereinafter cited as *SEC-English*.

5. Maurice Blanchot, "La littérature et le droit à la mort," in *La part du feu* (Paris: Éditions Gallimard, 1949). English translation: Maurice Blanchot, "Literature and the Right to Death," in *The Gaze of Orpheus and Other Literary Essays*, trans. Lydia Davis (Barrytown, N.Y.: Station Hill, 1981).

6. *SEC*, 19.

7. *SEC*, 45.

8. "C'est que cette unite de la forme signifiante ne se constitue que par son itérabilité, par la possibilité d'être répétée dans l'absence non seulement de son "referent", ce qui va de soi, mais en l'absence d'un signifié determine ou de l'intention de signification actuelle, comme de toute intention de communication présente" *SEC*, 31–32. "Because this unity of the signifying form only constitutes itself by virtue of its iterability, by the possibility of its being repeated in the absence not only of its "referent", which is self-evident, but in the absence of a determinate signified or of the intention of

actual signification, as well as of all intention of present communication."
SEC-English, 10.

9. *SEC*, 26.

10. Is there a careless association of iterability with repetition in Derrida's writing? "Il faut qu'elle soit répétable—itérable—en l'absence absolue du destinataire" *SEC*, 27.

11. *SEC-English*, 7–8. "Il n'y a pas de code—organon d'itérabilité—qui soit structurellement secret. La possibilité de répéter et donc d'identifier les marques est impliquée dans tout code, fait de celui-ci une grille communicable, transmissible, déchiffrable, itérable pour un tiers." *SEC*, 28.

12. *SEC*, 28–29.

13. *SEC*, 27.

14. *SEC*, 49.

15. *SEC*, 30.

16. *SEC-English*, 17–18. "Il faut d'abord s'entendre ici sur ce qu'il en est du 'se produire' ou de l'événementialité d'un événement qui suppose dans son surgissement pretendument present et singulier l'intervention d'un énoncé qui en lui-même ne peut être que de structure repetitive ou citationnelle ou plutôt, ces deux derniers mots prêtant à confusion, itérable." *SEC*, 45.

17. *SEC-English*, 18. "Il faut donc moins opposer la citation ou l'itération à la non-itération d'un événement que construire une typologie différentielle de formes d'itération, à supposer que ce projet soit tenable, et puisse donner lieu à un programme exhaustif, question que je réserve ici." *SEC*, 45.

18. *SEC-English*, 10; *SEC*, 46.

19. *SEC*, 19.

20. *SEC*, 19–20.

21. *SEC*, 27.

22. *SEC*, 28.

23. *SEC*, 30.

24. Catherine Pickstock, *After Writing: On the Liturgical Consummation of Philosophy* (Oxford: Blackwell, 1998), 3.

25. Pickstock, *After Writing*, 29.

26. "Toute signe, linguistique ou non-linguistique, parlé ou écrit (au sens courant de cette opposition), en petite ou en grande unite, peut être cité, mis entre guillemets, par là il peut romper avec tout contexte donné, engendrer à l'infini de nouveaux contexts, de façon absolument non saturable. Cela ne suppose pas que la marque vaut hors contexte, mais au contraire qu'il n'y a que des contexts sans aucun centre d'ancrage absolu." *SEC*, 36.

27. Translating the elusive French word *vaut* in "Cela ne suppose pas que la marque vaut hors contexte." *SEC*, 36.

28. Blanchot, "La littérature," 306–7.

29. Blanchot, "La littérature," 307.

30. Blanchot, "La littérature," 307.

31. Blanchot, "Literature and the Right to Death," 330. "Elle est tournée vers le mouvement de négation par lequel les choses son séparées d'elles-mêmes et détruites pour être connues, assujetties, communiqués." Blanchot, "La Littérature," 332.

32. Blanchot, "Literature and the Right to Death," 330. "La littérature est alors le souci de la réalité des choses, de leur existence inconnue, libre et silencieuse: elle est leur innocence et leur présence interdite, l'être qui se cabre devant la revelation, le défi de ce qui ne veut pas se produire au dehors." Blanchot, "La Littérature," 332.

33. *"contenu sans forme."* See Blanchot, "Literature and the Right to Death," 330.

34. Blanchot, "Literature and the Right to Death," 330.

35. *"Il n'y a pas de hors texte."* Jacques Derrida, "Force et signification," in *L'écriture et la différence* (Paris: Éditions du Seuil, 1967), 45.

36. Dissemination is used here much in the way Derrida uses dehiscence– as a rupture producing life.

37. Caruth, *Unclaimed Experience,* 69.

38. Iterability as a nonrepetitive structure will be further pursued in chapter 4 and primarily in chapter 5.

39. WA 8:564–669 and LW 44:245–400 and the letter/preface in English LW 48:329–36.

40. Heiko A. Oberman, "Luther Contra Medieval Monasticism: Friar in the Lion's Den," in *Ad fontes Lutheri: Towards the Recovery of the Real Luther. Essays in Honor of Kenneth Hagen's Sixty-Fifth Birthday,* ed. Timothy Maschke, Franz Posset, and Koan Skocir (Milwaukee: Marquette University Press, 2001), 211–12.

41. Oberman, "Luther Contra Medieval Monasticism," 211.

42. WAT 4, no. 5034:624, 19f.

43. Oberman, "Luther Contra Medieval Monasticism," 196–97.

44. ". . .sed plane ignoravi haec ita habere." WA 8:573, 18, and LW 48:331.

45. WA 8:576, 30, and LW 48:336. After the Diet of Worms, Luther had been clandestinely whisked away for his own protection and safekeeping to the Wartburg Castle by the elector Frederick.

46. Luther's suggestion, of course, that vows do not make one holy implies that the vow itself is not different from choosing some other walk in life. The person taking a vow cannot despise the ways of others. The whole idea of vows has been devised to ensnare the conscience and hold it captive to the bondage of the law. It actually takes pride in so doing. For who among the religious would allow himself to be put in the same class as a married man, a farmer, or a workman in the sight of God? Do not the religious in fact take their vows for

the express purpose of appearing to serve God with a more devoted obedience than anybody else? Why do they despise as they do all other ways of living and esteem this one only? These people do not say with the prophet, "Thy mercy is better than all the ways of life" [Ps. 63:3]. The opinion that "one life is better than all others" may be true as far as men are concerned, but it is not true as far as God is concerned. So let us reveal here the thoughts of their hearts. What would the nuns and monks do if they heard that in the sight of God they are not a bit better than married people and mud-stained farmers? Will they not murmur against the householder that they are being treated the same as those who worked for but one hour while they alone have borne the burden and heat of the day? (LW 44:304 and WA 8:610, 17–27)

47. LW 44:252.

48. "La première consequence en sera la suivante: étant donné cette structure d'itération, l'intention qui anime l'énonciation ne sera jamais de part en part présente à elle-même et à son contenu. L'itération qui la structure a priori y introduit une dehiscence et une brisure essentielles." *SEC*, 46.

49. LW 44:252. Luther applies this judgment to liturgy as well.

50. WA 8:584, 31–32, and LW 44:263.

51. WA 8: 578, 5, and LW 44:252.

52. LW 36:73. "Vows should either be abolished by a general edict, especially those taken for life, and all [people] recalled to the vows of baptism, or else everyone should be diligently warned not to take a vow rashly. No one should be encouraged to do so; indeed, permission should be given only with difficulty and reluctance. For we have vowed enough in baptism, more than we can ever fulfill; if we give ourselves to the keeping of this one vow, we shall have all we can do."

53. *SEC*, 36.

54. ". . . sed terrore et agone mortis subitae circumvallatus vovi coactum et necessarium votum . . ." WA 8:573, 32–574, 1, and LW 48:332.

55. "Breviter, cum virginitas in scriptures non laudetur, sed tantum probetur, praeconiis coniugalis castitatis ceu alienis plumis vestitur ab istis, qui ad pericula salutis animas prompti sunt inflammare." WA 8:575, 6–9.

56. WA 8:575, 30, and LW 48:335.

57. WA 8:575, 30, and LW 48:335.

58. WA 8:575, 32, and LW 48:335.

59. WA 8:574, 32–33, and LW 48:333.

60. WA 8:575, 23, and LW 48:334.

61. ". . . sed plane ignoravi haec ita habere." WA 8:573, 18, and LW 48:331.

62. WA 8:574, 2–3, and LW 48:332.

63. WA 8:574, 9–10, and LW 48:332.

64. WA 8:575, 24–27, and LW 48:335.

65. WA 8:575, 29, and LW 48:335.

66. WA 8:575, 32–33, and LW 48:335.

67. WA 8:576, 8, and LW 48:335.

68. "La première consequence en sera la suivante: étant donné cette structure d'itération, l'intention qui anime l'énonciation ne sera jamais de part en part présente à elle-même et à son contenu. L'itération qui la structure a priori y introduit une dehiscence et une brisure essentielles." *SEC*, 46.

69. WA 5:239, 3.

70. For a fuller discussion of the notion of the body not being "at home," see Geoffrey Bennington, *Lyotard Writing the Event* (New York: Columbia University Press, 1988), esp. 77.

71. Martin Brecht, *Martin Luther Band 2: Ordnung und Abgrenzung der Reformation 1521–1532* (Stuttgart: Calwer Verlag, 1986).

72. Brecht, *Martin Luther Band 2*, 194–95.

73. WA 8:576, 15, and LW 48:336.

Chapter 4. Writing Trauma

1. Cathy Caruth, *Unclaimed Experience: Trauma, Narrative, and History* (Baltimore, Md.: Johns Hopkins University Press, 1996). And for the purposes of this study, the pages 57 and following will be of particular interest.

2. Caruth, *Unclaimed Experience*, 60.

3. Sigmund Freud, *Moses and Monotheism* (New York: Knopf, 1967); Sigmund Freud, *Der Mann Moses und die momtheistische Religion in Gesammelte Werke* XVI (Frankfurt am Main: S. Fischer, Verlag, Fünfte Auflage 1950), 101–246.

4. Caruth, *Unclaimed Experience*, 60.

5. Caruth, *Unclaimed Experience*, 61.

6. Caruth, *Unclaimed Experience*, 61.

7. Caruth, *Unclaimed Experience*, 62.

8. Caruth, *Unclaimed Experience*, 62.

9. Caruth, *Unclaimed Experience*, 63.

10. Caruth, *Unclaimed Experience*, 11.

11. Caruth, *Unclaimed Experience*, 11.

12. Caruth, *Unclaimed Experience*, 71.

13. Caruth, *Unclaimed Experience*, 71.

14. Caruth, *Unclaimed Experience*, 71.

15. Caruth, *Unclaimed Experience*, 18.

16. Caruth, *Unclaimed Experience*, 66.

17. Caruth, *Unclaimed Experience*, 63.

18. Caruth, *Unclaimed Experience*, 67.

19. Caruth, *Unclaimed Experience*, 63.

20. Sigmund Freud, *The Standard Edition of the Complete Psychological Works of Sigmund Freud*, ed. and trans. James Strachey, 24 vols. (London: Hogarth, 1958), 5:232. Cited also in Caruth, *Unclaimed Experience*, 92.

21. Caruth, *Unclaimed Experience*, 107.

22. Caruth, *Unclaimed Experience*, 112.

23. Caruth, *Unclaimed Experience*, 18.

24. Caruth, *Unclaimed Experience*, 64.

25. Caruth, *Unclaimed Experience*, 101–102.

26. Sigmund Freud, *Beyond the Pleasure Principle*, ed. and trans. James Strachey (New York: Norton, 1961), 12; Sigmund Freud, *Gesammelte Werke* XIII (Frankfurt am Main: S. Fischer, Verlag, Fünfte Auflage 1967), 11.

27. Freud, *Beyond the Pleasure Principle*, 15. "Wie stimmt es also zum Lustprinzip, dass es dieses ihm peinliche Erlebnis als Spiel wiederholt?" Freud, *Gesammelte Werke*, 13.

28. Freud, *Beyond the Pleasure Principle*, 4.

29. Freud, *Beyond the Pleasure Principle*, 4.

30. Freud, *Beyond the Pleasure Principle*, 14. Though it must be noted that the English "obvious" is much stronger than the German "*nahe.*"

31. Freud, *Beyond the Pleasure Principle*, 15.

32. Freud, *Beyond the Pleasure Principle*, 15.

33. Freud, *Gesammelte Werke*, 11–12.

34. Freud, *Beyond the Pleasure Principle*, 17.

35. Freud, *Beyond the Pleasure Principle*, 4.

36. Freud, *Gesammelte Werke*, 4.

37. Caruth, *Unclaimed Experience*, 68.

38. Freud, *Gesammelte Werke*, 13.

39. Freud, *Beyond the Pleasure Principle*, 14n6. "Diese Deutung wurde dann durch eine weitere Beobachtung völlig gesichert. Als eines Tages die Mutter über viele Stunden abwesend gewesen war, wurde sie beim Wiederkommen mit der Mitteilung begrüsst: Bebi o-o-o-o! die zunächst unverständlich blieb. Es ergab sich aber bald, dass das Kind während dieses langen Alleinseins ein Mittel gefunden hatte, sich selbst verschwinden zu lassen. Es hatte sein Bild in dem fast bis zum Boden reichenden Standspiegel entdeckst und sich dann niedergekauert, so dass das Spiegelbild 'fort' war." Freud, *Gesammelte Werke*, 13.

40. Caruth, *Unclaimed Experience*, 66.

41. Cathy Caruth writes: "What strikes Freud as he tells the story of the *fort-da* is that the game of departure and return is ultimately, and inexplicably, a game, simply, of departure. I would suggest that if this game is resonant in BPP, it is not only because the child's play does or does not provide evidence of repetition compulsion. It is also because the symbolized pattern

of departure and return brings into prominent view a larger conception of historical experience." Caruth, *Unclaimed Experience*, 66.

42. Caruth, *Unclaimed Experience*, 64.

43. Freud, *Beyond the Pleasure Principle*, 51. "Der Weg nach rückwärts, zur vollen Befriedigung ist in der Regel durch die Widerstände, welche die Verdrängungen aufrecht halten, verlegt." Freud, *Gesammelte Werke*, 45.

44. Freud, *Beyond the Pleasure Principle*. "Er [der Kranke] ist vielmehr genötigt, das Verdrängte als gegenwärtiges Erlebnis zu *wiederholen,* anstatt es, wie der Arzt es lieber sähe, als ein Stück der Vergangenheit zu *erinnern.*" Freud, *Gesammelte Werke*, 16.

45. Jacques Derrida, "*Signature Événement Contexte,*" in *Limited Inc* (Paris: Galilee, 1990), 20. Hereafter cited as *SEC*.

46. Reading Nietzsche as himself interpreter of Luther would be the focus of such a genealogy.

47. WA 8:576, 4–6, and LW 48:336. "Itaque sub conscientiae meae periculo tibi non obedire non possem (ita sum modo persuasissimus), ubi ministerium verbu ultra monachatum non accessisset."

48. See Emmanuel Levinas, "*La trace de l'autre,*" in *En découvrant l'existence avec Husserl et Heidegger* (Paris: Librairie Philosophique J. Vrin, 1974).

49. Caruth, *Unclaimed Experience*, 71.

50. Martin Luther, *That These Words of Christ, 'This Is My Body,' etc., Still Stand Firm against the Fanatics,*" LW 37:99ff. and WA 23:64ff.

51. LW 37:29. "Denn ich thar auch wol darauff schweren, das dieser spruch Christi (das ist mein leib) ynn yhrem hertzen stickt, wie ein ewiger stefft, des sie nirgend mugen los warden." WA 23:88, 8–10.

52. LW 37:32. "Denn wer sich vnter steht, die wort ynn der schrifft anders zu deuten denn sie lauten, der ist schuldig dasselbige aus dem text desselbigen orts, odder durch einen artickel des glaubens zu beweisen." WA 23:92, 25–28.

53. LW 37:32.

54. LW 37:28–29. "Da stehet nü der spruch vnd lautet klar vnd helle, das Christus seinen leib gibt zu essen, da er das brod reicht, Darauff stehen, gleuben vnd leren wir auch das man ym abendmal warhafftig vnd leiblich Christus leib isset vnd zu sich nymbt, Wie aber das zu gehe, odder wie er ym brod sey, wissen wir nicht, sollens auch nicht wissen Gotts wort sollen wir gleuben vnd yhm nicht weise noch mas setzen, Brod sehen wir mit den aügen Aber wir horen mit den oren das der leib da sey." WA 23:87, 28–35.

55. WA 23:245, 35–246, 5, and LW 37:126.

56. WA 23:262, 33–35, and LW 37:137.

57. Luther writes that, through the outward (or literal) Word, "the Holy Spirit is given with all [the Holy Spirit's] gifts." LW 37:137.

58. LW 37:140. "Nu stehen da Gotts wort, die ynn sich begreissen vnd fassen den leib Christi, das er dasey, Drumb wie das wort vnd der glaube not ist,

so ist auch der leib ym wort verfasset vns not, auff das vnser glaube recht sey vnd mit dem wort sich reyme weil die beide, wort vnd leib nicht zu scheiden sind." WA 23:266, 22–26.

59. Irving L. Sandberg, trans., *The 1529 Holy Week and Easter Sermons of Dr. Martin Luther* (Saint Louis, Mo.: Concordia Academic, 1999), 69.

60. LW 22:519–520, Commentary on John 4:9.

61. "Et bene notandm est et maxime observandum, quod extra Cbristum non est Deus alius." WA 39 II:25,17.

Chapter 5. Writing Disruption

1. Martin Luther, "The Large Catechism," in *The Book of Concord: The Confessions of the Evangelical Lutheran Church,* ed. Robert Kolb and Timothy J. Wengert (Minneapolis: Fortress Press, 2000), 466.

2. The designation "eucharist" will be used, for it encompasses the variety of expressions employed in reference to the sacramental "event," such as "Sacrament of the Altar," "Holy Communion," "The Lord's Supper," and "Holy Mass."

3. Heiko A. Oberman, "Luther Contra Medieval Monasticism: Friar in the Lion's Den," in *Ad fontes Lutheri: Towards the Recovery of the Real Luther: Essays in Honor of Kenneth Hagen's Sixty-Fifth Birthday,* ed. Timothy Maschke, Franz Posset, and Koan Skocir (Milwaukee: Marquette University Press, 2001), 187.

4. See the earlier discussion of this in chapter 1.

5. Alexander Schmemann, *Introduction to Liturgical Theology,* trans. Asheleigh E. Moorhouse (London: Faith Press, 1966), 35.

6. A form of this remembering has recently been made very popular in Mel Gibson's film *The Passion of the Christ.* It witnesses to an ecumenical curiosity: this controversial example of a deep Catholic piety "remembering" the *Via Dolorosa* and its enthusiastic reception by more right-wing, fundamentalist Christians who "relive" for themselves the sufferings of Christ as "they happened."

7. If he did have to choose, however, he would have preferred the Catholic position, stating in one of his humorous moments, "I'd rather drink blood with the Romans than wine with the Swiss."

8. See chapter 3 and the discussion on Sartre.

9. See also my chapter "Eating, Drinking, Sending," in Dirk G. Lange and Dwight W. Vogel, *Ordo: Bath, Word, Prayer, Table. A Liturgical Primer in Honor of Gordon W. Lathrop* (Akron, Ohio: OSL Publications, 2006), 84–99.

10. LW 35:80–81. "Auff das nu Christus yhm bereyttet eyn angenhem liebes volck, das eintrechtiglich yn ein ander gepunden were durch die liebe, hat er auff gehaben das gantz gesetz Mosi, und das er nit ursache den secten und zurteylungen hynfuerter gebe, hatt er widderumb nit mehr den eyne weyß

odder gesetz eyngesetzt seynem gantzen volck, das ist die heylige Meß (. . .) das nu hinfuertter keyn ander eußerliche weyß solt sein, gott zu dienen, den die meß, und wo die geuebt wirt, da ist der recht gottis dienst." WA 6:354, 19–28. *Eyn Sermon von dem neuen Testament das ist von der heylige Messe.*

11. Gerhard Ebeling, *Luther: An Introduction to His Thought*, trans. R. A. Wilson (London: Collins, St. James's Place, 1970), 110. ". . .damit es den Leser gegenwärtig angeht, ihn trifft, in seinem Herzen lebendig wird." Gerhard Ebeling, *Luther Einführung in Sein Denken* (Tübingen: Mohr, 1965), 120.

12. Ebeling, *Luther Einführung,* 125.

13. Ebeling, *Luther: An Introduction,* 114. "Was heisst hier eigentlich 'Unterscheidung'?" Ebeling, *Luther Einführung,* 125.

14. Ebeling, *Luther: An Introduction,* 115–16. "Unterscheidung meint hier nicht einen ohne weiteres bestehenden und nun eben bloss zu konstat-ierenden, einzusehenden, zu erkennenden Unterschief. Das ist ja gerade der Ernst der Sache, dass dieser Unterschied faktisch nicht besteht, vielmehr nur als vermengt und verwirrt zur Erfahrung kommt, und dass er selbst dort, wo er klargestellt ist, immer neu klargestellt werden muss, nur gegen eine dau-ernd anstürmende Wirrnis geltend gemacht werden kann." Ebeling, *Luther Einführung,* 127.

15. Ebeling, *Luther Einführung,* 126.

16. Ebeling, *Luther: An Introduction,* 125. "Die Unterscheidung von Gesetz und Evangelium hat eine Unterscheidung in bezug auf das Gesetz selbst zur Folge." Ebeling, *Luther Einführung,* 137.

17. Gerhard Ebeling and Timothy J. Wengert, *Law and Gospel: Philip Melanchthon's Debate with John Agricola of Eisleben over Poenitentia* (Grand Rapids, Mich.: Baker, 1997), 191. Luther rejects the classical theological use of the law as pedagogical.

18. Ebeling, *Luther: An Introduction,* 126. "Denn "frohe Botschaft" [Evangelium], das heisst froh machende, befreiende, Mut machende, Hoffnung eröffnende, Glauben schaffende Verkündigung muss doch, wenn sie nicht etwa bloss ein Intermezzo sein soll, das ein vorübergehendes Aufatem, eine Ablen-kung, ein wenig Illusion, ein zeitweises Vergessen, etwas Opium vermittelt, sondern aller Zukunft überlegen, aller Anfechtung gewachsen sein, alle Wirrnis lösen, alle Finsternis überstrahlen soll, ein solches Wort sein, das schlechterd-ings klar, wahr und gewiss ist, an dem nicht zu deuteln und zu rütteln ist, ein Wort ohne Wenn und Aber, ein verlässliches und eben darum Vertauen schenk-endes Wort, das den, der es sich gesagt sein lässt, erleuchtet, aus dem Bann der Lüge zur Wahrheit befreit, aus der Verzweiflung zur Gewissheit, aus dem Tod und der Hölle zum Leben und zur Seligkeit." Ebeling, *Luther Einführung*, 138.

19. ". . .*ut legem credendi lex statuat supplicandi*"—this phrase, found in the "Official Pronouncements of the Apostolic See on Divine Grace and Free Will" by Prosper of Aquitaine apparently establishes a relation between a

rule of believing and a certain rule of supplication. See Prosper of Aquitaine, *Defense of Saint Augustine,* trans. P. De Letter (Westminster, Md.: Newman, 1963), 183.

20. "It is true that Montaigne used an interesting expression, which Pascal takes up for his own purposes and which I'd also like to reinterpret and to consider apart from its most conventional and conventionalist reading. The expression is *"fondement mystique de l'autorité,"* 'mystical foundation of authority.'" Jacques Derrida, "Force of Law: The 'Mystical Foundations of Authority,'" in *Deconstruction and the Possibility of Justice,* ed. Drucilla Cornell, Michel Rosenfeld, and David Gray Carlson (New York: Routledge, 1992), 11.

21. Derrida, "Force of Law," 14.

22. Michael G. L. Church, "The Law of Begging: Prosper at the End of the Day," *Worship* 73, no. 5 (1999): 442–53.

23. Conversation with Gordon W. Lathrop, March 2004.

24. See Mark D. Jordan on the significance of the term *invention"* Jordan, *The Invention of Sodomy in Christian Theology* (Chicago: University of Chicago Press, 1997).

25. Derrida, "Force of Law," 15.

26. This displacement of law by the eucharist challenges the very framework of current ecumenical and intradenominational debate on the "meaning" or theological significance of the eucharist.

27. Mark D. Jordan, *Rewritten Theology: Aquinas after His Readers* (Oxford: Blackwell, 2005).

28. "You must trust that Christ is the Fountainhead of life, and that God has poured all [God's] gifts, [God's] will, and eternal life into Christ and has directed [all people] to [Christ]. There we are to find all. If you take hold of [Christ], you have all; you have taken hold of the entire Godhead. (. . .) This calls for a humble and helpless, a hungry and thirsty soul, which relies on the words and seeks God nowhere but in the Christ who lies in the manger, or wherever [Christ] may be—on the cross, in Baptism, in the Lord's Supper, or in the ministry of the divine Word, or with my neighbor [or sister] or brother. That is where I will find [God]." LW 23:55–56 (Commentary on John 6).

29. "And you must run directly to the manger and the mother's womb, embrace this Infant and Virgin's Child in your arms, and look at Him—born, being nursed, growing up, going about in human society, teaching, dying, rising again, ascending above all the heavens, and having authority over all things. In this way you can shake off all terrors and errors, as the sun dispels the clouds. This vision will keep you on the proper way, so that you may follow where Christ has gone." LW 26 (Gal. 1:4).

30. "Verba enim spiritus sunt annunciata de re absente et non apparente, per fidem apprehendenenda" WA 5:239, 3.

31. Cathy Caruth, *Unclaimed Experience: Trauma, Narrative, and History* (Baltimore, Md.: Johns Hopkins University Press, 1996), 11.

32. See Schmemann, *Introduction to Liturgical Theology.*

33. Alexander Schmemann is also aware of the complexity of the event and what actually "happens" around the bread and the wine. See his *For the Life of the World* (New York: St. Vladimir's Seminary Press, 1973).

34. This question hides within it a christological question. For if, in Christ, the whole fullness of deity dwells bodily (Col. 2:9), then is the incarnation already the beginnings of the dissemination of God?

35. Michel de Certeau, *The Capture of Speech and Other Political Writings,* trans. Tom Conley (Minneapolis: University of Minnesota Press, 1997), 20.

36. Caruth, *Unclaimed Experience,* 92.

37. Caruth, *Unclaimed Experience,* 92.

38. The *Didache* was only discovered by Archbishop Philotheos Bryennios in 1873 and published in 1883. For more detailed analysis of this document, see Jonathan Draper, ed., *The Didache in Modern Research* (Leiden: Brill, 1996), and Kurt Niederwimmer, *Die Didache* (Göttingen: Vandenhoeck & Ruprecht, 1989).

39. But only published in 1883, the importance of the discovery having been initially ignored! Draper, *The Didache in Modern Research,* 1.

40. See, primarily, Willy Rordorf et André Tuilier, *La doctrine des Douze Apôtres (Didachè),* vol. 248 bis of *Sources chrétiennes* (Paris: Les Éditions du Cerf, 1978).

41. Robert Taft summarizes these finding in a recent article. Robert F. Taft, "Mass without the Consecration," *Worship* 77 (2003): 482–509.

42. Even after more than a century of critical and worthy analysis, the text of the *Didache* is still subject to an abundance of disputed assertions. Dating the *Didache* is problematic. Jean-Paul Audet and Enrico Mazza, examining what they regard as pre-*Didachistic* fragments, especially *Didache* 9–10, place these chapters prior to the fall of the temple in 70 CE. Jean-Paul Audet, *La Didachè Instructions des Apôtres* (Paris: Librairie Lecoffre, J. Gabalda et Cie, Éditeurs, 1958), 199. Mazza goes even further than Audet, placing them before the Council of Jerusalem, that is 48–49 CE. Enrico Mazza, "Didachè IX-Christ: Elementi per una interpretazione Eucaristica," *Ephemerides Liturgicae* 92 (1979): 393–419. Translated in Draper, *The Didache in Modern Research,* 276–99, see also 282. Willy Rordorf and André Tuilier, in their very helpful *Sources chrétiennes* edition of the *Didache,* posit an archaic date for component parts (in accordance with Audet) but a later date for the redactional form. A *terminus ante quem,* they believe, is all that can be really established. (Rordorf et Tuilier, *La doctrine des Douze Apôtres,* 94–95.) Kurt Niederwimmer, on the other hand, acknowledges the archaic nature of three components (the "Two Ways tractate," the liturgical

formulae, and the questions around the reception of itinerant charismatics and other disciplinary issues) but places them much later than Rordorf and Tuilier. He attributes them to the late first century CE. The most recent scholarly work by Enrico Mazza is gaining in acceptance placing chapters 9 and 10 around the middle of the first century (50 CE)—only fifteen to twenty years after the crucifixion of Jesus of Nazareth. It would be, therefore, the earliest witness to what has become known as the "Christ event" preceding even the written Gospels.

43. Enrico Mazza, *The Origins of the Eucharistic Prayer* (Collegeville, Minn.: Liturgical Press, 1995), 40–41.

44. Mazza, *The Origins*, 30, 35, and 38–39.

45. Mazza, "Didachè IX-Christ," 291.

46. Mazza, "Didachè IX-Christ," 292.

47. Mazza, "Didachè IX-Christ," 292.

48. Mazza, "Didachè IX-Christ," 295.

49. Kurt Niederwimmer, *The Didache: A Commentary,* trans. Linda M. Maloney, Hermeneia (Minneapolis: Fortress Press, 1998), 155.

50. Mazza, "Didachè IX-Christ," 298.

51. Mazza, "Didachè IX-Christ," 298.

52. See Gordon W. Lathrop, *Holy People: A Liturgical Ecclesiology* (Minneapolis: Fortress Press, 1999), 188–91. See also David Power, *The Eucharistic Mystery* (New York: Crossroad, 1992), 31–32; Gail Ramshaw, *Treasures Old and New: Images in the Lectionary* (Minneapolis: Fortress Press, 2002), 186–87; and Samuel Torvend, *Daily Bread, Holy Meal* (Minneapolis: Augsburg Fortress, 2004), 44–48. Though the idea is already present in the classic liturgical study by Yngve Brilioth, *Nattvarden i evangeliskt gudstjanstliv* (Stockholm: SKDB, 1926, 2nd ed., 1951). Yngve Brilioth, *Eucharistic Faith and Practice,* trans. A. G. Hebert (London: SPCK, 1965), 18–19.

53. John Dominic Crossan, *Jesus: A Revolutionary Biography* (New York: HarperCollins, 1989), 70.

54. For further discussion of cosmology and its reorientation through the liturgy, see Gordon W. Lathrop, *Holy Ground: A Liturgical Cosmology* (Minneapolis: Fortress Press, 2003).

55. I am indebted to Gordon W. Lathrop for pointing out to me this further dissemination.

56. For a finer analysis and reading of this radical commensality, see the work of Marianne Sawicki, *Crossing Galilee: Architectures of Contrast in the Occupied Land of Jesus* (Harrisburg, Pa.: Trinity Press International, 2000), and *Seeing the Lord: Resurrection and Early Christian Practices* (Minneapolis: Fortress Press, 1994).

57. These words, "This is my body," can also, of course—as we will see in Luther—contain a radical dissemination, especially when the celebration says

to each individual: "Receive what you are, the body of Christ," or when each one says of himself or herself: "This is 'my' body."

58. Mazza, "Didachè IX-Christ," 295.

59. Is there the possibility that in the remembering that occurs through dissemination a new definition of ritual is possible?

60. See Lathrop, *Holy Ground*, 179–182.

61. To what extent, it may be asked, is every promise a demand and every law a question?

Chapter 6. Rewriting Promise

1. Gerhard Ebeling, *Luther: An Introduction to His Thought*, trans. R. A. Wilson (London: Collins, St. James's Place, 1970), 118. "Nicht dann also ist das Evangelium rein und unversehrt da, wenn es un ungestörtem Frieden für sich allein steht und die Beziehung zum Gesetz gar nicht in den Blick kommt. In solcher Isolierung könnte das Evangelium gar nicht Evangelium sein. Denn nur da tritt das Evangelium in Aktion, wo es unterscheidend dem Gesetz gegenüber in Aktion tritt und darum auch das Gesetz erst wirklich als Gesetz erkennen lässt." Gerhard Ebeling, *Luther Einführung in Sein Denken* (Tübingen: Mohr, 1965), 129–30.

2. Ebeling, *Luther: An Introduction,* 116.

3. Ebeling, *Luther: An Introduction,* 116.

4. Ebeling, *Luther: An Introduction,* 116.

5. Ebeling, *Luther: An Introduction,* 118.

6. Ebeling, *Luther: An Introduction,* 118.

7. Jacques Derrida, *Acts of Religion* (New York: Routledge, 2002).

8. LW 51:19.

9. LW 51:19–20.

10. LW 51:22.

11. Derrida, *Acts of Religion,* 233.

12. LW 51:19.

13. Gordon Lathrop points out, however, that in his own practice, Luther does seem to have used all of these "additions." Luther insisted on a use that he did not himself practice. "In the parish church we still have the chasuble, alb, altar and elevate as it pleases us." WA 18:113 and LW 40:131. See Gordon Lathrop, *Holy People,* 161–63.

14. LW 35:82.

15. "Christian, Evangelical Worship," 4.4.2. http://www.wordalone.org/docs/wa-chris-worsh.shtml.

16. "Christian Evangelical Worship," 4.4.4.

17. Eric W. Gritsch and Robert W. Jenson, *Lutheranism: The Theological Movement and Its Confessional Writings* (Philadelphia: Fortress Press, 1976), 51.

18. "Verba enim spiritus sunt annunciata de re absente et non apparente, per fidem apprehendenenda" WA 5:239, 3.

19. WA 30 II:637, 5–7.

20. WA 30 II:640, 33–641, 1.

21. WA 30 II:637, 10–20.

22. WA 30 II:636, 12–13.

23. WA 30 II:637, 1–4.

24. LW 35:195. "Aber nu hab ich nicht allein der sprachen art vertauet und gefolgt, das ich Roma. 3 'solum' (Allein) hab hinzu gesezt, sonder der text und die meinung S. Pauli foddern und erzwingens mit gewallt, denn er handelt ja daselbs das hauptstuck Christlucher lere, nemlich, das wir durch den glauben an Christum on alle werck des gesetzs gerecht werden, und schneit alle werck so rein ab." WA 30 II:640, 33–641, 2.

25. WA 30 II:641, 9–10.

26. In the liturgical celebration, the Gospel had been previously "announced" through singing.

27. I am indebted to Gordon W. Lathrop for this insight that arose out of our mutual conversation.

28. LW 35:196. "Sage mir doch ob Christus tod und auffersteen unser werck seh, dass wir thun oder nicht?" WA 30 II:642, 7–8.

29. WA 30 II:642, 11–13. "What is the work by which we lay hold of Christ's death and resurrection?" LW 35:197.

30. Of course, there is yet another use of the term *liturgical language*: as words about the liturgy, as liturgical theology.

31. "I give so that you might give." "We may even understand our giving as establishing the ancient religious exchange *do ut des* . . . the obligation for God to give us good things in return for our gifts." For a strong critique of this metaphor, see Gordon W. Lathrop, *Holy Things: A Liturgical Theology* (Minneapolis: Fortress Press, 1993), 140. See also Gordon W. Lathrop, *Holy Ground: A Liturgical Cosmology* (Minneapolis: Fortress Press, 2003), 193, and Gordon W. Lathrop, "The Bodies on Nevado Ampato: A Further Note on Offering and Offertory," *Worship* 71, no. 6 (1997): 546–54.

32. In a broad brush stroke and certainly open to much critique, I will suggest that the traditional metaphor for public worship was a "receive and give back" or a "take and give" schema. The people receive something—a gift, a gift of liberation, a gift of forgiveness, a gift of bountiful crops, and so forth— and in return they give something back—a sacrifice, a commitment, a thanksgiving, praise. This metaphor remains popular at least in Christian theology. The New Testament witness, in its use of the term *leitourgia*, appears to move away from that metaphor. Something has been given—the gift of Christ—but the people can do nothing in return. The only possible action is a response of service to the other—in other words, to minister. This is underlined by

Emmanuel Levinas' use of the *leitourgia*. The "gift" that knows of no return gratitude is a gift that exceeds, that supersedes—to use the superlative—anything the human can offer. This gift is encountered in the face of the other. The only response—if we can call it a response—is an ethical response or what Levinas calls *leitourgia*. The response is not a work but a liturgy, which is, as Levinas writes, "ethics itself." Emmanuel Levinas, *"La trace de l'autre,"* in *En découvrant l'existence avec Husserl et Heidegger* (Paris: Librairie Philosophique J. Vrin, 1974.)

33. See also Mark 16 and Luke 24.

34. This is particularly pertinent in relation to the Gospel of Mark. There is a growing consensus among New Testament scholars that Mark 16:8 is the ancient ending of the Gospel. But this ending only sends the reader back to the beginning of the Gospel once again. For a development of this analysis and its implications for liturgical theology, see Lathrop, *Holy Ground,* 37 and 128.

35. Anselm of Canterbury, *The Major Works,* ed. Brian Davies and G. R. Evans (Oxford: Oxford University Press, 1998).

36. Cathy Caruth, *Unclaimed Experience: Trauma, Narrative, and History* (Baltimore: The John Hopkins University Press, 1996), 65.

37. Caruth, *Unclaimed Experience,* 105.

38. Caruth, *Unclaimed Experience,* 107.

39. Caruth, *Unclaimed Experience,* 100.

40. Caruth, *Unclaimed Experience,* 105.

41. Don E. Saliers was the first to point out, in discussion, that the Words of Institution have the character of an *epiclesis*. This insistence by Luther on these ords would also then disrupt our notion of consecration or the consecratory moment. The *epiclesis* is classically understood as the invocation of the Holy Spirit upon the elements of bread and wine during the eucharistic celebration. It is considered by some theologians an essential part of the consecratory action that constitutes the eucharist.

42. The connection between Word and Spirit, or the blurring, in the liturgy, of their absolute distinction, suggests a question for further research: How does the liturgy disrupt historically embedded, theological taxonomies? Don Saliers has suggested that here, in this liturgical text and in the liturgical theology of Luther, we find a retrieval of something hinted at in the pre-Nicene notions that see Word *(Verba)* and Spirit much more intimately interrelated.

43. On the day of Pentecost, the King James Bible translates an intervention in these words: **"And they were all filled with the Holy Ghost, and began to speak with other tongues, as the Spirit gave them utterance."**

44. In an essay on German literature and literary theory, Thomas Mann invokes the question Lessing hypothetically poses to Luther: "Grosser, verkannter Mann! Du hast uns von dem Joche der Tradition erlöset, aber wer

erlöset uns von dem unerträglichen Joche des Buchstabens! Wer bringt uns endlich ein Christentum, *wie Du es itzt lehren würdest,* wie es Christus selbst lehren würde!" Thomas Mann, "Rede Über Lessing," in *Gesammelte Werke* IX (Frankfurt am Main: S. Fischer Verlag, 1960), 243.

45. WA 2:743, 7–10, and LW 35:50–51.

46. WA 2:743, 27–31, and LW 35:51.

47. WA 6:354:19–28, and LW 35:80.

48. WA 2:745, 7–8, and LW 35:54.

49. WA 2:745, 8–9, and LW 35:54.

50. LW 35:60. "Auß dem allen ists nu clar, das dyß heylig sacrament sey nit anders, dan eyn gottlich tzeychen, darynne zu gesagt, geben und zu geeygent wirt Christus, alle heyligen mit allen yhren wercken, leyden, vordiensten, gnaden und guttern zu trost und sterck allen, die yn engsten und betrubniß seyn, vorvolget vom teuffell, sunden, welt, fleysch und allem ubell, und das sacrament empfahen sey nit anders, dan desselben alls begeren und glauben festiglich, es gescheh alßo." WA 2:749, 23–29.

51. LW 35:60.

52. LW 35:58. This quote continues: "And through the interchange of his blessings and our misfortunes, we become one loaf, one bread, one body, one drink, and have all things in common. O this is a great sacrament." WA 2:748, 15–17.

53. LW 35:58. "Widderumb sollen wir durch die selb lieb unß auch wandelnn und unßer lassen sein aller ander Christen geprechen und yhr gestalt und notdurfft an uns nehmen." WA 2:748, 20–22.

54. Irving L. Sandberg, trans., *The 1529 Holy Week and Easter Sermons of Dr. Martin Luther* (Saint Louis, Mo.: Concordia Academic, 1999), 69.

55. One could examine the use of hyperbole in liturgical texts as a witness to this excess of a promise and as a means to declare the accomplishment of transformation.

56. I would like to thank Mark Jordan for pointing out that the Greek χαρις is itself a word of transaction and exchange, a word of dissemination.

57. Don Saliers has suggested this strong link between the writing and the practice of liturgical theology.

58. Gordon W. Lathrop and Timothy J. Wengert, *Christian Assembly* (Minneapolis: Augsburg Fortress, 2004), 25.

59. Hypermnesia is a medical term designating an abnormally strong memory of the past.

60. WA 2:743, 7–10, and LW 35:50–51.

Index